Between the Seas

Between the Seas

Island Identities in the Baltic and Mediterranean Seas

Deborah Paci

BLOOMSBURY ACADEMIC
LONDON • NEW YORK • OXFORD • NEW DELHI • SYDNEY

BLOOMSBURY ACADEMIC
Bloomsbury Publishing Plc
50 Bedford Square, London, WC1B 3DP, UK
1385 Broadway, New York, NY 10018, USA
29 Earlsfort Terrace, Dublin 2, Ireland

BLOOMSBURY, BLOOMSBURY ACADEMIC and the Diana logo are
trademarks of Bloomsbury Publishing Plc

First published in Great Britain 2023
This paperback edition published 2024

Copyright © Deborah Paci, 2023

Deborah Paci has asserted her right under the Copyright, Designs and
Patents Act, 1988, to be identified as Author of this work.

For legal purposes the Acknowledgements on p. xii constitute an
extension of this copyright page.

Series design by Adriana Brioso
Cover image © Westend61/Getty Images

All rights reserved. No part of this publication may be reproduced or
transmitted in any form or by any means, electronic or mechanical, including
photocopying, recording, or any information storage or retrieval system,
without prior permission in writing from the publishers.

Bloomsbury Publishing Plc does not have any control over, or responsibility for,
any third-party websites referred to or in this book. All internet addresses given
in this book were correct at the time of going to press. The author and publisher
regret any inconvenience caused if addresses have changed or sites have ceased
to exist, but can accept no responsibility for any such changes.

A catalogue record for this book is available from the British Library.

Library of Congress Cataloging-in-Publication Data
Names: Paci, Deborah, author.
Title: Between the seas : island identities in the Baltic and Mediterranean seas / Deborah Paci.
Description: London ; New York : Bloomsbury Academic, 2023. |
Includes bibliographical references and index.
Identifiers: LCCN 2022038650 (print) | LCCN 2022038651 (ebook) |
ISBN 9781838606190 (hardcover) | ISBN 9781838606206 (pdf) |
ISBN 9781838606213 (epub) | ISBN 9781838606220
Subjects: LCSH: Islands of the Baltic–History. | Islands of the Mediterranean–History. |
Islands of the Baltic–Relations. | Islands of the Mediterranean–Relations. |
Group identity–Islands of the Baltic. | Group identity–Islands of the Mediterranean.
Classification: LCC DK502.7 .P34 2023 (print) | LCC DK502.7 (ebook) |
DDC 945.8–dc23/eng/20220923
LC record available at https://lccn.loc.gov/2022038650
LC ebook record available at https://lccn.loc.gov/2022038651

ISBN:	PB:	978-1-3503-6039-6
	ePDF:	978-1-8386-0620-6
	eBook:	978-1-8386-0621-3

Typeset by Integra Software Services Pvt. Ltd.

To find out more about our authors and books visit www.bloomsbury.com
and sign up for our newsletters.

Contents

List of illustrations	vii
Preamble: Comparing Islands by Godfrey Baldacchino	viii
Acknowledgements	xii
Maps	xiii

	Introduction	1
1	**The Baltic Sea and Mediterranean regions as spaces of expectations**	**15**
	Spatial imaginations of the Baltic Sea and Mediterranean region	16
	The Baltic Sea region as a space of expectations	19
	The Mediterranean Sea region as a space of expectations	28
2	**The views of the European Institutions on the island question**	**39**
	The islands within European institutions: Historical background	40
	The islands of the European Union today	50
	Islands and migration in the Mediterranean region	58
3	**Insular identity in the Baltic Sea region**	**61**
	The Ålanders: Swedish-speakers in Finland	62
	'Universi mercatores Imperii Romani Gotlandiam frequentantes'. Gotland as a strategic island for the security of the Baltic Sea region	78
	Saaremaa and Hiiumaa: A border zone between West and East	89
	Ruhnu, 'Pearl of the Gulf of Riga': The island disputed between Estonia and Latvia	104
4	**Autonomy and independence in insular Mediterranean areas**	**115**
	The *corda seria*: The tireless dialectic of the Sicilian elites	116
	The 'besieged citadel': Maltese nationalism between British imperialism and Italian irredentism	135

The inescapable choice of the island of 'demoniacal sadness':
    Sardinian autonomy   153
An island among many centres: Corsica and the continent   170

Conclusion   191

References   201
Index   229

Illustrations

1. The seat of the Ålands Lagting (Parliament of Åland). According to the Act on the Autonomy of Åland (also known as the Autonomy Act), the Ålands Lagting is the elected parliament. The Parliament of Åland by Magne Kveseth on norden.org via Wikimedia Commons — 75
2. A view of the Medieval Week in Visby in 2011. Medieval week, Östergravar, Visby, Gotland by Helen Simonsson on flickr — 85
3. Signs of the Soviet presence are still present in Saaremaa. Soviet WWII memorial, Tehumardi, Saaremaa, Estonia. 27 July 2007 by Mark A. Wilson on Wikimedia Commons — 101
4. Ruhnu women in folk costumes in 1937. Rahvariietes Ruhnu naised 1937. Aastal by an unknown author on Wikimedia Commons — 111
5. The Strait of Messina marks the territorial discontinuity between the mainland and Sicily. Villa San Giovanni and the Strait of Messina by Scott Barron on Flickr — 117
6. A panoramic view of the fortifications which were built to make Valletta an invincible capital city for the Order of St John. Le bastion Saint-Salvator de La Valette (Malte) by Jean-Pierre Dalbéra on Flickr — 136
7. The anthem *Su patriotu sardu a sos feudatarios* ('The Sardinian Patriot to the Lords'), is a poetry written by Francesco Ignazio Mannu on the occasion of Sardinian revolution. The mural reproduces an extract from the poetry: 'This – oh people – is the hour to eradicate abuses. Down with all evil customs! Down with dispotic power!'. Murales in Orgosolo by Heather Cowper on Flickr — 160
8. The battle of Ponte Novu has become a symbol of Corsican nationalism. Every year, on 8 May, the commemoration of this event takes place with the participation of many people. Ruines du pont Génois sur le Golo (Haute Corse) sur la commune de Castello-di-Rostino, hameau de Ponte-Novo. En cours de restauration by Piero Montesacro on Wikimedia Commons — 182

Preamble: Comparing Islands

For centuries, the Western tradition of cartographic map-making has played a pivotal role as a political technology of empire building, settler colonialism and the dispossession of Indigenous lands (Rose-Redwood et al. 2020). The power of the map lies in the application of scientific rigour to identify terrains as sites of conquest, establish boundaries and assign these to different hegemons, all with the stroke of a pen, and then legitimated via the printed form. Such deeply political representations of space are also powerful enablers of epistemology, conditioning how we look at our world, what we consider to be true and valid, shaping our understandings and constructions of the neighbourhood, the nation, the region and the planet (Brotton 2013; Lefebvre 1991). In recognition of the commanding influence of map as artefact, scholars and practitioners have responded by acknowledging and exposing the power dynamics that include resorting to such mapping techniques to establish and then consolidate and anchor their power in self-evident vistas, while others remind us about, and celebrate, maps conceived on the basis of alterative knowledge systems (e.g. Eckstein and Schwarz 2019). This is a necessary and ongoing practice, and not just for Indigenous peoples. There is another deliberate act that we need to invest in more seriously, in order to come to better terms with our world, and to wean (including decolonizing) ourselves of the perspectives and outlooks that current cartographic landscapes unwittingly induce. This is, *prima facie*, simpler since it asks for a deliberate appreciation of a comparative approach. Shorn down to its basic principles, the idea is to distil and expose patterns and similarities that may come to light by looking at spaces and places *relationally*. The difficulties, however, are palpable. First, by ordering the world, maps are by definition sticky and paradigmatic: their representations automatically negate counter-conceptualizations. There is something quite naïve, even dangerous, in assuming that maps are neutral and objective; no map is. One may argue cogently that all maps lie, since they invariably must frame and simplify their subject and thus wilfully eliminate (Monmonier 2018). Second, many scholars in the social sciences are wary and even sceptical of comparative research. The indulgence in 'deep' (including ethnographic) studies of single cases or milieux builds a steady resistance to methodologies where cases are double or multiple, and where they are presented for scrutiny, not just for their own intrinsic merits but also for the insights that they may provide to and about each other. The comparative field is riddled with objections and debates, mainly questioning the soundness and validity of the approach. Be that as it may, comparative research has its obvious rewards, since by definition (1) it throws up items for inspection and analysis *together* that may not have been thus considered; while (2) it proposes unifying concepts and lenses to revisit and unpack historical truths and re-stitching them in this new light. The freshness of the analytic frame renders the pursuit of the technique worthwhile, even as the critics moan and protest against illegitimate similarities and contrasts. This preamble is necessary to frame Deborah Paci's *oeuvre* that weaves together a new narrative inspired by the comparative approach. In the pages that follow, we have a serious and scholarly attempt to compare the two great seas of Europe: one to the north and one to the south, each with their islands and littorals, each with their histories of navigation, settlement, conquest and empire. Each with a historic nemesis threatening from the east: Russia (in the Baltic) and Turkey (in the Mediterranean). We need to continue to watch these dynamics. Having seen Paci's collection, I will be excused for stating that the invitation to look at the Mediterranean and the Baltic *together* is powerful and irresistible. Equipped with this frame of analysis, it is hard not to see the obvious scope for comparison whenever a geographical map of Europe is presented. (I deliberately say 'geographical' because a political map of Europe excises the Mediterranean as a 'sea' and presents it as a natural aquatic frontier, which, however, as we have been reminded, it historically and culturally is *not* (Braudel [1949] 1995). Of course, we are not saying that geography causes history, or anything else. However, geographical features and conditionalities do exacerbate certain historical trajectories, and therefore suggest certain outcomes. We accept and believe firmly that people make history; but they do so in circumstances inherited from the past (as Marx would insist) but also from their material condition. Which is why the concept of islandness is so fundamental in this pioneering Baltic–Mediterranean assessment (e.g. Hall 2012). The invitation is to consider islands on their own terms and merits, shorn of the negative and depressing baggage that comes with notions of insularity and isolation. The comparison is original and insightful, also because it is called for. Europe has had an obvious and ongoing history with both seas; watery expanses that lead to the hearts of the continent, even as they coddle along the shores of extra-European powers and expansive territories: the steppes of Russia to the east and the deserts of North Africa to the south. At the focus of the navigations in these two seas are the islands, from the smallest (Castellorizo; Muhu) to the largest

(Sicily; Saaremaa), often victims of the tide of empire, switching affiliation and hegemons through the decades. They also bear the legacies of a painful and unnatural division: only a dozen populated islands in the world are divided – *de jure* or *de facto* – between more than one country, and one each of these exemplars is found in the Mediterranean and Baltic, respectively (Κύπρος/ Kibris; Usedom/Uznan) (Baldacchino 2013). The comparative study of islands has an interesting pedigree. Some powerful 'natural experiments of history' permit critical reflections of, say, the impact of different environmental protection regimes in two states sharing the same island, so holding many variables constant. For example, Diamond and Robinson (2010) looked at satellite images of the two states sharing the island of Quesqueya/Hispaniola: Haiti and Dominican Republic, thus gauging the extent of their tree cover. On the contrary, in the humanities and social sciences, Richards (1982) compared political practices in the small island polities of Faroes, Isle of Man and Malta. Even earlier, Dommen (1980) curated a collection of papers that bravely selected islands as their focus, and some of these were genuinely comparative (e.g. Caldwell et al. 1980). I looked at 144 successful, export-oriented small firms from five European island regions to understand how they may have used their distinct small island base as part of their brand message (Baldacchino 2005a). Such scholarship has expanded, thanks also to the emergence of dozens of new small island states on the political stage, and the accompanying spurt of journals and publications (Baldacchino 2006; Suwa 2007). Meanwhile, scholarship on archipelagos has matured into a genre of its own, facilitating the study of multiple effects, often with various islands that have much in common (including jurisdiction, location, terrain, climate), serving as members of convenient 'experimental group versus control group' settings (Stratford et al. 2011). Consider here, for example, the study of the impact of bridges and tunnels that connect islands to mainlands (e.g., Scott and Royle 1996; Baldacchino and Starc 2021), or the manner that different island components of an archipelago respond to the promise of tourism, on the basis of current or proposed logistics and accessibility options (Baldacchino 2016). Zoology has pioneered the comparative study of islands *within* archipelagos: most notably, the Galápagos (modern-day Ecuador) by Charles Darwin and the Aru Islands (modern-day Indonesia) by Alfred Russel (Quammen 2012). The comparative study *across* archipelagos is, however, a rarer endeavour. DeLoughrey (2001) has proposed an 'archipelagraphy' of Caribbean and Pacific cultures. Apostolopoulos and Gayle (2002) profiled island tourism and sustainable development experiences in the Caribbean, Pacific and Mediterranean. Diamond (1997) looked for explanations to the markedly different histories of the Old and the New Worlds by ingeniously comparing the geography and evolutionary biology of the world's two largest island masses: Europe–Asia–Africa and America. The methodology is obviously fraught with serious challenges, since such pursuits must face the harsh criticism of validity: *how could one possibly compare A to B?* Yet, unlikely relationalities are not necessarily ill fated or ill advised all the more reason to be bold and experiment with such (apparently illicit) comparators. Thus, an obvious next step is to foster a deep and engaging comparison *between* two (or more) aquatic basins, and not just *parallel* sections and chapters. The island studies literature is still 'testing the waters' of the comparative method, often preferring the easier, deep immersion of specific islands, rather than the ambitious, perhaps preposterous, island-island adventure. The single case study remains by far the glorified methodological favourite. A text exclusively devoted to island studies methodologies is under production (Stratford et al. 2023). Nevertheless, there is a heartfelt need to extend and expand comparisons across waters, seas and oceans. Bringing together Hau'ofa's reading of Oceania, Abulafia's assessment of the Mediterranean and Walcott's poetic rendering of the Caribbean – just to mention an obvious yet underexplored marine triangulation – is likely and liable to throw up some welcome surprises (Abulafia 2011; Hau'ofa 1994; Walcott 2014), as well as some cherished salve in these days of nationalist and anti-migrant rhetoric. Much more of such work is needed, as we increasingly acknowledge the role of the sea in the history, development and (sustainable) future of *homo sapiens* on planet Earth, and of the role of islands as 'entangled worlds' therein (Chandler and Pugh 2021). Deborah Paci has her work cut out. So: dear reader, go on; read or browse, and enjoy this book. Do so for what it offers, and for inspiring the much more that is yet to come.

Godfrey Baldacchino
Valletta, February 2022

Acknowledgements

This book is the outcome of a research study that began in 2014 in the context of the project on 'Spaces of Expectation: Mental Mapping and Historical Imagination in the Baltic Sea and Mediterranean Region' (Södertörn University-Ca' Foscari University of Venice). First, I must thank my friends and colleagues Norbert Götz, Janne Holmén, Jussi Kurunmäki, Rolf Petri and Vasileios Petrogiannis. I do owe a special debt to Janne Holmén and Rolf Petri, who gave me useful input during the drafting stage.

I would like to thank them for our continuous exchange of ideas and pleasant days and evenings spent discussing mental maps and maritime imaginaries during the course of our encounters in the Mediterranean and Baltic.

I would like to thank the Foundation for Baltic and East European Studies, which has financed this research [grant number 41/13]. I also extend appreciation to colleagues who have offered their expertise throughout the process, providing important feedback on specific sections of the book. My thanks are due to Emiliano Beri, Marco Cini, Giulio Ferlazzo Ciano, Roberto Ibba, Fabrizio La Manna, Rosario Mangiameli, Giorgio Peresso, Giampaolo Salice, Gianluca Scroccu and Ivan Vassallo. Any shortcoming the manuscript contains is certainly no fault of theirs but rather rests with me alone.

This book is dedicated to my grandfather Emanuele, who saw the fiery sunsets of the Mediterranean and the boreal dawns of the Norden when he was a sailor. In the words of Simone Perotti, 'Maybe the only people who can really talk about islands are seafarers. Those travelling back and forth between their remote coasts have the time of memory and of imagination' (2017: 12). It is also dedicated to my parents, my brother and my little niece Amélie. A special thought to Mr. Klaus from Bussaghja: a chance encounter that showed me how an island can be a 'place of the soul' from which you can leave but also a place where you are always welcome to return.

I would like to thank my family: Jacopo for his continuous support and for re-reading my manuscript, Pietro, 'the Baltic boy', who learned to walk in Stockholm and on the Åland islands, and Ernesto, who wriggled around in my baby bump during my research studies and conferences in the Mediterranean. Thanks for putting up with my long absent presence: I owe this book to you.

Maps

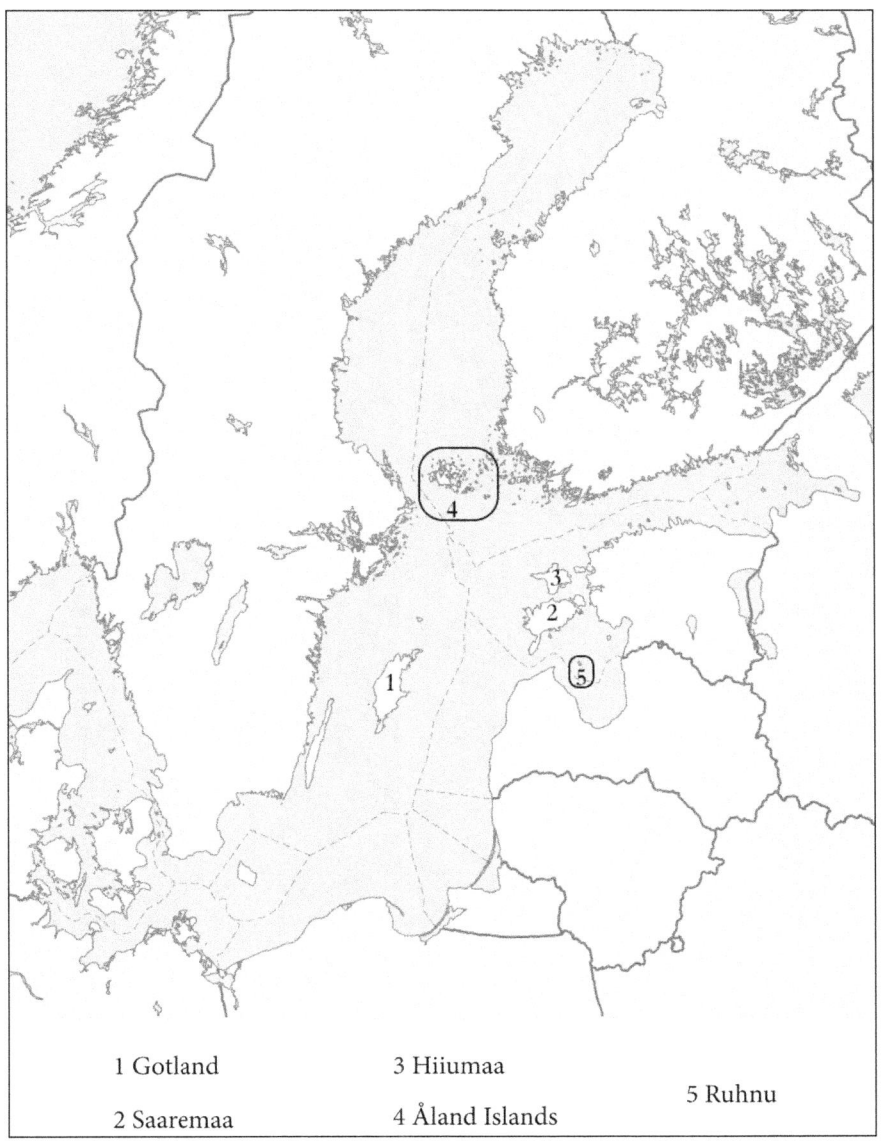

Map 1. Case Studies in the Baltic Sea region.

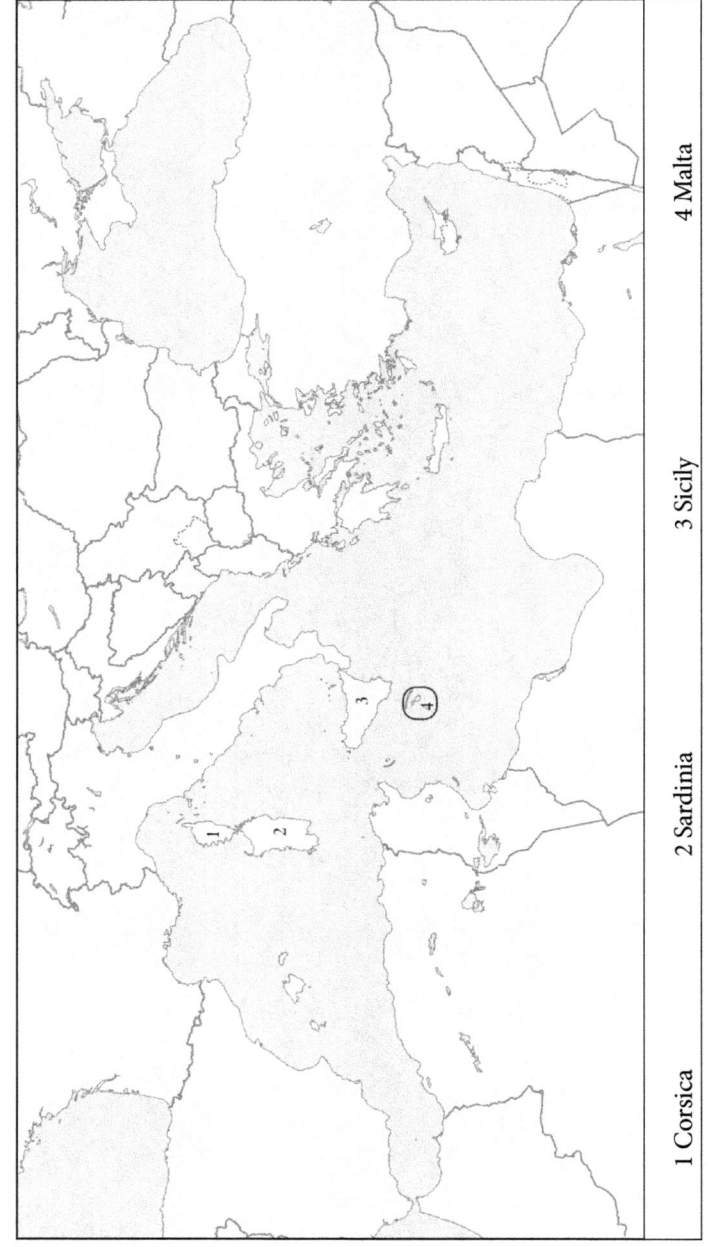

Map 2. Case Studies in the Mediterranean Sea region.

1 Corsica   2 Sardinia   3 Sicily   4 Malta

Introduction

The present book aims at providing a deeper understanding of the perception of island identity in the Baltic Sea and Mediterranean regions. It looks at islands not only as an undeniable geographic notion but also as objects of representation and expectation. A first question that leads the present study is whether there exist similarities in the ways Mediterranean and Baltic Sea islandness is constructed. A second question is how in the era of European integration, the EU has represented Mediterranean and Baltic Sea islands and determined the goals of its regional politics with regard to these islands.

A short answer to the first question will be that there exist commonalities such as the historical experience of domination of islands by continental forces and a lasting condition of structural peripherality; however, while Mediterranean islands' self-descriptions continue to ruminate self-victimizing representations of perduring dependency, Baltic Sea islands tend to speak more often of themselves as equal parts of a broader emancipated 'Nordic' reality. The short answer to the second question is that the regional politics of the European Union display shortcomings in regard to both declinations. Instead of a comprehensive concept of 'islandness' that takes into consideration also the effects of imaginative self-representation of islands, EU regional politics sticks to a more reductive vision of 'insularity' that tends to define the needs and prospects of islands in geographically deterministic terms, perhaps believing such an approach would be more impartial and objective. The co-determining and co-defining elements of imagination and self-imagination are not really considered as a part of an island's material reality and effective needs. The main purpose of the present book is to show that such a vision is flawed as the dimension of imaginative geography and self-representation matters indeed.

The above distinction between 'islandness' and 'insularity' therefore requires clarification and the positioning of the present research in the broader context of island studies. The choice of the subtitle *Island Identities in the Baltic and*

Mediterranean Seas underlines from the start that this book appreciates the Godfrey Baldacchino's approach regarding 'islandness', seen in its most generic meaning as 'a distilled and judgement-free sense of island living' (2018: XXIV). In order to reinforce the correct use of the various concepts, it may be necessary to dwell here on the very words 'insularity', 'islandness' and 'insularism'. According to Anne Meistersheim, insularity refers to the physical condition of isolation; islandness is linked to the perception of isolation felt by island inhabitants; insularism is the attitude of insularist elites calling for autonomy by virtue of their insularity (1988: 96–120). Insularity describes a geographic, biogeographic and socio-economic condition of isolation that can be determined by means of physical and biological criteria of isolation of a territory that allow us to classify and distinguish different islands from each other (Gallia 2012: 931). Contrary to Meistersheim's suggestion, although the notion of insularity evokes the physical condition of the island space, it also has significant implications on a psychological level. According to the *Oxford English Dictionary*, the term insularity refers to both the physical qualities of the island and the impact that such qualities have upon the islanders: '1. The state or condition of being an island, or of being surrounded by water; 2. The condition of living on an island, and of being thus cut off or isolated from other people, their ideas, customs, etc.; hence, narrowness of mind or feeling, contractedness of view' (Hepburn 2012: 126).

If we start with these considerations, we can see that insularity is, above all, a social phenomenon or concept used by islanders to assert their unique identity in the context of the centre/periphery dichotomy (Baldacchino 2002: 194). This book can be situated within a broader set of contemporary, vibrant, debates surrounding island insularity, relationality and connectivity in island scholarship. The theoretical contextualization of insularity within the centre/periphery paradigm put forward in 1980 by the Italian geographer Angelo Turco (1980) is corroborated by the words of Jean-Didier Hache, former secretary general of the Islands commission at the Conference of Peripheral Maritime Regions of Europe, who believes 'insularity tends to be the result of a process of economic, social, cultural and political peripheralisation that has affected these populations, a process made more acute, or more apparent, by their insular condition; insularity should be seen, first and foremost, as a political phenomenon, and especially as the product of evolving centre/periphery relationships' (Hache 1998: 60). The term insularity is often used with negative connotations alluding to the narrow-mindedness of islanders (Hepburn 2012: 126). For these reasons, those studying islands and this author as well, prefer to use the concept of 'isolanità' in Italian (Vieira 2016: 10), 'islandness' in English and 'îleité' in French.

The concept of islandness includes the field of perception, that is, the cultural imaginary of an island society (Brigand 1991: 2). It refers to the unique condition of the island frontier that represents a combination of opening/closure (Jackson 2008: 309). As pointed out by Eve Hepburn, islandness is a notion whose meaning lends itself to different interpretations in the specialist literature (2012: 127). While Stephen A. Royle considers it a summa of 'constraints that are imposed upon small islands by virtue of their insularity' (2001: 42), the definitions supplied by Joël Bonnemaison, Godfrey Baldacchino, Rebecca Erinn Jackson and Elaine Stratford are more complex because they draw upon the cultural and social dynamics of island spaces. According to Bonnemaison, this concept implies 'an interrupted link with the rest of the world and therefore a space existing beyond space, a place lying outside of time, a naked place, an absolute link' (1990: 119). For this reason, islandness belongs to the field of representations and metaphors. As seen by Baldacchino, 'islandness is an intervening variable that does not determine, but contours and conditions physical and social events in distinct, and distinctly relevant, ways' (2004a: 278). Rebecca Erinn Jackson follows in the footsteps of Anne Meistersheim by distilling the concepts of insularité, insularisme and îleité into the notion of islandness: 'I would like to define islandness as the dynamics of the natural boundary and the resulting island qualities, including elements geographical (for example, degree of separation from a mainland), political (often expressed through tensions between autonomy and dependence on a mainland jurisdiction) and social (such as islander identity and sense of place)' (2008: 47).

Elaine Stratford underlines the strong value of identity intrinsic to the concept of islandness, highlighting the 'strong perceptions of island-self and mainland-other, as well as potent connections to island communities and environments' (2008: 161). Equally significant is the neologism 'counter-islandness' coined by Nathalie Bernardie-Tahir and Camille Schmoll. It indicates an analytical perspective at odds with the idea of insularity distinguished by a condition of isolation. If by counterculture we intend a form of contestation of the dominant culture rather than 'an opposing culture', then in the same way counter-islandness is a way of considering the insular condition that rejects the paradigm of insularity. As the two authors point out: 'we use counter-islandness as a posture that enables us to rethink and challenge the set of characteristics habitually and cursorily ascribed to islands and island societies' (Bernardie-Tahir and Schmoll 2014: 44).

For this reason, islandness in the present book will be placed in the context of the discourses and the policies aimed at sustaining the idea of unity and civilization in the Baltic Sea and Mediterranean regions. In the first chapter, these are conceived of as spaces of expectations. The documentation on which the analysis concentrates is that produced by the regional, local and European institutions. The Euro-Mediterranean policy – as determined by the Barcelona Process after 1995 and the Union for the Mediterranean since 2008 – revolves around the idea that the countries of the European Union have a common interest in developing forms of cooperation and solidarity with countries bordering on the south of the Mediterranean. But thanks to the French initiative, in particular, such policies have been dictated by Western Eurocentric thinking. In fact, the question of migration, which has loomed larger with the events of the Arab Spring, has raised question marks about this idea. In the Baltic area it was following the dissolution of the Soviet Union that the regions of the Baltic Sea re-established links that had until then been determined by the hampering presence of the two blocs. The rhetoric of the unity of the Baltic area resurfaced, for example, in the form of 'The New Hanseatic League'.

I then will examine the 'island question' that has been dealt with in European capitals from the 1950s to today through an examination of the acts and documents produced by European institutions. In the act that gave birth to the European Community, interest in island regions was more or less non-existent (Chapter 2, 'The views of the European Institutions on the island question'). The attention of Europe was on the mainland, as seen in the treaties signed in that decade. The European Community started to take into consideration the needs and necessities of island societies only at the end of the 1980s, within a political climate that contributed to an awareness of the island question. The conditions that created a favourable environment for the introduction of Community policies attuned to the island societies were, on the one hand, the emergence of the regions on the European scene that led in 1992 to the creation of the Committee of the Regions, and on the other – in the context of actions tightly connected to the development of regional policy – the availability of structural funds destined for 'disadvantaged regions'. In the Mediterranean region the role of islands, as points of transit and through which migrants come, has also become a key factor in understanding the discourse around the unity of the Mediterranean.

Case studies of specific islands in the Baltic Sea and Mediterranean regions provide occasions for an appropriate investigation of the topics discussed in a practical manner. In Chapter 3, 'Insular identity in the Baltic Sea region', I reflect on the perception of island identity in the Baltic Sea Region, looking at several significant case studies (see Åland islands, Gotland, Saaremaa, Hiiumaa and Ruhnu). In some cases, the dialectic between islands and the mainland triggers processes seeking forms of autonomy or independence; in other contexts, the recovery of cultural heritage was used in these societies to validate a specific island identity that could justify the request for political and economic advantages. In Chapter 4, 'Autonomy and independence in insular Mediterranean areas', I focus on political claims by several pro-autonomy/independence groups in the Mediterranean and how the political claims have influenced the forging of the insular political institutions. Through the examination of several case studies (Sicily, Malta, Sardinia and Corsica) the rhetoric employed by the insularist groups will be analysed along with the politics practiced by these groups in the ambit of negotiations with the institutional centre.

The objective is to observe in historical perspective the 'insularist' rhetoric employed by pro-independence/autonomy groups and by insular institutions. A part of the island population may decide to found political claims upon the paradigm of insularity. The island/mainland combination – in a context in which island regions are institutionally dependent – presupposes a confrontation, which may sometimes take on dimensions that are conflictual – between the central State, which finds itself with the upper hand, given that it has decision-making power, and the island peripheries, who feel penalized by belonging to a national context they feel to be alien – if not downright hostile – from a cultural point of view. These power relations between island and mainland are confirmed by the definition provided by the *Oxford Dictionary*, which describes the term 'mainland' as 'a large mass of land forming a country, continent, etc., without its islands'. The mainland is the 'main land' against which to measure the island existence which finds itself 'with a role that is subordinate or dependent if not subjugated' (Sedda 2019: 25).

The hypothesis that I would like to put forward in this research study is that insularist groups, although claiming autonomy of decision-making within a rhetorical framework, knowingly assume a secondary role, leaving the responsibility of conducting island politics to those currents closer to the 'Continental'/'European' context. Realpolitik is a decisive factor that explains the behaviour of insularist groups. The analysis from an historical perspective of the dialectic between 'insularism' and regions of the nation state is what distinguishes this research and makes it innovative and able to incorporate, scientifically, the emergence of the increased prominence of islands in the context of the European Union. This analysis will take an historical and, simultaneously, comparative approach to two European regions, Baltic and Mediterranean – which, while different in terms of economic development, have in common the rhetoric of maritime unity. The focus on the islands in the two regions will be particularly useful because it will throw light on how the insularist groups follow a common course at the rhetorical level yet diverge in practice to respond to the logic particular to the respective maritime regions to which they belong.

Eve Hepburn maintains that islanders aspire to forms of administrative and legislative autonomy in order to meet the challenge they face due to their condition of islandness (Hepburn 2012: 127).

It is precisely this islandness that provides insularism with the tools to become a driver of political mobilization. The French geographer Roger Brunet coined the expression 'insularisme' (insularism) to describe the tendency by islanders to over-cultivate their insular specificity with the aim of affirming a specifically insular cultural identity or to benefit from more or less specific advantages (Brunet, Ferras and Théry 1993). When seen as a discourse on the cultural and geopolitical specificities of island spaces, insularism acts as a factor of political mobilization and defence of identity particularism. As we will see, in the Mediterranean area, in particular, but also in the case of the Åland islands, autonomist and independentist parties operating in island realities dependent upon a sovereign institutional centre use insularist discourses to bind a sense of belonging to an island space, with the ultimate aim of achieving autonomy or independence. Insularism is like a type of mechanism by means of which island populations are led to adopt forms of behaviour involving fragmentation and isolation. The insularist perspective is dominated by the idea that an island is a unique entity with an economic, identity-based and cultural personality that must be recognized in all of its uniqueness rather than from a legal perspective and in terms of political practices. Island movements seeking autonomy or independence often adopt the notion of insularity – as a paradigm of disadvantage – to justify the political claims made in their proclamations in the context of relations between centre and periphery. In the insularist rhetoric – that is, the rhetoric of insularism – the island is the disadvantaged periphery suffering from a condition of isolation and solitude in the face of the total disinterest of the institutional centre to which it refers. Autonomy or independence is presented as the cure for all ills. From this perspective, the recognition of insularity is what may allow the islanders to overcome their status as minors to take control of their existence. The term 'island' is a constant in the discourses made by movements for autonomy or independence, confirming the privileged relationship existing between subjectivity and spatiality.

The state of the art of work dealing with processes of state-building in an insular context is distinguished by the specific attention paid to forms of island governance (Baldacchino 2006; Depraetere and Dahl 2007; Hay 2006) as well as to the political and economic relationship between mainland and islands (Warrington and Milne 2007). Some scholars have proposed a series of reflections on island nationalism with the subnational island jurisdiction framework proposed by Godfrey Baldacchino (Baldacchino 2004b; Baldacchino 2010; Baldacchino and Hepburn 2012; Farinelli 2017; Fazi 2009; Hepburn 2012). With some exceptions, including the works by Samuel Edquist and Janne Holmén (2015) and by Marcel A. Farinelli (2017), there is a scarcity of purely historiographic works exploring relations between islands and mainland.

At first glance, islands appear to be isolated worlds by definition, that is, inward-looking and jealous of a cultural heritage that has stratified over time. As outlined by Nathalie Bernardie-Tahir, islands have lent themselves to different uses (2011). Chronotopes of the western geographic imaginary, islands are subject to a twofold representation causing them to appear, on the one hand, as claustrophobic, isolated, distant and dreamlike spaces, and like a time that is slowed down, if not frozen, on the other (Bernardie-Tahir 2010: 9). A universal geographic archetype, islands are bearers of a symbolic dimension that has produced an entire series of representations that have fed into a vision of island space that is both idyllic and frightening. This happens because islands are a space of expectations like no other: an idealized, aestheticized place that fascinates while clashing with reality; the island of fantasy is the desert island yet real islands are actually densely populated places (Castelain 2006: 402).

Islands are therefore a miniature world, a complete, perfect vision of the cosmos because they embody an intrinsic value. This concept approaches notions associated with temples and sanctuaries. The island is one of the chosen places of silence and peace (Diegues 1998: 15) as well as the archetype of the collective consciousness (Diegues 1997: 15). In his *Mediteranski breviari* Predrag Matvejević analyses the term 'insulomania' which refers to an unstoppable desire to travel to islands, an illness suffered by the author who recognizes its limits (1991: 253). After all, in the 1700s and 1800s, the Rousseauian myth of the good savage contributed to reinforcing the mythical conception of the island world, expressed in the figurative arts by Paul Gauguin during his Tahitian sojourn (Staszak 2003). According to Elaine Stratford, 'islands are constitutive of strong place-based identifications and emotional geographies' (Stratford 2008: 171). Many of them have been frequently conquered and represented a mirage for those who aspired to find a refuge or an idyllic place to establish experimental or utopian societies (Marimoutou and Racault 1995; Trabelsi 2005).

Islands are places to escape to and flee from the frenzy of everyday life, tax havens and places for illicit activities as well as prisons in which to remove individuals from society at large (Bernardie-Tahir 2011: 9). This finiteness typical of the island space means that islands lend themselves to becoming a place of reclusion, assuming the metaphor of imprisonment, on a symbolic level: for this reason, islands can result in manifestations of claustrophobic topophobia (Cavallo 2013a: 193). If we observe islands from the point of view of ecology, we can see that these places are distinguished by closure: just consider insular endemism and the evolution of the species in a spatially finite, insular territory (Cavallo 2013b: 1). Islands establish a constant dialogue between what is within, inside the insular space, and what lies without: 'islands have occupied such a power of local *and* global realities, of interior *and* exterior references of meaning, of having *roots* at home while also deploying *routes* away from home' (Baldacchino 2005b: 247–8).

According to Matvejević (1998), islands offer a key to interpreting the history of the Mediterranean. Fernand Braudel's masterful study describing the Mediterranean with reference to its deep structures has an entire section dedicated to islands ([1949] 1995 vol. 1: 148–60): in it, the French historian relativizes the scope of insularity, drawing attention to the dynamism of islands and their interaction with continental spaces. Braudel stigmatizes the definition of islands as 'objects', pointing out that certain islands are miniature continents, others form archipelagos, and yet others are mere rocks, so numerous as to be impossible to list. He does not fail to relativize the idea suggesting that islands are isolated worlds, stressing, instead, their function as a crossroads of peoples and ideas. In another passage, he dwells on the precarious nature of island life, reminding us that islands are constantly under threat from the sea ([1949] 1995 vol. 1: 151–4). This results in the need to develop effective defences by building more protection structures. The existence of rudimentary agriculture and the difficulties involved in obtaining supplies of the basic necessities are common to most islands. They all face a huge problem that has never been solved or badly resolved; that of living from their own resources. After considering the isolation and precarious conditions of the islands, Braudel puts forward a reflection on the location of islands 'on the paths of general history' ([1949] 1995 vol. 1: 154). He observes that regardless of all expectations, 'the islands lay on the paths of the great sea routes and played a part in international relations' (Braudel [1949] 1995 vol. 1: 154). Migration is the preferred way for islanders to interact with the external world. Braudel's reflection on islands therefore begins with the conviction that we need to reassess the scope of insularity. This aim can be pursued by focusing on their social and economic structures, and upon the role that islands have played in 'general history'. According to Braudel, economic interest – not insularity – drives the actions of islanders.

Although they have on occasion played a leading role in history, as noted by Braudel, island environments remained on the margins of historical reflection. It is only since the early 1990s that island scholars inspired by the 'spatial turn' in the social sciences (Cosgrove 1984) have drawn attention to the need to shift the focus away from the continent.

Making island spaces the focus of the historic discourse means observing how islanders represent themselves and how they interact with the outside world. It means taking a closer look at the mental map – outlined by the islanders – and comparing it with the geographic map. The collective perception is that island spaces are distinguished by geographic limits defining mechanisms of isolation from and openness towards the external world. Despite complying with a system of conventions defined as 'scientific', the geographic map is only apparently a flat, codified image: actual nearness to or distance from the continent – or another island space – is determined by the collective imaginary. In fact, the geographic map mirrors the mental map and cannot avoid the game of representations. To borrow the expression coined by Paul Ricoeur (1986: 389), the island can be considered as a text. Adopting a phenomenological approach to the island imaginary makes it possible to investigate the mental maps in the island *milieu*. Some researchers into island spaces have opted to use a similar textual and rhetorical approach to that of Michel De Certeau ([1980] 1984), who claimed that places were the outcome of operations defining borders carried out by means of literary processes, while others have adopted a pragmatic, procedural method highlighting social relations. This latter approach is the one preferred by geographers and, as Angelo Torre (2011: 45) has pointed out, it is indebted to the theory of Pierre Bourdieu (1980) regarding the discussion of Montesquieu's *Esprit des lois*.

Island scholars have begun to focus on the claim that islands should be studied on their own terms, and some have labelled this interdisciplinary field of study 'nissology'. In particular, Godfrey Baldacchino, one of the most authoritative voices in the field of island studies, called 'for a recentering of the emphasis from mainland to island, away from the discourse of conquest of mainlanders, giving a voice to and a platform for the expression of island narratives' (2008: 37). Baldacchino's suggestion breaks away from the colonialist vision that has dominated the field of social sciences for so long, privileging the view of the continentals and paying little attention to the perception that islanders have of themselves and to the way in which they approach the Other when making political demands.

The idea of a new 'island science' appeared for the first time in 1982 in 'Nissonologie ou Science des îles' by the French sociologist Abraham André Moles (1982: 281–9). In a book written together with Élisabeth Rohmer, Moles used psychogeography to explore the mechanisms underpinning the semanticization of space, observing that spatial representations are the social and symbolic expression of an ideological appropriation of space (1978: 69). Every territory is a space experienced by human beings sharing a history, culture, language and religion. This perspective attributes great importance to the geographical impact upon the collective consciousness of island populations. Moles brings together a phenomenological analysis of human behaviour with an analysis more closely connected to the psychoanalysis of the space. From this perspective, our vision of the world is conditioned by the physical place in which we grew up and where we spend our daily lives. There are topological structures of space that take on a negative or positive value according to the value attributed to them by each individual, drawing upon their own unique experience. According to the definition of the geographical sciences, the term 'island' literally refers to a portion of land completely surrounded by water, however, it has a far more profound meaning for islanders: this physical break with the continent determines an age-old awareness of their limits that are recognized to the extent to which the maritime boundary is crossed in order to reach the mainland. Islands only exist in the moment in which they impose themselves upon our perception (Moles 1982: 284). The determining criteria defining an island is 'consciousness of insularity', in other words, the islanders' perception of a specifically insular otherness going beyond physical and natural properties.

The awareness of living on an island depends first and foremost upon the collective perceptions of islanders and upon the manner in which they represent the space that they inhabit. 'An island is considered small when each individual living there is aware that they are living in a territory surrounded by the sea', suggests French geographer Françoise Péron (1993: 3). Despite possessing specific geographic and physical qualities, islands – like all territorial spaces – are the product of social imaginaries that refer to perceptions, lived experiences and, most importantly, to myths and spatial ideologies. An island is a geographic notion that is subject to a human and social construction: for this reason, its isolation or its links to the mainland are the result of a process of inscription in the cultural space. It is no coincidence that the island space is frequently represented by means of a labyrinth: a place that, because of its dimensions, reveals the illusion of its complete knowability but that also reveals its intrinsic quality of mystery (Brazzelli 2012: 7). Therefore, as outlined by Pete Hay, 'place phenomenology works as a coherent theoretical framing for island studies' (2006: 34).

A decade or so after the insights expressed by Moles, researchers incorporated the concept into island studies (Vieira 2010: 18), and it was then that 'nissologie' (Depraetere 1990–91: 126–34) or 'nissology' emerged (McCall 1994: 1–14). In 1994, Grant McCall proposed the latter concept to provide a better understanding of insular spaces and to encourage international cooperation and networking among islands (1994: 2). One objective of nissology is to reverse the 'continental bias' and (re)place the study of islands by treating them as interconnected units of a 'world archipelago' (Depraetere 2008:17–36; Shell 2014: 21). For this reason, island scholars should '(re)inscribe the theoretical, metaphorical, real and empirical power and potential of the archipelago' (Stratford et al. 2011: 113). Jonathan Pugh invites us to begin 'thinking with the archipelago': this makes it possible to 'denaturalize space', emphasizing networks, mobility and connectivity. So doing we will stop responding 'to that absurd cry "History", associated with such grand narratives as progress, development and colonialism' (Pugh 2013: 20). As seen by Philip Hayward, this world archipelago becomes a 'world aquapelago' or 'an assemblage of the marine and land spaces of a group of islands and their adjacent waters', in which the aquapelagic society takes on the appearance of 'a social unit existing in a location in which the aquatic spaces between and around a group of islands are utilised and navigated in a manner that is fundamentally interconnected with and essential to the social group's habitation of land and their senses of identity and belonging' (2012: 5).

In recent years, there has been growing interest in islands because they have become 'paradigms for planetary transformation' (de Angelo Laky and Angliker 2021a: IX): they are like laboratories in which we can observe phenomena like rising sea levels, the acidification of the oceans, migration and the disappearance of traditional cultures. In a recent interview, Jonathan Pugh explained that islands play a key role in the international debate on the Anthropocene, not just because island territories are emblematic of human abuse of nature but also because they evoke an evolution of modern thought. As Pugh explains, the concept of resilience ties in very well with the conditions that may be generated in islands: not surprisingly, island spaces were used in the first studies into resilience in line with the Darwinian belief that islands are emblematic sites of adaptive relation (de Angelo Laky and Angliker 2021b). According to Pugh, 'it is in the context of Anthropocene thinking, where modern, command and control approaches are waning, in which the interest in human–non-human entanglement comes to the fore, that the concepts of island and islandness become interesting' (de Angelo Laky and Angliker 2021b: 269).

The mid-1980s onwards saw a rise in associations, bodies and institutions, at both regional and international level, which had the objective of creating a platform for debate concerning issues relevant to island regions. As we shall see, a particularly active and influential role would be played by the Islands Commission, the oldest of the Geographical Commissions of the Conference of Peripheral Maritime Regions of Europe (1980), by the International Small Islands Studies Association (ISISA) (1992), and by the European Small Islands Federation (ESIN) (2001), which were all involved in promoting comparative initiatives, studies and research. Among the higher education institutions introducing degree courses specializing in island studies were the universities of Malta, Maui in Hawaii, Prince Edward Island in Canada and the University of the West of Scotland in the UK. Various specialist journals were also published, starting with *The Contemporary Pacific*, published from 1989 onwards by the Center for Pacific Islands Studies at the University of Hawai'i. 2006 saw the publication of the *Island Studies Journal*; brought out at the initiative of Godfrey Baldacchino, it was the first interdisciplinary academic journal to be entirely dedicated to islands. In the editorial of the first issue, Baldacchino expressed the hope that different studies from heterogeneous disciplinary areas in search of a 'home' might all be brought under one roof (Baldacchino 2006: 8). This gave rise to the inspired decision to establish a completely open-access peer-reviewed journal (a rarity in the world of Anglo-US journals). The sensational, innovative nature of the methods employed by island studies was again confirmed in an editorial that appeared in 2016 in the *Island Studies Journal* whose editors, Yaso Nadarajah and Adam Grydehøj, underlined the fact that Island studies are first and foremost a 'decolonial project' (2016: 437–46).

2007 saw the birth of the journal *Shima*, in the context of the Division of Research at the Southern Cross University in Australia. These institutions and editorial initiatives take the shape as places where scholars of island regions can meet and share knowledge. As we will see in parallel with this renewed attention to island spaces in the human and social sciences, since the 1990s there has also been a growing interest of the EU in this spatial reality. Conceptually, however, the EU policies almost ignored nissology, preferring a more traditional understanding of island realities (Paci 2016b: 15–16).

The adoption of an interdisciplinary approach will allow the advancement of the field at European level. Island studies give us a frame of reference for the object of study, i.e., the island, seen as a space that is subjective and lived in, which is represented by a precise mental map.

Island studies help understand how islandness, i.e. the discourse about the geopolitical and cultural specificities, functions as a politically mobilizing factor. They also show how this affects the negotiations between insular peripheries and metropolitan centres, creating a special role for islands within national identity construction. However, the methods of island studies will be combined with those of history and political science. The investigation adopts the perspective of island studies, but goes on to extend the critical examination to their own islandness, assessing the extent to which the discourse about the 'isolated' territory and community of islanders itself becomes a tool for political consensus making, identity construction and power negotiation. In order to strengthen their position as tutors of insular interest and to legitimize themselves in the eyes of their electorate, local political elites frequently refer to islandness. They affect the cultural sense of belonging of their island fellows, sometimes attuning it to national narratives centred elsewhere, at other times shaping a self-referential centre of political attraction. The relation between the island peripheries and the mainland powers, with the sea as a liquid frontier between them, is therefore crucial for a region's mental mapping. The borders between island and mainland remain physically and conceptually fluid, requiring permanent negotiation and legitimization. This is why islandness cannot be understood solely by adopting the approach of island studies. As island identities are constructed by similar mechanisms as described by Benedict Anderson for nations, overarching perspectives of political and cultural studies are crucial ([1983] 1991). The inhabitants of an island form an 'imagined community' the geographic and mental delimitations of which remain ambiguous as they can easily shift from national to insular identities, and vice versa.

1

The Baltic Sea and Mediterranean regions as spaces of expectations

From the 1990s onwards, the historic Baltic and Mediterranean regions underwent a process of region building. In the wake of the dissolution of the Soviet Union, local political actors rediscovered a rhetoric of unity and regional cooperation inspired by the historic Hanse experience. In the Mediterranean region, the Barcelona Process and the Union for the Mediterranean sought to favour forms of cooperation with countries on the southern shores of the *mare nostrum*: these policies, which were pervaded with a Eurocentric rhetoric, proved inadequate in managing migratory flows. Although Baltic narratives presented the Baltic region as a model for the European Union's macro-regional strategy, the same cannot be said of the Mediterranean where the logic of the single states proved to be an insurmountable barrier. Imaginative geography allows us to observe how the Baltic region – and the Nordic states in general – tends to cultivate the expectations of cooperation within a geopolitical context, placing it within the European Union with Russia at the gates, while the Mediterranean region is struggling to glimpse unity and failing to manage migratory policies, thereby falling victim to a self-victimizing prejudice that relegates it to a peripheral role in the EU.

Spatial imaginations of the Baltic Sea and Mediterranean region

In geographical, geopolitical and cultural terms, the Mediterranean and Baltic islands lie within two historic regions – the Baltic Sea and Mediterranean regions – which have undergone a process of region building, as we will now see.

Narratives about the Baltic and Mediterranean are based on a dialectic of inclusion–exclusion. The area of research associated with the history of international relations that can be traced back to imaginative geography and discursive constructionism implies that, in as far as a territory exists, there will always be a representation and that the two areas of geography and imagination may not always coincide perfectly. For this reason, discourses on the Baltic and Mediterranean promoted by the political institutions also contribute to the construction process of a maritime imaginary. As a result, in order to describe a region we must ask ourselves why and how it is defined (Benigno 2009). The Baltic and Mediterranean are not objective autonomous physical cultural entities but the outcome of processes of mental mapping. These processes have undergone profound shifts and reconfigurations influenced by changing geopolitical situations like the Cold War, European integration and the 2008 financial and economic crisis.

The Baltic and Mediterranean are first and foremost symbolic spaces: their identities are shaped by suggestive ideas that 'seek to define or carve out a space but that actually end up by evoking images, sensations, and values' (Benigno 2013: 221). The imagination of space takes hold of physical conditions, but is bound up with power structures and strategies of legitimization. The sea has freed itself from its purely physical dimension to become a concept charged with symbols. Let us see how the historical narrative regarding a sea is completely detached from 'the determinisms of political stories – of a limited duration – and national stories – which are historicist and ideological in themselves' (Ivetic 2019: 18).

The spatial identification and mental mapping in the Baltic Sea and Mediterranean regions depend on changing historical circumstances. This interpretative approach, close to postcolonial studies, conducts us to a kind of imaginative geography, which refers to the vision of a spatiality conceived as a symbolic territory crossing all areas of social existence (Said 1978). In an attempt to denaturalize western mental maps regarding the Arab world, Edward Said noted how the nature of places is used to determine spatial images that reveal an Orientalist conception based on exclusion. According to Said, this type of creation of spatial images should be located within the interpretive structure of a dominant community seeking to legitimize its hegemony over other communities (Carta 2012: 55). Moreover, as outlined by Janne Holmén, in the 2000s, historians used the mental map concept 'to describe the worldviews of political leaders, the French colonial mind, or images of the Baltic Sea region' (Holmén 2020: 124–5). The imagination of space is based on physical conditions, but is connected with power structures, communication patterns, strategies of legitimization, ideological categorization and national projections.

If we follow the paths of imaginative geography, we will see how the space of experience and the horizon of anticipation, which should not be defined as complementary and symmetrical concepts according to Reinhardt Koselleck ([1979] 2004), are actually 'so tightly interrelated to represent reciprocal preconditions' (Petri 2016a: 8). If, as Koselleck suggests, experience is a present past in which events have been collected and reunified in order to be remembered while anticipation is a 'presentified' future looking towards something that cannot yet be experienced, we can catch a glimpse in EU policies of the desire to look towards a horizon of anticipation, which sees the 're'unification of these spaces as an improvement on the current situation. Therefore, by reunifying territorial regions like the Baltic Sea region, which according to the narrative once upon a time belonged to each other and had to break off their relations following the introduction of the Iron Curtain, it would have been possible to envisage a better future (Petri 2016a: 8–9).

Vasileios Petrogiannis, who carried out a study into the imaginaries and expectations of immigrants from Greece and Latvia in Sweden, showed how national belonging remains the foremost level of self-identification (2020). According to him, although migration is located within a fluid identity space, the political projects that have been launched with the aim of creating a Baltic Sea region have not been capable of giving rise to a sense of belonging to a macroregional space (2020: 292).

The Baltic Sea and Mediterranean regions are spatial constructs that have become the focus of political interest. However, the overall impact of macro-regional thinking has been limited given that these region-building projects have been overshadowed by the primacy of nation states and the European Union. Moreover, if we observe EU politics, we can see how the eastern coastal areas have been excluded from the Baltic area while the southern shore of the Mediterranean has been placed in a subordinate position within the Mediterranean overall. Smaller regions, such as the Baltic republics, the Nordic countries, Southern Europe, or the Balkans, play a greater role in people's imaginations. Moreover, when comparing these two sea regions, a certain asymmetry of our comparative framework becomes apparent: on the one hand, the Baltic Sea region is associated with the idea of cooperation and the economic growth of the European Union, while on the other, the Mediterranean Sea region, which is by definition the cradle of Western civilization, is the very expression of humanitarian emergency, uncontrolled migration and economic stagnation. The Mediterranean region experiences a duplicity that we can summarize, reformulating Chris Rumford's expression, as the coexistence of a 'network Mediterranean' and of the 'fortress Mediterranean' (2008). Therefore, it is precisely because of the porous nature of its frontiers that the European union will find the securitization of the maritime margins of Europe to be one of its main challenges. The macro-regionalization of the European space moves around two narratives: a 'seascape', 'a discourse that relies on the representation of the sea as an open space of networking' and a 'borderscape' 'a counter-discourse partially contradicting the seascape narrative while relying on it, for the very nature of maritime openness demands regulation and control' (Bialasiewicz, Giaccaria, Jones and Minca 2013: 65). And it is precisely in this 'inner tension between "seascapes" and "borderscapes"' that we find 'a distinctive spatial imagination and "meta-geography" that underpins the idea (and practice) of macro-regions' (Bialasiewicz, Giaccaria, Jones and Minca 2013: 65).

The Baltic Sea region as a space of expectations

Nine EU member states with different historic heritages and cultural and linguistic traditions – Denmark, Germany, Poland, Lithuania, Latvia, Estonia, Finland, Sweden and Russia – border the Baltic Sea, a semi-enclosed sea basin with a total area of 397,978 km². The Baltic Sea can be divided into the following subregions: the Gulf of Finland, the Gulf of Bothnia, the Gulf of Riga, Baltic Proper (which includes the Gulf of Gdansk), the Danish Straits and the Kattegat (European MSP Platform 2021). Together they form a unique spatial entity that is the so-called Baltic Sea region (Götz 2014). For many years, this region was the object of interest of various powers seeking dominion – often in conflict – since the sixteenth and seventeenth centuries when Sweden and Denmark clashed over the control of the Baltic sea. In the context of the *dominium maris Baltici* (Baltic Sea dominion), Sweden became a major European power and the Baltic became Sweden's internal sea. In the eighteenth century, the Russian Empire became Sweden's main contender and in the nineteenth century, Sweden lost its primacy over the Baltic. In the twentieth century, the Soviets had already envisaged a notion of a Baltic region that would create a connection between Russia and the Baltic.

On the occasion of a conference held in November 2014 at Ca' Foscari University of Venice with the title 'Comparative Area and Transregional Studies. A Framework for the Baltic and the Mediterranean', Jörg Hackmann outlined major narratives attached to spatial images of the Baltic Sea region within the nations bordering the southern and eastern shores. The first narrative referred to the *dominium maris Baltici*, that is, to the wars fought in the sixteenth and early seventeenth centuries by Denmark and Sweden in an attempt to gain dominion over the Baltic Sea. The expression *dominium maris Baltici* appeared as a notion criticizing first Danish control of the Öresund and Swedish early modern politics of domination. The second narrative regards the so-called 'German(ic) Sea' and therefore regards German dominion: this rhetoric took shape in the nineteenth century and emerged after the First World War against Slav nations and Russia / Soviet Union in particular. A third narrative is linked to the notion of 'access to the sea' which we can relate to the foundation of St. Petersburg by Peter the Great: this was an act against the Swedish domination of the Baltic Sea and of access to the sphere of European great poker. Access to the Baltic became a major political, economic and military strategy of interwar Poland as shown by Poland's symbolic 'wedding to the sea' (Zaślubiny Polski z morzem), a nationalist ceremony based on a Venetian ritual, which was held in

January 1920 in Puck at the initiative of General Józef Haller to evoke Poland's winning back access to the Baltic Sea, which had been lost after the 1793 partition. This ceremony was repeated at the Pomeranian shore in Kołobrzeg in 1945 after the Soviet-Polish advance in Pomerania. A fourth third narrative refers to the 'Sea of Freedom' and goes back to the end of the First World War when the Baltic riparian countries gained greater margins of autonomy after the 1917 Russian revolutions and Finnish Independence. This enabled them to normalize shipping and to do their best to collaborate in stabilizing the freedom of the Baltic Sea. It was then that the activist circles including German, Swedish, Finnish and Estonian nationalist region-builders began to nourish hopes of creating – at Russia's expense – a new post-war Baltic Sea region with Sweden as its leading regional power. They began to join their efforts to form a 'new Mare Nostrum Balticum' (Kuldkepp 2015: 249–86).

The last narrative, the so-called 'New Hanse' refers to economic co-operation as a factor of region building. In the twentieth century, the Iron Curtain, the boundary line running along the Baltic, separated East from West. The fall of the Wall and the end of the Cold War represented a hiatus in the history of the Baltic area. This saw the emergence of an idea of unity in the spirit of cooperation going back to the times of the Hanseatic League, in the thirteenth century, and that became tangible on a political level through the Union of Kalmar, which unified the kingdoms of Denmark, Sweden and Norway in a single sovereign entity in the fifteenth and sixteenth centuries.

The Nordic Council was set up during the early years of the Cold War (1952) at the initiative of Denmark, Iceland, Norway and Sweden. Finland joined in 1955, followed by the Faroe Islands and Åland in 1970, and Greenland in 1984. These three autonomous island countries – the Faroe Islands, Greenland and Åland – were to have an important impact on Nordic co-operation since the Åland Document was adopted by the Ministers for Nordic co-operation in Mariehamn, Åland, on 5 September 2007. This document also recognizes the right of these regions to equal participation in Nordic co-operation together with the other countries belonging to the Nordic Council (Nordic Co-operation 2007). During the Cold War, the countries in the Nordic Baltic area waved the flag of their 'exceptionalism' and of the Nordic model as a third way of democracy, peace and social well-being. The rhetoric of peace and prosperity became the driver of politics in the region: the political actors took on the role of mediators, 'as bridge-builders in the East-West conflict' (Browning 2007: 33). In 1961 the Finnish President Urho Kekkonen declared to the UN General Assembly that 'We see ourselves as physicians rather than judges; it is not for us to pass judgement nor to condemn, it is rather to diagnose and to try to cure' (Browning 2007: 33). Some years later, in 1966, the Baltic Sea Commission – one of six geographical commissions that make up the Conference of Peripheral and Maritime Regions (CPMR) – was founded as a forum for policy-oriented cooperation and a platform for cooperation amongst Regional Authorities in the Baltic Sea region. His main goal is to support and implement the EU Strategy of the Baltic Sea region.

The day of 31 October 1978 was a watershed moment in the history of the Baltic area: it marked the beginning of the rediscovery of the Hanseatic League. The city of Zwolle in the Netherlands called upon fifty-seven Hanseatic cities to revive the Hanseatic spirit and to draw inspiration for the future from a period of economic cooperation that extended beyond national borders (Escach 2011: 77). From 23 to 27 August 1980, the city of Zwolle (Netherlands) hosted the 'Hanseatic Days of Modern Times' which marked the rebirth of a network of cities known as the 'new Hanseatic world'. This led to the rediscovery of a tradition dating back to the time of the medieval Hanseatic League and inspired by the Hanse Day, which took place every year from 1356 to 1669 and provided the member towns and cities with an opportunity to meet and make joint decisions about matters of collective interest. Today, Hanseatic Days are again being held in various cities of the New Hanseatic League; Visby in Gotland hosted this initiative in 1998, the year marking the introduction of the concept of the youth Hanse, that is, the participation by young people aged between sixteen and twenty-five in the Hanseatic Days. We could also mention the 'Städtebund DIE HANSE', an initiative co-funded by the COSME programme of the European Union, which is a voluntary community of cities that aims at supporting tourism and continuing the tradition of the Hanseatic League of the Middle Ages and early modern times. Moreover, we should also point out that Bundeszentrum Lubeck is the seat of the new Hanseatic Office and the Mayor of Lübeck is the President of the New Hanseatic League (Graumann and Affeldt 2020: 12).

However, we have the then President of Schleswig Holstein Björn Engholm to thank for creating the concept of New Hanse in 1988. Fearing that the region under his administration would end up on the margins of Europe, he realized the urgency of establishing cooperation between the regions belonging to the Hanseatic League in order to maximize the value added that they could produce: high productivity, capacity for innovation and ecological awareness (Escach 2011: 77). According to Engholm, the constitution of networks of cities would play a crucial role in countering nationalistic tendencies, creating spaces for transnational cooperation route and this would have been facilitated by the so-called 'Hanseatic identity' (Escach 2011: 73). 1990 saw the organization of 'The New Hanse' conference in Kotka on the Gulf of Finland. This interesting choice of venue confirms that the New Hanse concept was interpreted and conceived as a metaphor to highlight the idea of cooperation: in fact, this Finnish town had never been a Hanseatic city but its position was useful in promoting the new concept (Gerner 2002: 53). The notion of New Hanse was rather ambiguous, in fact. In a speech given in Bremen on 29 May 1991, Engholm sought rather clumsily to place Germany at the centre of the New Hanse: 'I am not speaking about a weak Europe with a greater Germany in its centre but about a strong Europe in which Germany, which is now greater, makes a massive contribution' (Escach 2011: 79). This ambiguity emerges if we consider these matters from the perspective of Denmark or Norway: here the Hanseatic League evokes a period of German domination. In 1992, the then Danish Minister of Foreign Affairs Uffe Ellemann-Jensen stated, 'We Danes fought a war against the Hanseatic League. We should remember that the centre of the Hanseatic League was Lübeck, its language was German, and its sphere of influence stretched from Novgorod to London' (Escach 2011: 79).

The concept of the New Hanse connects to the post-modern definition of region: while the modern region was territorial and state-oriented, involved the presence of intergovernmental organizations, and was based on multilateral relations, the postmodern region revolves around the connections and relations established with actors from neighbouring countries, around cooperation between territories, and, last but not least, the will to build an advantageous relationship with civil society. As Nicolas Escach notes, when envisaging the New Hanse, Björn Engholm intended to refer to 'governance not government, to bottom up rather than top down [...] to cooperation rather than to coordination [...] to decentralization rather than concentration, in short, to a neo-medieval rather than a neo-West Phalian model' (2011: 78). In 1994, the expression New Hanse was replaced by the rather more neutral term of Baltic Sea region.

The fall of the Iron Curtain saw a variety of political actors affirming the existence of a regional Baltic Sea identity, which emerged increasingly emphatically on the occasion of public discourses. Therefore, the dismantling of the east–west border opened the way for a process of regionalization (Blanc-Noël 2002). It was then that a new type of space was imagined in which it would be possible to bring about real cooperation and integration. This was followed by the development of a series of political and academic projects proposing to 'transform these imaginations into reality' (Grzechnik 2016: 29) along with the emergence of a new regionalism standing as an antithesis to Cold War regionalism because of its rejection of the typical logic of the bipolarism that had distinguished the history of the area. On the contrary, it presented itself as a grass-roots response to challenges posed by globalization. As pointed out by Jussi Kurunmäki, this saw the diffusion of a series of ideas of de-territorialization, rescaling, cross-border cooperation, integration that connected to a regional framework. This narrative was present in the discourse of multilevel governance, which was considered an 'antidote to the democratic deficit the European political integration entailed, and thought of as being able to combine the local, national, and supranational spheres of democracy' (Kurunmäki 2016: 44).

The Baltic was defined as a 'historic region' thus giving rise to a series of discussions on the theme of identity and memory. The stories marking the history of the Baltic were therefore defined as transnational stories (Grzechnik 2016: 31). Baltic Sea regionalism became an alternative to the nation state. From that moment on, a series of research centres were set up, reflecting the desire to represent the Baltic region as a large unitary cooperative community distinguished by a marked cultural dynamism. Among the many examples of this, we might point out the Baltic University Programme founded in 1991 and coordinated at Uppsala. This programme stemmed from the idea of proposing an international programme of cooperation between universities and other institutions of higher education in the Baltic Sea region. As we can read on its website, 'the main aim is to enhance strong regional educational and research communities, but also to foster a greater awareness on our focus areas. The BUP focuses on questions of sustainable development, environmental protection, and democracy in the Baltic Sea region' (Uppsala Universitet 2021). In 1992, it was decided to establish the Council of the Baltic Sea States (CBSS), an intergovernmental political forum for cooperation in the Baltic Sea region. This was followed a year later by the establishment of the Baltic Sea States Subregional Co-operation (BSSSC), a political network for decentralized authorities in the Baltic Sea region. The organization was founded in Stavanger, Norway, in 1993. Its participants are regional authorities from Germany, Denmark, Finland, Sweden, Norway, Poland, Latvia, Lithuania, Estonia and Russia.

In 1994, the Östersjöstiftelsen (The Baltic Sea Foundation) was founded at the initiative of the Swedish government with the aim of providing economic support for research activities in natural, human and social sciences regarding the Baltic region. Two years later, the Södertörns högskola was set up. In 2005, a Centre for Baltic and East European Studies (CBEES), directly linked to the Östersjöstiftelsen, was established at Södertörn University in Stockholm with the aim of organizing workshops and seminars, and of carrying out research studies into the region.

The Baltic Sea region – seen by the collective imaginary as an area of peace and conflict resolution – is first and foremost an expression of identity strongly supported not only by the policymakers of the Baltic area but also by large swathes of its political experts and media. In fact, it is no coincidence that Sweden is home to the Stockholm International Peace Research Institute (SIPRI, founded in 1966), an independent international institute funded by the Swedish government and dedicated to research into conflicts, armaments and arms control in a global context. SIPRI has a representative in Beijing and works assiduously together with intergovernmental organizations including the United Nations and European Union; it also periodically invites and hosts researchers and academic and government delegations. Another study centre promoting research on issues linked to security, peace, conflicts and the rights of minorities is the Ålandsfredsinstitut. Established in 1992, in Mariehamn on the Åland islands, the Ålandfredsinstitut is an independent charitable foundation, which carries out numerous research activities in cooperation with other national and international organizations, beginning with the consideration that the statute of the Åland archipelago can be a useful model for other areas with similar characteristics: in fact, this is a Swedish-speaking demilitarized zone in the Finnish state, with a right to self-government endorsed by specific international guarantees going back to 1922. The scale and international relevance of the Ålandfredsinstitut is attested by its assiduous relationships with scholars, journalists and politicians from the southern Caucasus, Japan, China, Middle East, Balkans, Iran and Central America.

As Pauli Kettunen has pointed out, European integration has activated a context conducive to discussion about the models that should be followed in order to create a competitive Europe within the global economic market. In fact, the Nordic model has a whole series of characteristics evoking positive images connected to the progress, modernization, internationalism and Third Worldism (Kettunen 2006: 645). In particular, the status of the Åland islands is presented as a model of integration and peaceful resolution of conflicts that can be transposed elsewhere (Chillaud 2009; Paci 2016a). As pointed out by Sia Spiliopoulou Åkermark, political analysts, academics and politicians all use the term 'model' of the Åland islands to emphasize how the potential expressed by this Finnish archipelago can be a source of inspiration, a platform for reciprocal discussions leading to negotiations and crisis management (2009: 229). In 1992, Roger Jansson, the Deputy Speaker on the Åland Parliament, declared at the Second Parliamentary Conference on Co-operation in the Baltic Sea Area held in Oslo that the Åland islands – 'The islands of peace in the sea of peace' – represented a model for the other regions in the Baltic (Hägerhäll Aniansson 1992: 34).

Drawing upon the expressions used by Iver Neumann, Marta Grzechnik described how the Baltic region was 'written into existence': this means that academics as well as political actors took on the role of 'region builders', imagining a certain spatial identity and diffusing this imagined identity in the outside world. This operation, which was cultural and political at the same time, led to the affirmation of a shared identity based on a shared historical heritage. For this reason, this theory would have needed the support of historical narratives capable of highlighting the validity of this assumption and therefore of the existence of the historic Baltic region (Grzechnik 2016: 33). According to Grzechnik 'the Baltic Sea region has become an established unit of scholarly reflection, a frame of reference for projects and research in different fields, which attests to the fact that at least in some sense it has been talked into existence, and some of the expectations have been fulfilled' (Grzechnik 2016: 34). In fact, the Baltic Sea region is a cultural and political construct that places itself 'at an intersection of other regional frameworks of identification' (Grzechnik 2016: 41), that is, from the north with the Scandinavian or Nordic region and from the south with the region defined as central or central-eastern Europe, labels revealing definitional difficulties.

The notion of region makes it possible to understand the 'stable state of instability' of the Baltic space (Paci 2018: 195) and – as Norbert Götz points out – avoids falling into the trap of essentialism (2016: 55–6). Discourses about region building often refer to Fernand Braudel's *The Mediterranean and the Mediterranean World in the Age of Philip II* ([1949] 2008) given that the discourse on the 'Mediterranean of the North' seeks to dismantle stereotyped images like those suggesting that the history of the Baltic region was shaped by wars and that this maritime basin was for many years an arena of confrontation and rivalries for power. The expression 'Mediterranean of the North' acts as a narrative device whose purpose is to fully evoke the metaphor of peace, prosperity and cooperation. This political brand alludes to the ancient vocation of the region as a communication route between all of the countries bordering the Baltic (Grzechnik 2012: 334). As the Latvian diplomat and journalist Alfrēds Bīlmanis wrote in 1945, 'the Baltic Sea has a certain analogy with the Mediterranean: it separates and at the same time it unites the riparian Baltic countries – Germany, Denmark, Sweden, Finland, Russia, Estonia, Latvia, Lithuania, and Poland – just as the Mediterranean separates and unites the continents of Europe, Africa, and Asia Minor (3-4)'.

There is a strand of the historiography of the Baltic area, whose main exponents are Matti Klinge (1994) and David Kirby (1995), which claims that the 'Baltic World' constitutes a shared cultural sphere comparable with Braudel's Mediterranean. The books of both scholars carry a title inspired by Braudel. While Braudel's structuralist approach assigned the Mediterranean the function of living entity, the aforementioned historiography was convinced of the idea that the sea was an integrative factor for the states and societies around its shores. From this perspective, the Cold War represented an exception within an age-old integration process. Very different arguments were put forward by Bo Stråth (2000: 199-214), who warned the community of historians away from a kind of environmental determinism, that is, an approach implying a unitary vision of the history of the Baltic world, reminding them to bear in mind the heritage of disintegration and the continuous conflict around the Baltic rim (Stöcker 2018: 3).

Braudel's longue durée, in a perspective of cooperation, legitimized the vision of a united Baltic Sea region. 1991 saw the institution of the inter-parliamentary Baltic Sea Parliamentary Conference (BSPC), a forum for political dialogue between parliamentarians from the Baltic Sea region. It was given the role of promoter of transnational democracy. In 1992, the former President of the Nordic Council, Ilkka Souminem, declared at the Second Parliamentary Conference on Co-operation in the Baltic Sea Area that

> I find it surprising how quickly the Baltic Sea Area has been able to make a new start [...] Because of the new opportunities, the area has gained a position as one of the so-called "creativity corridors" in Europe. The results are already so striking that the region has been referred to as "the Mediterranean of the North", analogous maybe to Italy, with its magnificent history, which has now become one of the wealthiest countries in Europe.
>
> (Hägerhäll Aniansson 1992: 10)

If we dwell on the rhetoric employed by members of the BSPC, we will see that there was less a real desire to contribute to the formation of a civil society, a public opinion and a regional identity than the wish to favour 'the interests of their national constituencies, and represent the state of belonging as if the assembly were a diplomatic arena' (Petri 2016a: 10). The existence of the BSPC reveals that 'there is more nation state logic in regional democracy than what the theories of regionalism and transnational democracy usually recognize'

(Kurunmäki 2016: 55). It is precisely the predominance of the nation states and the presence of other regional divisions that prevented the Baltic Sea region from representing an 'attractive alternative' (Grzechnik 2016: 42).

The accession of Finland and Sweden to the European Union in 1995 followed by the entry, in 2004, of Estonia, Latvia, Lithuania and Poland, had a considerable impact on the political integration of the Baltic area. According to Götz, from 2004 onwards, regional cooperation in the Baltic became an 'exogenously designed project based in EU headquarters in Brussels' (2016: 62). He goes on to claim that 'Baltic Sea integration lost momentum after the 2004 enlargement of the EU, and has continued to do so over the past decade with the increasing estrangement and eventual rift between Russia and the West' (Götz 2016: 63).

The European Union Strategy for the Baltic Sea Region (EUSBSR) is the first macro-regional Strategy in Europe. The Commission presented its Communication on the EUSBSR on 10 June 2009 alongside a detailed Action Plan which was the result of extension consultation between the Member States and stakeholders. The 2010 document on EU Strategy for the Baltic Sea region set out to 'enable a sustainable environment, enhance the region's prosperity, increase accessibility and attractiveness and ensure its safety and security' (EUR-Lex 2015). The key objectives of the EUSBSR can be summed up in three appeals: 1) 'Save the sea'; that is, prevent the dumping of toxic waste in the sea and overfishing; 2) 'Connect the region' or, in other words, improve transport connections and energy security; 3) 'Increase prosperity' through the creation of partnerships and policies capable of favouring the successful integration of refugees into the labour market and society (Van Lierop 2020: 2). With regard to the islands, attention was drawn to the urgency of improving the maritime transport system; as specified in the 2009 Action Plan: 'links to islands and remote communities are a specific issue' (EUSBSR 2009: 43).

Although EUSBSR was the first macro-regional strategy to have been created, we are still waiting for a macro-regional strategy for the Mediterranean, the reason being that 'the developmental differences between the countries of the Mediterranean are such that the priorities of the countries of the southern Mediterranean differ significantly from those of their northern neighbours, making it difficult to agree on a set of common priorities for a possible macro-regional strategy in the Mediterranean' (Van Lierop 2021: 1).

The Mediterranean Sea region as a space of expectations

Eight EU member states – Italy, France, Spain, Malta, Slovenia, Croatia, Cyprus, Greece – have coasts on the Mediterranean basin. In 2002, the then President of the European Commission, Romano Prodi, gave a speech at the Université Catholique de Louvain tackling the thorny question of EU relations with the countries on the 'other' side of the Mediterranean that mentioned how Mercator had noted that the Mediterranean was given different names depending upon the shores it washed up against (2002). The various names given to the Mediterranean show how this sea adapts to different mindsets: 'our sea' (Mare nostrum) for the Romans; 'great sea' (Yam gadol) for the Jews; 'middle sea' (Mittelmeer) for the Germans; 'great green' for the ancient Egyptians; and 'white sea' (Ak Deniz) for the Ottomans (Abulafia 2011).

In his *Lectures on the Philosophy of History*, Hegel described the Mediterranean as 'the cradle of civilisation and as its raison d'être, that sea without which the Old World would never have produced Rome or Athens' ([1837] 2001: 105). These Hegelian views testify to the tendency to consider the Mediterranean as a place of civilization – a notion that makes of it a European space. It was on the back of this kind of reasoning that the conceptual development of the Mediterranean seen as a 'greater Mediterranean' or 'greater Europe' was elaborated. It is about the space of the Euro-Mediterranean Union: a naturally and culturally united space, one in which a collective humanity imbued with its own unique character lives. This tendency, which would last until the Second World War, sought to associate the term civilization with the civilization that had the Mediterranean as its cradle and whose 'roots' lay in the Christian Graeco-Roman-Germanic tradition (Bono 2016: 122).This idea has its origins in the late seventeenth century when explorers, merchants and navigators were outlining a 'new Mediterranean geography' through accounts drafted for their rulers.

The Mediterranean – intended as a 'rhetorical space' – has historically lent itself to different uses, coming to be employed as a rhetorical tool apt for determining the balance of geopolitical power. As Michael Drolet observed, the Mediterranean has become a 'new civilizational geopolitical space' (2015: 150): from geographical object, this sea has progressively assumed the appearance of a cultural entity charged with significant symbols and ideologies for the use and consumption of geopolitics. The metaphor of the Mediterranean and the representation of this maritime space as an arena of conflict and division has been the object of a deep reflection by Rolf Petri who has enquired into the geopolitical significance, in particular delving into the reasons why the idea prevails that history is a 'generator of spatial order' (2016b: 671–91). As Giancarlo Monina has observed 'the culture of "free seas", without national borders and not subject to territorial sovereignty, is definitively substituted by a conception of the sea as "territory"; the idea of control is substituted by that of conquest' (2008: 99). The idea of the Mediterranean as a unity is a creation of nineteenth-century intellectuals who represented, whether explicitly or implicitly, the ambitions of northern European powers in the Mediterranean. Napoleon's expedition to Egypt in 1798–1801 marked the beginning of the invention of the Mediterranean as a region organized following colonial principles. As outlined by Rolf Petri 'Napoleon, who evokes "history" to sanctify his action, is an excellent mouthpiece of the Mediterranean metaphor' (2016b: 675). Indeed, as Manuel Borutta and Sakis Gekas have noted, 'the Mediterranean has been a colonial sea since ancient times. It was "the first sea to be colonized"' (2012: 2).

The French concept of Mediterranean as an essentially European unitary geographic space was developed by historians, geographers, cartographers and anthropologists who contributed to the creation of colonist narratives through their description of this sea as the cradle of European civilization; Muslims and Arabs, on the other hand, were conceived as foreigners who had settled in the European space and colonization was greeted as the resurrection of Christian Latin Africa and reappropriation of the European space. In his *Nouvelle Géographie Universelle* (1876–95), the French geographer Élisée Reclus defined the Mediterranean not only as a geographic region but also as the cradle of Western civilization, attributing to it supremacy over all the other seas. The Mediterranean was described as a primordial site not only for Europe but for the entire world, the site of diffusion of European civilization. His description of the world started with southern Europe and the Mediterranean (Deprest 2002: 80). These ideas were expressed in the 1830s by followers of Claude Henri de Saint-Simon, whose ideals were clearly shared by Reclus. In particular, Reclus made frequent references in his work to the Saint-Simonian apostles who followed Émile Barrault to Egypt in 1833 on a quest to find the 'Femme-Messie' destined to join with their spiritual father 'Pere' Prosper Enfantin. These so-called 'compagnons de la femme' became involved in the building of the Suez Canal joining the Mediterranean and the Red Sea, an idea that tied in with the desire to join the East and West in matrimony. Reclus was fascinated by those phantasmagorical projects of social-economic renewal that came under the umbrella of a pacifist universalism (Ferretti 2011: 45).

This current of universalistic ideas found the ideal spokesman in the Saint-Simonian Michel Chevalier. The economist and future economic advisor to

Napoleon III became the obligatory point of reference for the Saint-Simonian's vision of the Mediterranean. Chevalier wrote a series of articles that were subsequently collected in a work entitled *Le Système de la Méditerranée*. Chevalier called for the development of intra-Mediterranean networks while all the time preserving the particularities of each state or each political sphere. The proposed system became symbol of the 'universal association': 'Now the Mediterranean must become like a vast forum of discussion on all the points that have divided the peoples. The Mediterranean will become the marriage bed of the East and the West' (Chevalier 1832: 126). Chevalier conceived of the Mediterranean as a place of communion between East and West, as the centre of a great system, a sort of 'human body' (Debrune 2001: 191–2). This idea of the Mediterranean as a unitary and homogeneous cultural space was at the origins of representations of the Mediterranean later devised by many French geographers. Paul Vidal de La Blache's *Géographie Universelle* (1927–48) caused the Mediterranean, which was also a 'terrestrial' world, to acquire a space of consecration. The homogeneity of the landscape and climate were a specific feature of the Mediterranean and the bordering lands, conditioning the daily lives of the people living there (Deprest 2002: 84). Fernand Braudel took up Vidal de La Blache's interpretative model, developing it further in his celebrated work in which he presented the Mediterranean as a unitary subject whose capacity to exert environmental conditioning impacts the lives of all of the populations dwelling on its shores (Benigno 2009). Braudel sought to divide the temporal complexities of history into three levels, 'les événements, which is the short political and military history of events, les conjunctures, the interrelated medium duration cycles (moyenne durée) of groups, institutions, economy and social structures and last, les longues durées, which is the history of the almost unchanging structures in mentality, technologies and landscape' (Rönnby 2007: 67).

In the 1930s, the Mediterranean was re-examined in the light of colonial projects and the advent of various forms of Fascism. A vision of the Mediterranean as the apex of the communion of peoples and of a Humanist renewal was developed primarily by French intellectuals associated with the literary journal *Cahiers du Sud*, which was founded by the writer Jean Ballard in Marseilles in 1925. In August 1937, its monthly bulletin *Jeune Méditerranée* featured the lecture given by the philosopher Albert Camus to mark the inauguration of the Maison de la Culture in Algiers. In it he condemns without reservation the nationalistic and fascistic theories embodied by Charles Maurras and his followers who transmitted a 'twisted' bleak vision of Latinity (Foxlee 2010). In

1936, on the occasion of the opening of the Centre Universitaire Méditerranéen, the poet Paul Valéry claimed that Mediterranean humanism had been provided him with inspiration for his 'General Programme of Mediterranean studies' (Canale Cama, Casanova and Delli Quadri 2009: 328). A similar line of thought was espoused by essayist Gabriel Audisio from Marseille in his article *Vers une synthèse méditerranéenne*, published in *Cahiers du Sud* in March 1936: 'I am a citizen of the Mediterranean, on condition that my fellow citizens are all the peoples of the sea, including Jews, Arabs, Berbers, and blacks' (Temine 2000: 60). At the other extreme, a reactionary fascistic view emerged between the wars, which focused on the civilization process originating with the Roman Empire. The concept of *mare nostrum* referring to the ostensible Italian supremacy in the Mediterranean was to be the ideological and strategic backbone of fascist Italy's foreign policy (Paci 2015a). Mussolini transformed this sea into the stage of Italian foreign policy, building 'the great theatre of an imaginary Mediterranean, a zone of natural influence determined by history and by the demands of a nation in arms' (Frascani 2008: 131).

The Mediterranean was characterized as a site of exchange and conflict. 1996 saw the publication of *The Clash of Civilizations and the Remaking of World Order* in which political scientist Samuel P. Huntington predicted a clash between the 'Islamic civilization' and 'western civilization', portraying the Mediterranean as a border between Christianity and Islam (1996). Henri Pirenne himself believed Arab expansion to be responsible for bringing about the interruption of flows of exchange in the Mediterranean basin (1937). Theories of the clash of civilizations were criticized by those pointing out that religious conflict had not produced a separation between the two shores of the Mediterranean (Guarracino 2007). For example, in her analysis of the case of Malta, Anne Brogini noted that the Mediterranean was characterized by its fluid nature and by the coexistence of conflicts, exchanges and relations (2005). The Mediterranean is a transit route for trade that transcends cultural or religious diversities (Paci, Perri and Zantedeschi 2018: 10–11). It is also an urbanized space, a 'terraqueous landscape' (Cuppini 2018: 33–45), distinguished by the connections between people, goods and ideas that reveal as baseless the distinction between earth and sea put forward by Carl Schmitt ([1942] 2002: 18). In fact, Fernand Braudel described the maritime expanses making up the Mediterranean as 'liquid plains' ([1949] 2002: chap. 2). The liquid nature of the coastal territories, which represents the distinguishing feature of the Mediterranean, is the element that characterizes our modern society (Bauman 2000) and that brings with it all the contradictions associated with the desire to propose lasting, stable definitions, come what may.

This liquidity means that the Mediterranean must be continuously reconfigured. We should not forget, moreover, that the Mediterranean is also a space of migration and of migrants, appearing as a space of confluence acting as a bridge to Elsewhere. It is here that a shift in perspective takes place, transforming the Mediterranean from a Eurocentric space to a space capable of telling the stories of those dwelling on the opposite shore.

As pointed out by Francesco Benigno (2013: 226–9), we need to make a distinction between the Mediterranean of historians, on the one hand, and the Mediterranean of anthropologists, on the other, particularly those belonging to the Anglo-Saxon school. Between the 1960s and 1970s, the latter conceived the Mediterranean as a 'laboratory of identities', drawing criticism from numerous sides, starting with Michael Herzfeld (1984) who referred to *Mediterraneism* in similar terms to Said's *Orientalism* (1978). According to Herzfeld, the stance taken by this anthropological current reflected the western imaginary of the Mediterranean. In fact, Mediterraneanism proposed a stereotyped vision of Mediterranean countries, seen as victims of congenital backwardness, barbarisms and irrationality ingrained in its peoples who were shackled by the concept of patronage and shared a culture unlike that of north-west European countries. This Mediterraneanist stance therefore suffered from a 'flaw' resembling that of Orientalism, which placed science at the service of colonialism (Benigno 2009). And it is precisely this intrinsic flaw that caused the passion for the Mediterranean to be adopted as a reason substantiating the occasionally unmannerly Mediterranean 'temperament', which was sometimes distinguished by inefficiency and political incompetence (Petrusewicz 2018: 16). Moreover, as remarked by Paolo Giaccaria and Claudio Minca, Mediterraneanist narratives are based on the belief that it is possible to affirm the '"objective" existence of a geographical object called the Mediterranean' (2010: 348). Therefore, anyone putting forward this type of narrative is merely affirming the value of an 'interpretative framework that tends to essentialize and naturalize an otherwise intricate set of spatial processes and understanding' (Giaccaria and Minca 2010: 348).

The Mediterranean of the historians evolved from an object of historical interpretation, following the Braudelian paradigm, distinguished by different economic, social and political times, to a 'corrupting sea' (Horden and Purcell 2000), which created a system that was unitary – despite its diversities – in which convergences between the differences took place – by means of a system of interdependence of local contexts, distinguished by specificities and exceptions (Ivetic 2019: 13). The Braudelian Mediterranean is the one proposed by the

French historian through a description of long-term history around and on a sea. The classicist Nicholas Purcell and medievalist Peregrine Horden revisited the Braudelian idea of the natural and cultural unity of the Mediterranean space by developing an analytical method considering the Mediterranean basin as a 'fragmented topography of microregions', that is, a dynamic space with multiple interconnections, a fragmented world united by its very connectivity (2000).

The Mediterranean is a territory narrated. It is a place of intellectual communication. The authors emphasize how the diversity and fragmentation of the Mediterranean region are accompanied by a general connectivity made possible by the ease of communication. This involves imagining the Mediterranean as a 'corrupting sea', in other words, as a sea influencing the different local contexts and that 'unites them through countless interdependencies, dictated by a generic sense of precariousness and by the need to move, so many minimal realities' (Ivetic 2019: 13). The approach to research proposed by Horden and Purcell is not one that seeks to 'make history' in the Mediterranean by reconstructing the stories of the nations and land empires that interacted in this great basin, one of the history of the Mediterranean, seeking instead to view this sea as a 'maritime body with its own unique characteristics that must be understood in their functioning in time' (Ivetic 2019: 13).

In 2003, the historian David Abulafia coordinated a collective volume entitled *The Mediterranean in History* that sought to distance itself both from the Braudelian paradigm and the interpretive approach proposed by Horden e Purcell, rejecting what he considered to be Braudel's environmental determinism (2003). Abulafia highlighted the incisiveness of human action, conferring absolute centrality upon the sea and upon those who crossed it, putting the surrounding land masses in second place.

Let us take a look at how the Mediterranean takes shape as a 'fluid, changing [space] subject to negotiation' (Benigno 2013: 234). It is this very narrative that provided inspiration for the political policies of the European Union torn between the desire to guarantee security, on the one hand, and the wish to promote the economic and social development of the countries on the southern shores by implementing policies intended to help build a 'shared tangible and intangible Euro-Mediterranean heritage' (Capasso, Corona and Palmieri 2020: 18). The events marking the beginning and the epilogue of the European Mediterranean were the opening of the Suez Canal in 1869, which gave the Mediterranean basin a global strategic relevance, and the nationalization of the canal in 1956 by Gamal Abdel Nasser, the Egyptian president at the time, which decreed the end of the colonial period in this great sea (Bono 2016: 123). Decolonialization and the birth of the European economic community in 1957 put pay to this idea of Mediterranean unity: the birth of this new supranational organism, whose headquarters all look towards Atlantic Europe, was accompanied by a process of distancing from the Mediterranean while also establishing, from the early 1989s onwards, economic agreements with the Maghreb countries, although it was not until 1995 that they were established with the Barcelona Declaration (Bono 2016: 128).

From the very start, the political debate in the European Economic Community (EEC) focused on issues regarding relations with the Mediterranean countries. It was not until 1972 that an attempt was made to create a comprehensive legislative framework to regulate Euro-Mediterranean relations. The launch of the global Mediterranean policy favoured free circulation in the EEC of goods produced in the Mediterranean basin countries as well as an overall increase in cooperation. Nevertheless, the Israeli-Palestinian conflict of the period, the economic recession, and the 1973 energy crisis combined to push into the background the need to implement a policy of cooperation and development the area. The end of the Cold War and the fall of the Berlin Wall in 1989–90 marked the beginning of a new phase defined as redirected Mediterranean policy: this saw the launch of the Med Programmes promoted by the European Commission to fund projects developed by various institutional actors and to create networks of collaboration between Member countries and Mediterranean non-member countries (MED) in the context of matters relating to the environment, to education and research, as well as the promotion and protection of cultural heritage. In the early 1990s, the European Union engaged in a strategy of international cooperation with Mediterranean shore countries that would lead to the institution in 1995 of the Euro-Mediterranean Partnership, the so-called Barcelona Process. The 1995 Barcelona Declaration set out to create a 'common area of peace, stability, and security' between the Member States of the European Union and Mediterranean countries (Morocco, Algeria, Tunisia, Egypt, Israel, Jordan, Lebanon, Syria, Turkey). This partnership was based on three pillars known as 'baskets': the first – the Political and Security Basket – involved a commitment to seek stability in the Mediterranean area through the creation of a common area whose function was to bring about peace; the second – the Economic and Financial Basket – referred to the promotion of economic relations between the countries on the two shores through an economic and financial partnership and the gradual establishment of a free-trade area; the third – the Social, Cultural and Human Basket – made explicit reference to the need to increase cultural dialogue within the Mediterranean region.

In the wake of the eastward enlargement of the European Union in 2004, the entry of Malta and Cyprus that same year followed, in 2007, by that of Romania and Bulgaria, there was a comprehensive reformulation of the southern part of the EU. There was the increasingly pressing issue of relations with Turkey, a densely populated Islamic country that is the ally of the United States in that geographical area. During his two presidential mandates from 1995 to 2007, the then President of France Jacques Chirac made numerous overtures towards Turkey and its entry into the European institutions. However, under the presidency of Nicolas Sarkozy, questions were raised with regard to European identity, religious beliefs, the failure to respect civil rights and Turkey's refusal to recognize the Armenian genocide. In July 2008, forty-three heads of state met in Paris to establish the Union for the Mediterranean, with strong support from Sarkozy, who had already launched the idea of creating an area of cooperation intended to create solid infrastructures protecting both the environmental and cultural heritage of the region and involving the countries on the shores of the Mediterranean (in February 2007 in Toulon and in October that same year in Tangiers (Ratka 2010: 35–51). Sarkozy's proposal was not met with any great enthusiasm because it was perceived as a tool intended to promote French interests in a region which the then President of France held to be a traditional sphere of influence of his country. This context also raised the question of immigration, which led to deep polarizations in both the public and political debate, undermining aims linked to promoting policies of cooperation between the two shores of the Mediterranean.

While the Baltic narratives evoke an area of expectations in which the Baltic Sea region supplied the model for the European Union's macroregional strategy, this is not the case in the Mediterranean. Many maintain that such a strategy is urgent because the countries bordering this sea face the same challenges: digital transformation, climate change, migration and mobility, and environmental protection (Van Lierop 2021: 1). However, in order for this to come about, a number of premises must be fulfilled: 1) the cooperation of neighbouring countries; 2) a transnational agreement on the terms of this strategy and on the advantages that this could bring; 3) respect for the '"three NOs principle": no new funding, no new administrative structures created, no new regulation necessary' (Haase and Maier 2021: 25). As pointed out by Thomas Perrin, macroregionalization is the result of developments representative of a territorial postmodernity, both in terms of spatial visions and public action (2021). It is based on the notion of state rescaling, which implies that decentralization into substate micro-regions and their inclusion in superstate macroregions are the main factors reshaping geography and the distribution of the power of the states, without causing them to be weakened (Perrin 2021). For the moment, all this sounds stranger to Mediterranean realities.

The Mediterranean narratives, contrary to the harmonious Baltic Sea region's macro narrative more feasible for political rhetoric, in fact display a far less tractable dichotomous image: on the one hand, the Mediterranean is conceived as a protective buffer within an area distinguished by growing social and religious tensions; on the other, 'it is seen as a 'new South' that should be considered as a space expressing a point of view critical of modernity' rather than as a space failing to meet the standards of north-western Europe (Benigno 2009). This is the southern thought referred to by sociologist Franco Cassano (1996) who believes we need to reverse the trend by refusing to see the South in the light of modernity, but rather rethinking modernity in the light of the South. The South reinterpreted as Mediterranean is a space providing a new starting point for proposals for political and cultural projects promoting plurality and rejecting all forms of ethnocentrism. As Cassano pointed out 'the first Mediterranean commandment is to *translate traditions*, to ensure that people not only become friends despite their differences but also thanks to them' (2004: 108). In his latest work *The Fishing Net and the Spider Web. Mediterranean Imaginaries and the Making of Italians*, Claudio Fogu (2020: 5) borrows Irad Malkin's idea of the Archaic Mediterranean of *emporia* (trading colonies) considered as a 'multidirectional, decentralized, nonhierarchical, boundless and proliferating, accessible, expansive and interactive system of self-organization' (Malkin 2013: 25) in order to introduce a key element of the Archaic Mediterranean, that is, the connection within a decentralized network system. This was followed, in the wake of Roman dominance, by a centralized network resembling a spider web. The Mediterranean was territorialized by Rome, becoming *mare nostrum*: 'the territorialized reconfiguration of the Mediterranean into a Roman *Mare Nostrum* transfigured the fishing net into a spider web, and produced an *Imperium* matrix that has proven to be historically dominant over the *emporion* imaginary (in all its forms)' (2020: 6). According to Fogu the 'Southern Question' was, from the beginning until today – also a 'Mediterranean Question', one of a dialectic between *Imperium* forms of imaginary that have aimed at 'making southerners into northerners by actively repressing their Mediterranean be-longing, and forms of fishing net imaginary that either originated in southern culture, or mobilized the *emporion* matrix in the service of alternative conceptions of Italian-ness' (Fogu 2020: 6). Francesco Benigno wonders how two such diametrically opposed images – of the 'sun and the sea' and of the 'clash of civilizations' – can coexist, reaching the conclusion that 'a space progressively acquires an emotional meaning followed by a rational meaning. The Mediterranean thus ceases to be a physical place, becoming a place of the soul' (2009).

This 'Mediterranean of the emotions' referred to by Benigno emerges from the pages of Predrag Matvejević's successful work *Mediteranski breviari* (1987) in which the Croatian classicist explained how the Mediterranean and the discourse around the Mediterranean were inextricably linked ([1987] 2006). The narrative inherent to the unity of the Mediterranean becomes a geographical and mental identifying bond, a trait that unites contrasting political visions. In this sense, the Mediterranean may represent the *grandeur* of a Nation (the rhetoric of *mare nostrum*) or the ideal synthesis of the encounter between peoples (metaphor of *mer amie*) (Temine 2000: 61). Presenting the Mediterranean as a unitary spatial subject and seeking not to contemplate the existence of continuities but, above all, of discontinuities plays a key role in putting forward ideological interpretations. Representations of the Mediterranean vary from country to country according to their cultural positions and national aspirations. As Petri has pointed out, what French geographers have in common with German or Italian geographers is their teleological vision of history, the idea of a universal mission associated with a place to which historical and cultural relevance is attributed:

> What interests us here is not such national or personal variants of the same narration, but the coinciding origins of Europe and the Mediterranean which it always contained, depicting both as products of an original transmission of culture or civilization from the east to the west. The degree of culture defines the "historical importance" of a place, that is, how far or close "this place" is to the teleological fulfillment of history.
>
> (2016b: 684)

Adopting a postcolonial gaze means, on the contrary, reconsidering this great sea within the historical framework of a greater Mediterranean distinguished by changing, fluid traits. The antidote to a representation of the Mediterranean as a unitary container of polysemic concepts responds to an ideo/teleological vision. The identity of the Mediterranean – as indeed of any other sea – is defined by precisely this idea of fluidity, manifested by its changing, fluid character.

2

The views of the European Institutions on the island question

Let us examine European policies with regard to insular regions from the 1950s to the present day. It is evident that such policies tend to reproduce a deterministic vision of the conditions and needs of islands, placing the emphasis on insularity instead of grasping the relevance of the imaginative self-representation of islands expressed in the concept of islandness. In the Mediterranean area, in particular, in the wake of the humanitarian emergency caused by the migration of peoples from war-torn countries and elsewhere, it has now become clear that developing EU policies using the yardstick of insularity is mistaken. Far from being isolated worlds, the Mediterranean islands, places of passage for migrants, are an integral part of a network system between islands and between islands and the continent.

The islands within European institutions: Historical background

Today, island regions operate within the European geostrategic context; decisions that affect them in many different ways are made not by their nation state of belonging, but by Brussels. Nonetheless, during the first two decades after the birth of the European Community (1958–78), Europe's peripheral and ultra-peripheral islands were left in a kind of political and juridical no man's land (Sanguin 2007: 15). In fact, they did not appear on the new supranational body's political agenda and the treaties signed in that period – the European Coal and Steel Community (ECSC), the European Economic Community (EEC), the European Atomic Energy Community (EAEC) – revealed an almost complete lack of interest regarding the backwardness of these islands. Although Italy had recognized the autonomous status of Sicily and Sardinia some years earlier, it did not bother bringing the insular question to the attention of the European Community. The special status of the two Italian islands made no provisions regarding international agreements thereby preventing them from making any requests (Hache 2000: 54).

It was not until 1973, in the wake of the establishment of the Conference of Peripheral Maritime Regions of Europe (CPMR) at Saint Malo, that the islands obtained their first recognition: this organization, which still exists today, comprises six geographical commissions including the Islands Commission, which was set up in 1980 with the specific remit of islands. In the 1970s, nissology adopted a phenomenological approach to insularity directly linked to the emergent sector of humanist geography. This period saw a significant shift taking place in the methodological foundations of geography: away from the theoretical-quantitative approach that was the expression of a Cartesian neutral space and from the typical descriptive approach of possibilist historicist geography towards 'the study of lived space, of subjective territories' (Lando 2012: 267). This involved 'understanding the world through the objective vision of the scientist with the aim of interpreting the action of the human inhabitant with their feelings, ideas, and hopes. The focus of this scientific analysis was the behaviour of humans in their territories' (Lando 2012: 268). The philosophical reference of this humanist current was Husserlian phenomenology based on 'the exploration and description of the world in the way that we experienced it originally, directly, and immediately, leaving prejudices and assumptions aside' (Lando 2012: 270).

During the 1980s, this phenomenological approach provided the scientific basis for the definition of the specificities of islands in an institutional context.

As noted by Joseph Martinetti, this insularist social determinism enabled the 'legitimization of the natural constraints to which islands are subject, encouraging them to organize themselves as a territorial lobby within European institutions' (2014). While Corsica ended up by representing the archetype of a European regionality seeking to free itself from national states, the Åland islands became the most successful example of an insular autonomy that lent itself to transposition to all European insular territories (Martinetti 2014: 8).

In 1975, the creation of the European Fund for Regional Development (EFRD) and of the notion of 'disadvantaged zone' in agricultural regulations led the European Community to recognize the existence of backward, disadvantaged areas, including insular areas: from this moment onwards, efforts were made to rectify these inequalities, at least as far as European Community proclamations were concerned (Hache 2000: 57). In 1982, the UN Conference on the Law of the Sea defined an island as 'a naturally formed area of land, surrounded by water, which is above water at high tide' (Olausson 2007: 25).

On 17 November 1987, the intergroup of the islands of peripheral maritime regions was established within the European Parliament at the initiative of the then Vice Chair of the group of the European Democratic Alliance, the Corsican MEP François Musso, in order to reflect on common problems such as energy, taxation and environment (Olivesi 1995: 58–9). The aim of the group was to contribute to the definition of policies supporting and accompanying the development of insular regions, drawing inspiration from the POSEI programme adopted by a number of ultra-peripheral islands (Overseas France, Azores islands, Madeira, Canary islands) (Olivesi 1995: 59). The following year, an explicit reference was made at European institutional level to the socio-economic limits affecting insular regions, specifically, in the European Council meeting held in Rhodes on 2–3 December 1988, which stated: 'the European Council recognizes the particular socio-economic problems of certain island regions in the Community. It therefore requests the Commission to examine these problems and submit, if appropriate, any proposals which deems useful, within the financial possibilities offered by the Community's existing policies as they have been decided' (The European Council 1988: 10).

In a speech given at Ajaccio in 1989, Jacques Delors, the then president of the European Commission, explained the pressing need for a general framework at European political level that would allow insular regions to overcome their natural structural limits (Sanguin 2007: 15). Some years later, in 1992, article 129b of the Maastricht Treaty referred to the need to implement connections between the islands and peripheral regions and the central regions of the European

Community: 'within the framework of a system of open and competitive markets, action by the Community shall aim at promoting the interconnection and interoperability of national networks as well as access to such networks. It shall take account in particular of the need to link island, landlocked and peripheral regions with the central regions of the Community' (Council of the European Communities, Commission of the European Communities 1992: 51). 1994 saw the establishment of the European Committee of the Regions (CoR), an assembly of local and regional representatives that provides subnational authorities that is numbered 'among the most important European institutions from the perspective of sub-national island jurisdictions designated as "regions" in their respective member states' (Warrington and Milne 2018: 180).

On 19 July 1994, the European Commission drew up the Single Programming Document for Corsica (DOCUP) (1994–9), defining a development and intervention plan intended to promote the island's resources. A further development of this renewed attention is revealed by the decision made in 1994 to lay down a number of criteria for the definition of an island. Eurostat identified four: the population of an island may not be below fifty units to have a minimal impact in socio-economic terms; an island may not be linked to the mainland by a permanent structure (bridge, tunnel, etc.); the distance between an island and the continent must be at least 1 km; lastly, an island may not be home to the capital of a European Union member state. The latter condition inevitably excluded islands such as Malta, Cyprus and Ireland. This was an attempt by the EU statistical office to 'materialize' the islands by using fixed parameters (Taglioni 2011: 48). This definition not only excludes Island states from being considered to be islands, and it also implies that with 'mainland' only the national reference territory is contemplated.

The entry of Sweden and Finland to the EU in 1994 brought the status of insular regions to the negotiating table. The Åland government obtained the adoption of a protocol authorizing the archipelago, should it have decided to adhere to the Community, to adopt particular provisions regarding the right of domicile and the supply of services. The Åland islands were able to benefit from even more favourable measures than those obtained by Madeira and the Azores in 1985. Yet when the Gotland (Gotlands Kommun 1994: 54) authorities submitted a draft protocol to the Swedish government requesting limited concessions on the occasion of the same negotiations, it was turned down (Hache 2000: 58).

In 1995, Lino Briguglio (1995: 1615–32), director of the Islands and Small States Institute of the University of Malta, drew up a vulnerability index for island regions based on economic, physical and cultural parameters, which was used without modification by the Economic and Social Council of the UN General Assembly (Development of a vulnerability index for small island developing States 1998).

The underlying idea at EU level is that islands experience delays in development, when compared to other regions, due to their insular condition. According to the European Union, there are certain characteristics that are common to islands and which can affect the conditions for their development. These characteristics usually relate to their degree of 'peripherality', which is associated with physical parameters such as insularity. The emphasis given to the fragility resulting from insularity led to the request for a specific programme, such as POSEICOR 'programme spécifique à l'éloignement et à l'insularité pour la Corse (Poseicor)' established in January 1995 (Olivesi 1995, 57).

In 1997, Declaration 30 on island regions underlined the urgency of introducing specific measures targeting island regions given the presence of objective structural constraints hindering the economic and social development of these areas:

> The Conference recognises that island regions suffer from structural handicaps linked to their island status, the permanence of which impairs their economic and social development. The Conference accordingly acknowledges that Community legislation must take account of these handicaps and that specific measures may be taken, where justified, in favour of these regions in order to integrate them better into the internal market on fair conditions.
>
> (Treaty of Amsterdam 1997: 115)

The Amsterdam Treaty represents a watershed moment in the evolution of the way island regions are perceived: from that moment onwards, a supranational organization like the European Union turned its attention to insular regions, focusing less on their historic heritage than on the effects of their geographical condition of insularity on a social and economic level (Hache 2000: 61). According to the European Commission, 'institutional recognition of the problem of the islands is important because it opens up the possibility of establishing new European programmes centring on the reduction of "permanent structural handicaps" and suggests that a special effort may be directed towards areas suffering from such structural handicaps linked to natural or geographic factors' (Foschi, Peraldi and Rombaldi 2005: 5). As outlined by Edward Warrington and David Milne, 'this outlook has fundamentally affected the Union's strategies and policies for islands, permitting it to accept non-reciprocal arrangements with many islands, without compromising the larger goal of integration' (2018: 180).

During the two decades following the fall of the Iron Curtain, Europe's geography was characterized by the emergence of an integrated supranational economic and political space. Also the islands were involved into the integration effort that went under the name of macro-regions (Mirwaldt, McMaster and Bachtler 2010: 1–20). The concept of macro-region was developed to respond to two challenges: on the one hand, the globalization process, which revealed the ineffectiveness of the old nation state based administrative and political borders in the face of changes in the environment, in world politics and in the globalized economy; on the other, the need to find a defence mechanism or a new territorial cohesion that could counter re-nationalizing tendencies in the EU.

The entry of islands into the European institutional arena led to a shake-up in the balance of power: no longer mere appurtenances to national states, they now acquired the status of peripheral areas of a continent (Hache 2000: 77). The negotiations were no longer exclusively with a national continental power but also with a supranational structure, within which bargaining mechanisms operated in different ways and the rules had yet to be established. For example, the European Union granted an exception to the right of domicile (*hembygdsratt*) in effect on the Åland islands that contravenes the fundamental principles of the Community's legal system according to which any form of discrimination with regard to nationality or in the context of economic freedom is prohibited (Hache 2000: 157). The Åland islands, joined the Union along with Finland, 'after securing permanent concessions permitting duty free transactions on Åland ships within EU waters and confirming restrictions on the right of non-residents to own property' (Warrington and Milne 2018: 179).

The European Spatial Development Perspective (ESDP) adopted in May 1999 at Potsdam stressed the urgency of drawing up regional planning focusing on environmental and landscape issues. Camille de Rocca Serra, president of the regional council of Corsica between 2004 and 2010, followed a political line that sought to sell land to private citizens in order to boost the economy but met with the opposition of the moderately regionalist ecological associations calling for compliance with legislation on coastlines and mountainous regions, diffusing alarmist messages about speculative construction. In 2002, at the initiative of the majority of the political exponents of the Collectivité territoriale de Corse, a Plan d'aménagement et de développement durable de la Corse (PADDUC) (Collectivité Territoriale de Corse 2015) was drawn up to redefine local planning and ease the constraints imposed by the 1986 Loi littoral regulating the protection and promotion of the French coastline.

In 1990, the European Commission earmarked structural funds intended to reduce the economic gap between regions within the Union: this led to the launch of the INTERREG Community Initiative which included a series of measures promoting cross-border cooperation. The INTERREG programmes (I between southern Corsica and northern Sardinia; II between southern Corsica and northern Sardinia, on the one hand, and between northern Corsica and Tuscany, on the other; III between Corsica, Tuscany and Sardinia) sought to integrate these regions, following the principle laid down in the document 'Europe 2000 + – Cooperation for European territorial development' which expressed the need for promotion, at EU level, of spatial, social and economic cohesion at regional level, implementing a series of actions intended to protect the most undeveloped areas that began by safeguarding the environment and their traditional cultural heritage (Dühr, Colomb and Nadin 2010: 201–2). On 29 September 1993, the Assemblée de la Corse adopted a development plan providing for the determination of a series of cultural and trade links with Italy, Catalonia, the island of Mallorca, and, more in general, with the Arab world, with the aim of turning the island into a hub for encounters and for the circulation of ideas in the western Mediterranean (Olivesi 1995: 55).

By way of example, we might mention the third edition of the INTERREG III A Italy-France 'islands' programme (2000–6), which sought to reduce the hardships resulting from the isolation of border areas, removing the obstacles represented by national borders through the adoption of a common strategy in interventions targeting the regions concerned, which shared specific needs and similar problems. Priority 2 concerned the environment, tourism and sustainable development (INTERREG III A): the aim was to develop and implement actions of cooperation in the tourism sector in order to promote sustainable economic development in Corsica, Tuscany and Sardinia (Di Falco 2003: 43). The INTERREG Italy-Maritime France 2014–20 programme was distinguished by a special focus on the environment, sustainable tourism and heritage considered as a 'common good' (Italy-Maritime France programme).

It was in this framework that in the mid-1990s the islands of the Mediterranean and Baltic Sea areas began to formulate new cooperation strategies in order to attain a more central position within the new geopolitical scenarios created after the end of the bipolar world and the acceleration of the European integration and enlargement process. They underlined that in view of the increasing role of the maritime spaces it was important to bring islands together to address common concerns and challenges. In analogy to the insularity/islandness theoretical divide, from an analytical viewpoint we can interpret this type of argumentation as an example for the social and symbolic practices developed in relation to the sea which have been delineated by the Brazilian anthropologist Manuel Diegues (1998: 259). Here the accent is on the sea space as a connecting medium, whereas the insularity-related paradigm points out the 'objective' problems created by the physical presence of water around islands. Island networks can be seen as a synergetic fund raising effort of a sum of 'disadvantaged' territories, or as a synergy effort of populations that practically redefines the maritime space they inhabit, placing their islands at its centre (Grzechnik and Hurskainen 2015).

The early 1990s saw the emergence of cooperation networks between island regions in both the Mediterranean and Baltic areas: the B7 Baltic Islands Network and the IMEDOC. The B7 Baltic Islands Network – a cooperation group involving the seven islands in the Baltic area (Bornholm, Gotland, Hiiumaa, Rügen, Saaremaa, Åland and Öland) – was established in 1989, at the start of the process that would have led to the dissolution of the Soviet Union. It was in this context of shifting geopolitical balances that the Baltic regions sought to rebuild the contacts that had been previously conditioned by the looming presence of the two blocs. Until then, the only islands to have had annual contacts regarding political matters were the Åland islands, Gotland and Bornholm. As pointed out by Knud Andersen, mayor of Bornholm County from 1990 to 2002, the creation of the B7 Baltic Islands Network produced the conditions necessary for a new order based on cooperation (B7 Baltic Islands 2014: 27). Moreover, the Network allowed the islands to develop shared projects regarding exchange of best practices in education and to unite their forces to meet the challenges arising from sustainable tourism.

As we have seen, the demise of communism provoked a redefinition and rewriting of the narratives associated with the Baltic Sea Region (Götz 2016: 55–67). The establishment of contacts with countries formerly belonging to the communist bloc, and their future integration, was presented as a historical necessity (Götz 2014). Cooperation between the islands in the Baltic area corresponds to a strategic vision that aimed to 'put the islands more in control of their own destiny' (B7 Baltic Islands 2014: 9). The rhetoric focused on the importance of acquiring a key role in the Baltic area, which would have been able to 'make the islands' more resilient and their population richer, smarter and happier' (B7 Baltic Islands 2014: 9). Andersen believed that the Baltic islands would have lost some of their bargaining power with their central governments if they turned to national organizations to safeguard their rights: 'island-questions are not high on the agenda of National organizations, simply because they have a different scope for their activities. That's why the islands will lose their power of influence if we let national organizations represent our rights and responsibilities instead of doing it ourselves' (B7 Baltic Islands 2014: 5).

The entry of the Estonian islands of Saaremaa and Hiiumaa to the B7 Baltic Islands Network helped to alleviate the isolation of these regions lying on the eastern shores of the Baltic. Hiiumaa joined the network in 1991, on the occasion of the annual meeting, which saw the following three points placed on the order of the day: the environment, sustainable tourism and democracy. The latter point, which was very high on the agenda, represented a particular challenge for the islands on the eastern coast of the Baltic. Hiiuma's representatives had to request a special permit to attend the Bornholm meeting from the Russians, who occupied the island until 1994. Through dialogue and an exchange of experiences benefitting all participants in the meetings organized by the B7 Baltic Islands Network, these insular regions had the opportunity to observe and actively participate in the dynamics of the democratic process. The then B7 Secretary Reet Kokovkin noted that 'the learning sessions and seminars in Bornholm and Gotland guided our politicians and municipal officials, teaching us the basics of the functioning of the municipality level' (B7 Baltic Islands 2014: 27).

The year 1992 saw the founding of the Association of Estonian Islands (AEI), a non-profit organization representing the Estonian islands within their respective states. Currently there are members from twenty islands: Piirissaar, Manõja (Manilaid), Kihnu, Ruhnu, Abruka, Vahase, Vilsandi, Saaremaa, Kõinastu, Kesselaid, Muhu, Hiiumaa, Heinlaid, Kassari, Vormsi, Osmussaar, Pakri Islands, Naissaar, Aegna, Prangli. The AEI has set itself the following aims: 'maintenance/ preservation of democratic and ongoing/lasting, continuous, durable, prolonged, permanent living environment and development of cooperation of the network between islands; representation of the communities living on the islands of Estonia on nation-wide and international levels; supporting the enactment of communities inclusive, including science-based legislation; assurance of the rights and interests of Estonian islanders' (EESTI SAARTE KOGU 2017).

In 1995, in the Mediterranean area, the Balearic islands, Corsica and Sardinia created a shared platform of cooperation, giving rise to IMEDOC, a body representing the islands of the western Mediterranean. Subsequently Sicily also joined. IMEDOC intended to create a stable space of cooperation for the exchange of experiences and the promotion of common interests in the European Union with the aim of ensuring that the needs of island regions would be heard at European level, in the hope that the insular dimension would be included in community policies (Olivesi 1995: 55). Similar aims were shared by the EGTC of the Mediterranean Archipelago – ARCHIMED, which was founded in 2010 as a partnership between the government of the Balearic islands, Sicily, the district of Larnaca and, from the following year onwards, also Crete.

May 2001 saw the founding of the first cooperation network at the initiative of the Danish, Finnish, French, Irish, Scottish and Swedish governments with the intent of promoting successful cooperation between small islands communities. In 2005, the decision was made to formalize the network, giving rise to the European Small Islands Federation (ESIN). In 2006, ESIN expanded to include the Association of Estonian Islands, the Association of Italian Minor islands and the Hellenic Small Islands Network. In 2009, the Åland islands became a member of ESIN and in 2014 the Croatian Islands followed suit. ESIN has twofold objectives: at local level, ESIN 'aims at strengthening islands cultural identity, facilitating the circulation of information between its members. It allows comparison on how different countries cope with issues and it gives support to each other through the sharing of knowledge'; while at European level, 'ESIN also aims at informing relevant EU institutions and at influencing EU policies and rules by increasing awareness and understanding of small islands issues' (ESIN 2021).

The new relevance of the island regions came about within an institutional framework dominated by the principle of 'multilevel governance' which promoted shared decision-making among institutional actors at local, national and regional levels. Despite their experience of cooperation networks, island regions slipped back into the rhetoric of insularity and, therefore, of isolation, also in the wake of a shift in geopolitical equilibriums. We know that the words 'isolation' and 'insular' derive from the Latin word for island, *insula*, whereas the Greek word 'for island is *nissos* or *nesos*, etymologically rooted in *nau-, meaning ship, and related to navigation of vehicles' (Clark and Clark 2009: 315). However, the insularity concept prevailing in EU policies preferred the Latin meaning over the Greek one. This is not just an academic question without practical relevance. In fact, it is in the practical dimension that all islands prove to be both, isolated *insula* and connected *nesos*.

In the Mediterranean, the recent humanitarian emergency caused by waves of mass immigration has revealed how mistaken it is to treat islands only as isolated spaces. In 2014, Bornholm and Öland left the B7 island network and since then, the network became progressively weaker to the point of almost vanishing. This is borne out by the fact that its website is now inaccessible and its Facebook page has not been updated since September 2014. The B7 island network emerged in a post-Cold War context when the idea of Baltic cooperation represented a model to be exported to other regions, at a time when it could count on the support of the European Union. As Jörgen Samuelsson, one of Öland's leading figures, pointed out in an article published in December 2014 in the Swedish weekly newspaper *Ölandsbladet*, 'it was inevitable that the European Union's interest in cooperation in the Baltic region would disappear in favour of North-South and East-West cooperation' (Ståhl 2014).

The islands of the European Union today

According to the European Spatial Planning Observation Network (ESPON), insularity, i.e. disconnection from a mainland, is the common and inherent characteristic of islands (ESPON 2019: 55). The final report presenting the interim results of a Targeted Analysis conducted within the framework of the ESPON 2013 Programme describes the concept of insularity in the following terms:

> [This notion] is the connecting link, the common characteristic of all islands regardless of their size, population and development level. Insularity expresses "objective" and measurable characteristics, including small size (area and population), isolation and remoteness, as well as unique natural and cultural environments. However, it also involves a distinctive "experiential identity", which is a non-measurable quality expressing the various symbols that islands are connected to.
>
> (ESPON 2013: 34)

In the vision of European institutions, insularity is no mere geographic condition but a permanent factor of economic and social peripheralization that is the true obstacle preventing islands from reaching the same levels of economic development as the mainland. Three interconnected dimensions concur to define insularity: smallness, remoteness and vulnerability. These features of insularity affect economic development.

The official documents estimate that there are around 2,400 inhabited islands in the European Union with a population of around 20,500,000 inhabitants, belonging to thirteen states (Poland, Germany, Denmark, Sweden, Estonia, Finland, Netherlands, Italy, France, Greece, Spain, Portugal, Croatia) (Haase and Maier 2021: 7). In addition to these territories there are Ireland, Malta and Cyprus which are insular Member States. Moreover, we must also include further islands, the so-called Outermost Regions (ORs), which are situated in the Atlantic and Indian Oceans but belong to France, Spain and Portugal. These islands are classified as NUTS 3 level island regions on the basis of cataloguing criteria for territorial units developed by Eurostat for statistical purposes linked to the territorial redistribution of EU Structural Funds. There are also a number of islands that are statistically classified as NUTS 2 – e.g. the Balearic Islands, Sicily and Corsica – and there are also two island Member States (Malta and Cyprus). We should point out that this is an estimation based on NUTS 3 island regions, which excludes islands that are part of continental Europe NUTS 3 regions (Haase and Maier 2021: 11).

Eurostat's Methodological manual on territorial typologies (2018 edition), defines island regions as territories having a minimum surface of 1 km^2; a minimum distance between the island and the mainland of 1 km; a resident population of more than fifty inhabitants; no fixed link such as a bridge, a tunnel, or a dyke between the islands and the mainland (EUROSTAT 2018: 12). EU legislation contains a body of specific laws regarding islands given that the criteria of insularity and distance is one of the main factors contributing to situations of social and economic disadvantage in comparison with other EU areas. Articles 174 and 349 of the Treaty on the Functioning of the European Union (TFEU) specify that islands are territories with particular geographic characteristics that require specific measures. Article 174 underlines the need to implement cohesion policies capable of reducing social and economic disparities between EU regions capable of promoting 'overall harmonious development' (European Union 2012: 127). It also indicates the physical conditions of the most disadvantaged regions as a factor explaining the delayed development of these areas. It is no coincidence that the problems affecting islands are the same ones experienced by 'rural areas, areas affected by industrial transition, and regions which suffer from severe and permanent natural or demographic handicaps such as the northernmost regions with very low population density and island, cross border and mountain regions' (European Union 2012: 127). Although it does not contain a specific definition of islands, it points out that 'the Conference considers that the reference in Article 174 to island regions can include island States in their entirety, subject to the necessary criteria being met' (European Union 2012: 326).

Article 349 refers to ORs, that is, Guadeloupe, French Guiana, Martinique, Réunion, Saint-Barthélemy, Saint-Martin, the Azores, Madeira and the Canary Islands, which are subject to a number of permanent conditions ('by their remoteness, insularity, small size, difficult topography and climate, economic dependence on a few products') making it necessary for the EU, in particular, the European Structural and Investment Funds (ESIF/ESI Funds) to adopt specific measures in their regard (European Union 2012: 195). In the 2021-7 programming period, the European Union intends to earmark funds to meet strategic objectives while at the same favouring territorial cooperation between ORs.

The document *Islands of the European Union: State of play and future challenges* produced in March 2021 by Policy Department B for Structural and Cohesion Policies within the European Parliament specifies that the development of a common European strategy is hindered by precisely the diversity of these islands;

nonetheless, it refers to macro-regional strategies aimed not only at islands but also at coastal regions. The aim of the drafters was to propose measures that would allow the following objectives to be attained: 'smart and resilient islands, energetic sustainability, better connectivity with the mainlands/continents, increased quality of life and opportunities for inhabitants and striving towards tailor-made/dedicated European policies' (Haase and Maier 2021: 8).

The aforementioned document contains a paragraph with the title 'Current challenges and Recommendations' that focuses on the purely geographical aspects of islands and on their physical separation from the continent as a key of interpretation to identify problems and propose solutions. This physical separation from the continent gives rise to a permanent situation of dependence upon maritime and air transport. These problems normally concern the rail network, water supply and waste disposal management; in fact, when such services are absent, there is a sharp fall in the quality of living on islands and a tendency to immigrate (Haase and Maier 2021: 8). On the one hand, islands must attempt to operate in such a way that real economic development can take place while, on the other, they must meet environmental sustainability needs on a daily basis: these conditions create a number of problems relating to management of resources and economic strategies.

Given that environmental sustainability is an issue that cannot be compromised because neglecting it would threaten the island ecosystem, islands must avoid importing fossil fuels. For this reason, the European strategy regarding islands integrates with the EU Green Deal and the communication on the Blue Economy which intended to reduce marine pollution, preserve biodiversity, support climate adaptation and resilience of coastal areas, promote sustainable food production and develop sustainable plans for managing the use of marine areas (European Union 2021). The communication on the Blue Economy replaces the previous 2012 Communication on Blue Growth. The European Union intends to launch a series of measures to bring about 'a proper transition towards a green, digital and resilient future' (Haase and Maier 2021: 8). However, these official documents also underline that the Member States are responsible for deciding how to implement such measures, which will be established by policy documents at national and regional level. Emerging from between the lines is the EU's intention to act as coordinator from European to macro-regional, national and regional level to ensure that 'policy measures are not a matter of privilege, but a mean of ensuring their survival as unique landscapes, preserving their heritage as well as the communities that have inhabited them for centuries' (Haase and Maier 2021: 8).

In 2016, the European Parliament adopted a resolution (European Parliament 2016) regarding the particular condition of islands, which demands the clear formulation of a strategy designed to define insular challenges and actions to be undertaken. This commitment arose from the conviction that the potential of island regions plays a role in enhancing the EU's sustainable development. The resolution lists ten structural conditions explaining the urgent need to develop a comprehensive strategy for the islands: 1) islands have shared, permanent characteristics making them unlike continental areas; 2) there are 'permanent natural and geographical handicaps specific to the situation of islands'; 3) the island question exists in an institutional framework where one of the main objectives of the European cohesion policy is 'the reduction in economic, social and environmental disparities between regions and polycentric harmonious development'; 4) the economic crisis has had dramatic repercussions for disadvantaged regions, including islands, 'resulting in increased poverty and social exclusion and preventing the achievement of the Union's long-term objective of economic and territorial cohesion'; 5) islands are particularly vulnerable to a number of phenomena affecting the European Union, including 'globalisation, demographic trends, climate change, energy supply and, especially for the southern areas, exposure to increasing migration flows'; 6) islands represent an opportunity for the European Union overall given their rich contribution in both environmental terms – 'specific habitats and endemic species' – and cultural terms – 'architectural heritage, sites, landscapes, agricultural and non-agricultural features and geographical identities'; 7) islands can contribute to the EU's sustainable development because their exposure to sunlight and winds means that they have enormous potential in terms of energy production from renewable sources; 8) in order to attract business investments, island areas must be easily accessible by means of maritime and air transport for people and goods that have a low sustainable cost in environmental terms; 9) agriculture, breeding and fisheries, which are the main economic driver of island regions, 'suffer due to lack of accessibility, particularly for SMEs, a low level of product differentiation, and climate condition'; 10) intensive tourism is a key aspect of island economies but is not environmentally sustainable. This resolution asks the European Commission to provide a number of measures listed below. Above all, it stresses the need for the Commission to provide 'a clear definition of the type of geographical, natural and demographic permanent handicaps that insular regions can suffer from, with reference to Article 174 of the TFEU' and to explain the measures taken to achieve economic, social and territorial cohesion.

Another aspect raised regarded the urgency of providing support to cope with the significant depopulation trend affecting islands as well as with the effects of climate change. The Commission was asked to launch an in-depth study regarding 'the extra costs incurred as a result of being islands, in terms of the transport system for people and goods, energy supply and access to markets, in particular for SMEs' while at the same time creating 'a homogeneous group made up of all island territories'. Moreover, the resolution also invited the Commission to take into account other statistical indicators, in addition to GDP, providing information on the specific condition of islands 'arising from natural permanent handicaps'. It also repeated the importance of maintaining special tax arrangements, 'in accordance with Council Directive 2006/112/EC', that would help to offset the permanent natural and demographic disadvantages.

The improvement of sustainable mobility and of the efficiency of transport (airplanes and ports) was described as a decisive element in bringing about the 'balanced territorial development of island regions by promoting innovation and competitiveness in these regions, which are remote from the major administrative and economic centres and do not benefit from ease of access to transport, and by strengthening local production for local markets'. Moreover, digital investments were held to be key in facilitating the connectivity of island regions and 'to ensure broadband access on islands and the full participation of islands in the digital single market'. Nor did the resolution neglect the migration flow to islands that would require 'a holistic EU approach', that is, joint support from all Member States in dealing with this phenomenon. While taking into account the problems affecting island regions, the resolution also emphasized their potential, which needed to be exploited to create employment opportunities to attract investments of foreign capital, explaining the importance of development sustainable tourism and alternative energy sources. The latter investment was held to be particularly urgent because it would also have made it possible to 'guarantee cheaper energy supplies for their inhabitants'.

The objective of reaching climate neutrality by 2050 is expressed in the EU Green Deal of December 2019, which aims 'to transform the EU into a fair and prosperous society, with a modern, resource-efficient and competitive economy where there are no net emissions of greenhouse gases in 2050 and where economic growth is decoupled from resource use' (European Commission 2019). In this case too, we find a clear reference to the islands: 'The Commission will take forward the work on the Clean Energy for EU Islands Initiative to develop a long-term framework to accelerate the clean energy transition on all EU islands' (European Commission 2019).

The 2016 Resolution called upon Member States and regional and local authorities to determine specific strategies for sustainable development in line with the principle of subsidiarity so that the measures implemented would be as responsible as possible to citizens and that the European Union would only intervene in sectors where it had exclusive competence unless its actions were to prove more effective than those taken at national or regional level.

The Cohesion Policy considers islands as being subject to particular provisions but groups them together with mountain regions and sparsely populated areas under the heading of 'less developed regions'. The European Union considers European Structural and Investment Funds (ESIF/ESI Funds) as the main instrument for the promotion of local and regional development through the funding of a series of measures aimed at supporting all EU territories, including islands.

In December 2019, at the initiative of the Conference of Presidents for the 9th legislature of the European Parliament, it was decided to form The Seas, Rivers, Islands and Coastal Areas Intergroup (SEArica), which brings together more than 100 MEPs from seven different political groups and twenty-three Member States. With regard to the Baltic area, we find a particular focus on the effects on marine biodiversity caused by climate change: among the initiatives taking place we would like to mention the webinar 'Marine biodiversity in a changing climate: How do we best enable the Baltic Sea ecosystem to be part of the solution?', which was held in November 2020 and was inspired by a scientific study into the 2018 heat wave in the Baltic Sea, the highest recorded since 1926, in order to tackle the thorny issue of which measures to take 'for increased marine resilience in a European and international policy context' (SEArica 2020). Equal importance was given to the role that ports can play 'in connecting regions, creating jobs and growth, they can also contribute to delivering carbon neutrality and the European Green Deal' (SEArica 2021a). More in general, there was a focus on the development of an EU strategy for sustainable tourism (SEArica 2021b).

It is interesting to note that while, on the one hand, European legislation groups islands with mountain areas, sparsely populated areas and Outermost Regions because of the particular challenges these all face, on the other, in, macro-regional strategic documents, we find them to be 'addressed by water basin, because together with the coastline regions and with the surrounding countries and waters, they act as a wider functional area' (Haase and Maier 2021: 24). During an interview in October 2020, at the height of the public health crisis caused by the Covid-19 pandemic, Francina Armengol, President of the Balearic Islands, drew attention to the need to develop a new EU strategy for

Mediterranean islands 'to build higher resilience to health and environmental crises' on the grounds that 'the exceptional richness of Mediterranean ecosystems and their particular vulnerability to socioeconomic development and climate change make the sustainable management of these islands' scarce natural resources a key challenge' (European Committee of the Regions 2020).

2019 saw the establishment of the 'Med Insulae partnership' between the Balearic Islands, Sardinia, Corsica and Gozo, which set out to find shared common solutions to meet the challenges of environmental sustainability. As stated by Armengol 'We believe that this new strategy for Mediterranean islands should incorporate specific action plans in key areas such as the agrifood sector and the improvement of our production structure, the improvement of sustainable fisheries management and the creation of new marine protected areas so as to protect biodiversity and increase the sustainability of the natural resources of the Mediterranean islands' (European Committee of the Regions 2020). More in general, we can see that 'there is no common European islands strategy, or any islands strategy based on geographical location, except for the Outermost Regions' (Haase and Maier 2021: 26). With the exception of the Mediterranean islands, which cannot be included in any form of macro-regional strategy given the absence of any such strategy for the area, 'insular territories are most commonly addressed in water basin macro-regional strategies and in national/regional strategic documents' (Haase and Maier 2021: 26).

As we have seen, the European Union has launched a series of measures targeting island regions with the support of economic resources on a scale that will compensate for any structural disadvantages resulting from their condition of insularity. Isolation is perceived as a key to reflect on the disadvantaged conditions of island regions. However, according to the emerging discipline of island studies, the isolation felt by islanders is not due to the physical separation from a mainland as such, but to the perception of their concrete living conditions as disadvantageous due to a more complex entanglement. There is no doubt that the European Union conveys a supranational view that mobilizes the island worlds in the effort of interregional integration and region building. In the event, however, there is a tendency to draw on the paradigm of insularity: 'the connectivity of islands appears to be constantly underestimated, both as a potential for the development of more seaward and outward looking economic and cultural initiatives and for the prevention of tensions and crises that manifest themselves on the islands not because of their isolation, but because of their connectedness' (Paci 2016b: 27–8).

The island networks are not perceived as 'archipelagos' that possess their own endogenous synergies, but continue to be seen as a sum of problematic 'insularities' that merit charitable help from the centre. The underlying idea in the official EU documents featuring the term 'insularity' is that the physical condition of the islands, and therefore their supposed isolation is the decisive factor in determining their delay in socioeconomic development. Both European and local decision makers have shown that they do not wish to adopt a more island-centred and connectivity-oriented approach that would improve the obsolete internal infrastructures of Mediterranean islands such as Sicily, Sardinia and Corsica, incentivize intra-islands transport and communication networks, and foster common marketing initiatives in tourism, wine and food production under a 'Mediterranean Islands' brand. We will end up with a Sicilian brand drawing upon the symbolism of the early Mafia with their *coppola* hats and sawn-off shotguns or the Corsican and Sardinian brand tied to a similar 'primordial component' associated with the islands' banditry. In the same way, we encounter the medieval brand in Gotland and the brand defining the Åland islands, 'islands of peace'. However, we do not encounter a comprehensive branding of the islands of the Mediterranean or of the Baltic.

Islands and migration in the Mediterranean region

In recent years, the immigration emergency in the Mediterranean area has impacted the geopolitical role of island spaces. Situated near the southern boundary of the northern coasts of the Mediterranean, the Mediterranean islands act both as the closed and relatively porous borders of the European Union and, at the same time, as the preferred point of passage and place of transit of migrants from north Africa, from sub-Saharan Africa and from the Middle East (Martinetti 2014: 12–3). The islands also filter and redistribute the flow of illegal migrants in the face of measures implemented by Frontex, the European Border and Coastguard Agency responsible for the system of management and control of the external borders of the Schengen Area.

The islands are therefore at the centre of a media-driven social construct of immigration which emphasizes aspects to do with humanitarian urgency and fuels 'geographies of fear' in the European public sphere (Bernardie-Tahir and Schmoll 2015: 4). They fall within the complex dynamics of the 'teichopolitique' (Ballif and Rosière 2009) – a neologism coined by Florine Ballif and Stéphane Rosière to denote the space control policies originating from the idea that the construction of barriers is sufficient to counter 'liquid modernity' (Bauman 2000).

Within the European space, there are territories situated on the edges of the Schengen area – the Mediterranean islands, which act as sentinels/prisons (Lemaire 2014: 143–60) – and territories where migrants hope to settle, including Baltic countries like Sweden (Bernardie-Tahir and Schmoll 2015: 7). In the European imagination, the island of Lampedusa has become the embodiment of the idea of border and the symbol of Euro-Mediterranean border: from 2011 onwards, in particular, in the wake of the Arab Spring, this Sicilian island came to resemble an open-air prison (Cuttitta 2012). The 'frontierization' process means that the islands – as bridgeheads for migrants – become the stage on which the 'border show' (Cuttitta 2012) is mounted. Islands such as Lampedusa – and likewise Lesbos – is therefore only a stage set created by the use-and-consume politics of the 'society of the spectacle' (Debord 1983) in order to represent the spectacle of mass invasion, reception and emergency.

As we have seen, the Mediterranean Sea is a liquid space constantly reconfigured by the movement of peoples, but it is also, and especially a space of passage for those who traverse it. In recent decades, from *mare nostrum* the Mediterranean has become *mare aliorum* (a sea of others) (Fogu 2010: 1–23). According to Claudio Fogu 'this de-Mediterraneanized image of European-ness has become hegemonic not only in Italy but across Europe. It has driven hard wedges between normative Europe and "Mediterranean Europe" (Spain, Italy, and Greece), and externally, of course, between a European union institutionalized along a West to East axis and the Mediterranean "of others'" (2020: 245).

Hence also the islands in the Mediterranean have become 'fortresses' unprepared to cope with the flow of migrants. The islands are located along migratory routes that are fluid and constantly recomposed by specific events, such as wars or agreements between countries on controls. The migrants who land on the islands express the desire to circulate freely in Europe. However, they collide with restrictive immigration policies designed to inhibit, if not to halt, the free movement of people.

The humanitarian rhetoric is used by European governments, and by the European Union itself, to reinforce the state of exception and emergency, thus giving the question of citizenship rights secondary importance. When the migrants – who lead a 'naked life' in the sense described by Giorgio Agamben (1996) – manifest their distress with public protests, they commit 'acts of citizenship' (Isin and Nielsen 2008) and in so doing become citizens, i.e. citizens who claim rights or the right to be right-holders. The humanitarian issue has been the focus of the European public discourse on immigration and border controls since 2004. In July of that year, the Cap Anamur, the ship of a German humanitarian organization, rescued thirty-seven Sudanese refugees originally from Darfur aboard a rubber dinghy drifting between Libya and Lampedusa. The Italian government did not authorize the ship to dock either in Lampedusa or Porto Empedocle, claiming that the Cap Anamur had entered Maltese waters. Italy therefore demanded the transfer of the migrants to Malta and gave Germany responsibility for the refugees because the ship was of German nationality. After a series of diplomatic negotiations, the ship declared a health emergency and was granted permission to enter the port of Porto Empedocle. Upon landing, the captain, the first officer, and the head of the aid agency were arrested on charges of aiding illegal immigration, only to be released a few days later.

Humanitarianism is used instrumentally to justify policies intended to deter migrants from travelling to Europe. It is a rhetorical mode designed to justify police operations by citing humanitarian arguments. In 2003, the Italian government signed an agreement with Libya on a joint strategy against illegal immigration. In 2007 Italy and Libya, reached an agreement for the joint patrolling of the Libyan coast to prevent 'tragedy at sea'. There is also a form of volunteer tourism on the islands, as in the case of the island of Lesbos, which reveals the capacity of tourists to imbue the insular space with symbolic meanings, confirming their role in the humanitarian borderscape of the island (Cavallo and Di Matteo 2021: 19–38).

The Mare Nostrum Operation was presented by the Italian government in 2013 as a humanitarian mission to save lives in the Strait of Sicily by relying on the humanitarian duties of Europe. It was replaced by the Frontex Triton Operation aimed at supporting the Italian authorities in border controls to prevent the illegal trafficking of migrants. While not presenting itself as a mission for eminently humanitarian purposes, Frontex Triton also falls within that rhetoric.

The protagonists of this history are the migrants and the island of Lampedusa, to which the label of 'island of solidarity' has been assigned. The political and media discourses depict a permanent state of emergency that forms the background to the solidarity of the island's population. On 5 July 2004 the then President of the Italian Republic, Carlo Azeglio Ciampi, awarded the town of Lampedusa and Linosa and the harbour master's office the gold medal for civil merit for the humanity shown by the Sicilians in coping with the emergency. In more recent times, the inhabitants of Lesbos and Lampedusa were nominated for the Nobel Peace prize after the massacres at sea of 2013. The nomination was officialized in 2014. As Joseph Martinetti has remarked, 'ramparts on the European shores of the Mediterranean, the Mediterranean islands are trapped in a territorial aporia' (2014: 13): they are strategic points of passage acting as a natural link between the two shores and, as peripheral areas of the European Union, they depend upon global geopolitical strategies, using a local identity as their defence. And coming to our aid here is the concept of borderscapes that express the spatial and conceptual complexity of the border as a space that is fluid and shifting (Brambilla 2015: 19), making it possible to investigate migration governance.

Observing the migration crisis in the Mediterranean and the post-1989 geopolitical reshuffle in the Baltic we notice that 'a sea not only separates islands from the mainland, but also connects them to realities inside and outside national and continental borders. A major awareness that these borders remain physically and conceptually fluid, and require permanent negotiation and legitimisation, could help a better handling and prevention of crises' (Paci 2016b: 28).

3

Insular identity in the Baltic Sea region

Let us take a closer look at a series of case studies in order to understand how islandness was built up in the Baltic region. The narratives produced in the Åland islands have transformed the archipelago into a model for the peaceful resolution of conflicts within the Nordic/Baltic area, where cooperation represents the main argument of self-representation. Similarly, the story of Gotland not only refers to the strategic importance of the island but, above all, to the way in which tourist marketing has presented the island, and Visby, the seat of Gotland Municipality, in particular, as the symbol of a new Hanse. The history of the small Estonian islands of Saaremaa, Hiiumaa and Ruhnu focuses our attention on their location between east and west: in terms of imaginative geography, these are the telltale signs of how these territories aspire to rediscover unity within the Baltic space in the wake of the Soviet occupation.

The Ålanders: Swedish-speakers in Finland

We are a people of the sea
the sea is our way
We live together with the sea, thanks to it and as part of it
We know that the sea gives and the sea takes,
that it isolates and connects
the sea is our past and our future
the sea is here and now.

Ålands sjöfartsmuseum (2016)

The archipelago of Åland is an autonomous Finnish province that can boast a centuries-old maritime tradition. The annual Prostrodden rowing competition – held in mid-June every year since 1974 – recalls the crossings that the Ålanders used to make between Sweden and Finland via Åland from 1638 to 1910. The aim of this reenactment is 'to remember Åland's rather meaningful position as a communication intermediator, the event "Postrodden" serves as a kind of cultural performance' (Grießner 2012: 89). What distinguishes the archipelago is its Swedish monolingualism, autonomous government recognized by international treaties and demilitarization (Edquist and Holmén 2015: 143–241).

Ålanders have developed a strong sense of identity (Holmén 2014: 135–54) that distinguishes them from the Swedish-speaking Finns of the continent who, contrary to the islanders, have not failed, on a number of occasions, to assert their allegiance to the Finnish state (Daftary 2000: 14–5). The Swedish-speaking population in mainland Finland strongly identifies itself with Finland. The Swedish language dominates all spheres of public life in Åland: the media, television, and the cultural offer are entirely in Swedish. Ålanders appear more 'realistic than the king' given that they usually affirm their belonging to Swedish culture in a more pervasive manner than Swedes born in Sweden (Eriksson, Johansson and Sundback 2006: 79).

Åland's geographical position has made it a place of strategic, above all, military relevance for centuries, as the archipelago could be used as a base for military operations in the north of the Baltic. Both Sweden and Russia, which controlled Finnish territory, had a particular interest in the islands for territorial defence. The invasion of Åland by a hostile state would have directly threatened Stockholm and the east of the country. If the archipelago had fallen into enemy hands, Russia would have feared for St Petersburg and the Russian Baltic fleet (Hannikainen 1994: 615). But in his doctoral thesis of law at the University of

Helsinki, the Swedish political liberal Johan Otto Söderhjelm maintained that until 1809 the Åland islands had had no great relevance to international politics. Two factors contributed to changing the Island's strategic value:

> The export of timber from the north of Sweden, that began in this period, followed a route that passed by Åland and touched on one of the supply routes of the British Empire. The construction of the fort of Bomarsund, not on the west side of the island of Åland, in the direction of Sweden, but on the east side [...] demonstrated that Russia understood the real importance of the island, from where it could threaten not only the West but could still dominate the entire Baltic.
>
> (1928: 323)

Because of their strategic position, the Åland islands became the focal point in the territorial disputes of Sweden, Russia and subsequently, Finland. (Daftary 2000: 13).

From the Kingdom of Sweden to the Russian Empire

The Åland islands were only absorbed into Swedish territory during the Swedish Crusades against the Finnish tribes in 1249 and 1293 (Padelford and Andersson 1939: 466). Their jurisdiction remained unresolved until 1634, when Axel Oxenstierna, the Chancellor of Sweden, reorganized the Vasa territories. It was then that the Åland islands were incorporated into the county of Turku-Pori, which was located in the south-west of Swedish Finland with its capital in Turku (Gregory 1923: 66).

In 1808, Czar Alexander I invaded Finland, evoking the treaty of Tilsit signed together with Napoleon on 7 July 1807 in which Russia and France established their respective spheres of influence (Jussila, Hentilä and Nevakivi 2004: 17). At the end of March 1808, the Russians occupied the entire southern coast of Finland and invaded the Åland Islands with an army of 840 men (Chillaud 2009: 22). Although they were subjected to food requisitions (Gregory 1923: 66), the Ålanders initially put up no resistance. However, on 6 May 1808, there was a popular uprising led by the local provost and by a clergyman that ended up decimating the Russian army five days later.

These conditions facilitated the Swedish counter-attack against the Russian forces deployed in the south-western part of Finland (Chillaud 2009: 22). In the meantime, a popular assembly declaring its loyalty to Sweden was set up on the Åland Islands (Gregory 1923: 66). As a result of the royal decree of 8 July 1808, the Åland Islands were incorporated into the county of Uppland, in Sweden (Padelford and Andersson 1939: 466). By the autumn of 1808, although it was by now obvious that Finland was in Russian hands, Sweden placed the defence of the Åland Islands at the centre of Swedish safety. In order to safeguard Swedish sovereignty on the archipelago, Sweden raised an army of 7,200 soldiers under the command of General Georg Carl von Döbeln. In the meantime, the Russians took advantage of the frozen Baltic to cross the archipelago to Sweden (Chillaud 2009: 22). This was a period of internal unrest for Sweden: King Gustav IV Adolf was deposed following a bloody coup d'état and on 17 March 1809, the Swedish troops abandoned the Åland Islands, which passed into Russian hands. Alexander I considered Finland to be a strategic rather than an ethnic entity as shown by the fact that he included the Åland Islands, which were Swedish in language and tradition, in the new state (Klinge 1994a: 58–9).

The first phase of the Russian occupation of the islands involved a large-scale deployment there of troops, officials and businessmen – but also craftsmen – causing the population of the Åland Islands to increase by 25 per cent. Civilians and military did not live in separate accommodation, however; between 1809 and 1839, Russian troops spent long periods living in the homes of Ålanders (Chillaud 2009: 19).

At the end of Swedish domination (1157–1809), the archipelago – situated 'in the centre of the Swedish lake' (Eriksson, Johansson and Sundback 2006: 9) – became, together with Finland, Russian territory. In the popular imagination of contemporary Ålanders, the period of Russian sovereignty is seen as a rupture between the long periods of Swedish domination and the phase inaugurated by Finland's declaration of independence in 1917 (Chillaud 2009: 19). Finland, including Åland, became a grand duchy with wide autonomy within a Czarist empire, retaining the constitution conceded by Sweden.

Åland played a secondary and peripheral role until they joined the Russian empire and became a strategic pawn on the international chessboard. This 'peripherality' also features in the inhabitants own self-perception: one could say that only when the archipelago assumed international relevance and no longer functioned as a bridge between Czarist Russia and the more central parts of Europe did claims for autonomy and separation emerge. During Russian domination, the inhabitants made no special claims for autonomy. The Russian empire did not have a repressive policy towards the archipelago, so much so that the Swedish language was preserved. It was only following the construction of the fortress of Bomarsund and the growing military presence that local peasants began worrying about their living conditions. As Pertti Joenniemi observed, the islands did not aspire to be decolonized and add to their subjectivity; rather, they aspired to shed the particularity imposed upon them and return to their previous existence as an ontologically safe entity, part of Sweden [...] Given that the islands had been integrated, as part of the Grand Duchy of Finland, into imperial Russia in 1809, the question of belonging re-emerged with full force with the demise of Czarist Russia and Finland gaining independence in 1917 (2014: 83).

From 1834, Sweden embarked on a route of neutrality, based on a policy of accommodation with the Czarist empire in the Baltic Sea and maintaining a particular stance regarding British interests in the area (Borioni 2005: 11). Annexed to the Russian empire as a buffer state with its own Diet (Klinge 1994a: 50), the new political entity created the Grand Duchy of Finland, kept up a solid economic relationship and cultural ties with Sweden. Finland's new territory (ex-Swedish Finland) remained in the Swedish orbit, while contact with Saint Petersburg was rather limited. General governor Zakrevskij called Finland 'my Siberia' (Jussila, Hentilä and Nevakivi 2004: 31). Despite Finland being of strategic importance to Russia for its proximity to Saint Petersburg (Klinge 1994a: 51), they controlled only the eastern part of the archipelago, while the western side was exposed to possible attack (Chillaud 2009: 23).

Between 1803 and 1825, the Russian Empire invested large sums to defend its realm: the forts of Brest-Litovsk, Dünaburg and Bobruisk protected the western front, while on the southern boundary the defence of Sevastopol was further reinforced, as was the fort of Kronstadt (Chillaud 2009: 25) in the Baltic. In 1830 the work, started in 1812 then interrupted, recommenced on the imposing granite fort at Bomarsund. Bomarsund's location was of strategic importance when Kronstadt, the Russian naval base on the Baltic, became icebound and practically unserviceable for many months of the year (Padelford and Andersson 1939: 467). The forts of Bomarsund and Sevastopol would have served as a base for the Czar's fleet charged with 'transforming the Baltic and Black Sea into a Russian lake' (Chillaud 2009: 27). The construction of the fortress of Bormasund was a concrete manifestation of the island's new role: that of a strategic outpost within the Russian Empire. On 15 August 1854, during the Crimean war, an Anglo-French fleet bombarded the Russian post at Bormasund. The following day, 2,000 defenders were arrested, the fort capitulated and was razed to the ground (Weibull 1996: 100); Åland was proclaimed 'free under the protection of the Western powers' (Rotkirch 1986: 360).

In 1854, a slim volume entitled *Les Îles d'Åland avec une carte et deuxgravures*, by Louis Léouzon Le Duc was published by the Parisian Librairie L. Hachette, bearing the incipit 'Bomarsund has fallen: the Åland islands are under the aegis of the joint forces of France and England. All eyes [...] are, as a result, on this region' (Léouzon Le Duc 1854: 1). At the outbreak of the war, French General Bernard Saint-Hillier went to Stockholm to offer Åland to Sweden in exchange for assisting the Franco-British fleet blockaded at Kronstadt. King Oskar I, fearing Russian reprisal, refused the offer (Padelford and Andersson 1939: 467). At the end of the Crimean war France and Britain invited the Swedish government to occupy the island, but Oskar refused it, not wanting to undermine the neutrality assumed in January 1854. Nonetheless, Sweden continued to pressure the French and British governments to restore the islands or at least render them neutral under the collective protection of France, Great Britain and Sweden. Great Britain supported the Swedish proposal, France did not (Rotkirch 1986: 360).

During the Congress of Paris, at the end of the war, the allied powers asked Russia not to establish any military or naval bases on the island (*The American Journal of International Law* 1908: 398). As a footnote to the Treaty of Paris, 30 (1856), which sanctioned the end of the war and the defeat of Russia, and signed by France, Great Britain, Russia, the Ottoman Empire, Austria, the Kingdom of Sardinia, and Prussia, was a convention establishing the demilitarization of Åland:

> In the name of almighty God, His Majesty the Emperor of All Russia, His Majesty the Emperor of France, and Her Majesty, the Queen of Great Britain and Ireland, desiring the extension to the Baltic Sea of the accord felicitously re-established between them and the East, in such a way as to secure the benefits of a general peace [...] declare that the Åland islands will not be fortified and that no military or naval base will be maintained or created.
> (Eriksson, Johansson and Sundback 1995: 11)

The convention comprised two articles: in the first, the Czar undertook, at the request of the French and British, to not fortify the island nor construct any naval bases; the second article declared the convention annexed to the peace treaty, as seen in article 33 of the general treaty signed at Paris the same day. It meant that even if Åland passed into other hands the Convention remained valid (Rotkirch 1986: 360). According to Jean Popovici, Great Britain pressed for the archipelago to not be fortified so as to hinder the construction of a Russian naval base in the Finland sea. 'Great Britain had always known how to reserve for itself maritime areas of greater strategic interest, leading to positive servitude: Gibraltar, Malta, etcetera..., flagrant breaches of international law, knew how to prevent the other powers doing the same' (1923: 22–3).

In reality, it came down to a 'declaration' which, according to article 33 of the convention, was intended to have the same binding force as the very Convention itself (Padelford and Andersson 1939: 467). The convention made no reference to neutrality and above all contained no detailed information about the area in which the obligation of demilitarization applied (Rotkirch 1986: 360). The moment that general indications became relative to a terrestrial area, nothing stood in the way of mining the waters of the archipelago. It was also unclear if Russia would be able to exercise the right to defend the islands in case of war (Rotkirch 1986: 361). The possible construction of fortifications by the Russians in time of war could be justified, starting in 1856, when Russia made a de facto 'declaration of intent' in reply to a desire shown by France and Britain, that the terrestrial and maritime area of Åland be demilitarized (Padelford and Andersson 1939: 468).

Russia and the demilitarization of the Åland islands (1904–14)

The territorial demilitarization of the Åland islands represented a sort of model: in the wake of the Crimean War, a concept of 'bloodlessness', of neutrality, took shape, and the idea began to emerge in the bourgeois circles of the coastal towns and in the liberal groups around the newspaper *Helsingfors Dagblad* that Finland should become a neutral country (Jussila, Hentilä and Nevakivi 2004: 57). 1905 saw the dissolution of the union established between Sweden and Norway in 1814 making it necessary to abrogate the treaty of guarantees concluded between France, Great Britain and Sweden in 1855 during the Crimean War. Under this treaty, France and Great Britain had undertaken to defend the Swedish and Norwegian territories from an eventual Russian attack (Rotkirch 1986: 361).

The Baltic Sea was a strategic space for the Russians: crossed by 50 per cent of the country's foreign trade and overlooked by the imperial capital, it was also a space where the German fleet was becoming a threatening factor (Padelford and Andersson 1939: 468). It is no coincidence that the concept of 'geopolitics' came into being in the context of the dissolution of the union between Sweden and Norway. Worried about the Russian Empire's threatening presence in northern Europe, the Swedish politician Rudolf Kjellén believed that the union with Norway was a necessary condition in order to safeguard the kingdom of Sweden and that an alliance with western countries – with Germany, in particular – would hinder Russian expansionism (Paci 2016a: 46).

In the 1906–8 period, the Åland islands lay at the heart of the Nordic and Baltic question. In that period, Russia drew up a pact with Great Britain regarding Tibet, Afghanistan and Iran, reassuring the German Government that it had no aggressive designs on Germany. On 29 October 1907, Russia and Germany signed a secret treaty at St Petersburg with the aim of maintaining the status quo in the Baltic area and of abolishing Russian obligations in the Åland islands – the so-called 'Åland servitude' – provided Sweden agreed to this (Padelford and Andersson 1939: 468). At the same time, Sweden hoped that the 1856 Convention would be maintained through an international agreement. This led, in fact, to the *Baltic Sea Declaration*, signed on 23 April 1908 in St Petersburg by Germany, Denmark, Russia and Sweden, which committed the four Baltic powers to maintaining the status quo in the region (Padelford and Andersson 1939: 468).

In the course of the First World War, the convention of 1856 remained in force despite the wish of the three committed parties, which had established an alliance in the course of the war (Rotkirch 1986: 366). However, at the start of 1915, fearing that Germany wanted to attack the islands, Russia took defensive measures by fortifying the archipelago. Fortification continued, albeit sporadically, during the course of the war, and by the end Åland became an immense fort (Rotkirch 1986: 362) In August 1915, German troops launched an attack on Utö, a small island in the eastern reaches of the archipelago (Rotkirch 1986: 362-3). The event caused an outcry in Sweden at the prospect of Swedish action in case of German occupation of the Island (Rotkirch 1986: 363). In an article entitled 'La Suède et la guerre' and published in *Le Figaro* on 11 August 1915, Swedish pro-entente publicist Erik Valentin Sjoestedt, argued for ceding the archipelago to Sweden as part of a rapprochement between Russia and Sweden against Germany (Chillaud 2009: 54).

A report sent by Francesco Tommasini, Italian Minister at Stockholm, to the Italian Minister of Foreign Affairs, Sidney Sonnino, on 14 April 1916, referred to the anti-Russian campaign carried out by the pro-German Swedish press and focusing on the matter of fortifications on the Åland islands (*I documenti diplomatici italiani* 1916a: 518–19). In May 1916, a question was raised in the Swedish Riksdag regarding the fortifications built by the Russians in the Åland islands. Reporting to Sonnino, Tommasini wrote:

We are clearly in the presence of an intensification of German plotting [...]. The parliamentary question has almost exactly the same contents as a very recent article in the *Deutsche Tageszeitung* regarding Åland. [...] The matter was undoubtedly chosen to provoke agitation given that Swedish public opinion had always been interested in this issue and during the 1908 negotiations for the agreement on the territorial status quo in the Baltic, the heads of the democratic parties explicitly declared that Sweden would not accept permanent fortifications in the archipelago.

(*I documenti diplomatici italiani* 1916b: 568)

Following the war, Åland was at the centre of a territorial dispute between Sweden and Finland. During the conflict, the Scandinavian press called for restituting of the archipelago to Sweden, claiming a parallel between Åland's situation and that of Schleswig or Alsace-Lorraine (Denier 1919: 10). As Jean Denier, pseudonym of Raymond Migeot, stated: 'Åland irredentism never really developed until the world war; it could be said that it was born because of the war' (Denier 1919: 13).

The origins of Ålandic irredentism (1917–22)

When civil war in Russia broke out in 1917, the Russians troops stationed on the islands tainted their reputation with grave abuses against the local peasants (Padelford and Andersson 1939: 469). On 20 August, a group of islanders representing the 'people of Åland' met in a popular high school (Folkhögskola) at Finström and adopted unanimously a resolution stating their desire to be reunited to Sweden. These representatives of the 'people of Åland' were peasant men without high levels of education who claimed to express the interests of all the population. They placed their hopes in Julius Sundblom and Carl Björkman, district prosecutors for the Swedish-speaking community of Finland, who appointed themselves interpreters of islanders' aspirations (Eriksson, Johansson and Sundback 2006: 82).

The islanders movement harked back to the romantic national Scandinavian movement, which in turn was inspired by German cultural nationalism. Language was considered the source of the nation's spirit just as nature and climatic conditions were considered to be the factors of significant impact on the formation of national character and temperament of the people (Eriksson, Johansson and Sundback 2006: 36). Åland's Swedish-speaking youth movement, influenced by national Scandinavian movements, organized musical festivals in the islands – known as Bygdesvenskhet (Eriksson, Johansson and Sundback 2006: 86–8). Bygdesvenskhet means 'rural Swedishness', a form of national romanticism focused on the Swedish peasant population in Finland that was contrasted to the kultursvenskhet (cultural Swedishness) of the Swedish-speaking elites in Turku and Helsinki.

One of the figures at the forefront of the Ålandic cultural movement was Otto Andersson, distinguished expert of Swedish music in Finland. In 1906, he founded the Brage society, which aimed to conserve and promote Swedish poetry, music and popular dances in Finland (Andersson 1920: 2). Andersson spent many years collecting songs and melodies from popular culture in the Swedish-speaking communities in Ostrobothnia, the Åland islands and in the provinces of Turku and Uusimaa. He collected 3,000 samples, roughly 2,000 of which are in the archives of the Society of Swedish Literature in Finland (Andersson 1920: 1).

Andersson was not in agreement with some of the premises on which the movement was grounded, beginning with the claim that the Ålanders were culturally closer to the Swedish than to Swedish-speakers in Finland. This opinion, along with other ideas, led to Andersson's removal from the official representatives of the movement and caused him to be labelled as a persona non grata who was damaging to the irredentist cause (Eriksson, Johansson and Sundback 2006: 88). The 1890s saw the emergence in Sweden of a nationalist movement known as Allsvensk Samling, led by the philologist Vilhelm Lundström under the motto of 'Swedes of the world unite'. Based in Uppsala and Göteborg, Lundström's movement sought to unite Swedes scattered all over the world through the primacy of the Swedish language, thereby addressing not only Swedes in Sweden but also Swedish emigrants in America and the Swedish-speaking communities in Finland and Estonia. The movement reached its height between 1919 and 1923, also giving rise to the national association for the preservation of Swedish culture outside Sweden (Eriksson, Johansson and Sundback 2006: 90).

The Ålandic movement authoritatively guided by Julius Sundblom had various aspects in common with the Allsvensk Samling, especially with regard to the idealistic concept of a language community living in harmony in its social context (Eriksson, Johansson and Sundback 2006: 91). Following the proclamation of the Soviet Republic on 7 November 1917, and the declaration on the rights of nationalities to take care of their own affairs, the hopes of the Ålanders grew that their request would find fertile terrain. However, no action was taken. A pamphlet printed in Helsinki in June 1920 underlined that before the war, the same leaders of the separatist movement expressed no desire to separate from Finland (*The Åland Question* 1920: 4). It was acknowledged that Sundblom had deemed the Ålanders as belonging to the 'Swedish race' of Finland, considered as the common homeland of the Finnish and the Swedish (Hermanson 1921: 82).

At a youth rally at Mariehamn on 22 June 1898, Sundblom explained:

> We must cultivate the legacy of our fathers. We must give our best for the Fatherland whose legacy they bequeathed; we must work with alacrity for the native soil which we are entitled to consider our own [...] *Swedish and Finnish*

fighting side by side when the struggle was fierce and heroic blood reddened the snow. There was only one homeland, one people. This is true today and will be so for eternity. Providence has judged well, in its wisdom, to place side by side in this country two groups with different tongues. United in working for the possession of the fatherland [...] *The Swedish race in Finland is one*, even though it is scattered over many hundreds of miles of coastline, our objective is common.

(Hermanson 1921: 82–3)

In another speech at Turku on 17 June 1906, at a choral performance, Sundblom reaffirmed the need for a common front – Ålanders and Swedish-speakers of Finland – because 'united is the fatherland, the land of our fathers and our sons, so dear and precious to each of us, whatever the language or social position' (Hermanson 1921: 83).

On 28 June 1908, Sundblom, guest at a musical festival, reiterated yet again the shared goals of the Finnish and Swedish-speakers of Finland, rejecting the accusation that the Swedish-speakers, including the Ålanders 'lacked patriotic sentiment, because we retain our special character and safeguard our mother tongue as the most precious thing we possess after the fatherland, our most prized legacy' (Hermanson 1921: 84). Sundblom's declarations between 1898 and 1908 reveal how the concept of sovereignty implied achieving a cultural autonomy shared with the Swedish-speakers of Finland. Most of the Åland population shared this position: what really mattered to the islanders was to preserve the Swedish language.

The idea of annexation emerged in 1917, when life conditions in Sweden were decisively better than in Finland. Terrorized by the brutality of the Russian soldiers and the Bolshevik regime in Finland, it made sense for the islanders to renounce sovereignty for an annexation that would have conferred a measure of protection against international interference. On 4 December 1917, Finland proclaimed itself an independent sovereign state and on the 31st was recognized by the Bolshevik government (Padelford and Andersson 1939: 469). Soviet Union's declaration recognizing Finland contained no mention of the Grand Duchy of Finland. If, on the contrary, the line of continuity between the Grand Duchy and the new Finnish state had been made explicit, it would have been possible to affirm with absolute certainty that the archipelago now came under Finland's authority. The Finnish declaration of independence thus raised again the question of the demilitarization of Åland. This posed the problem of compliance by the new state with the treaties concluded with Russia before independence.

Finland assumed a fairly clear position and took a resolute approach to the issue, opposing a simple refusal to recognize the obligations deriving from the 1856 convention. In turn, the Swedes observed that such obligations constituted a constraint that remained even when the territory became part of another state (Rotkirch 1986: 366). The Åland secessionists started to mobilize in favour of secession from Finland and for union with Sweden in August 1917, four months before the Finnish declaration of independence (Stanbridge 2002: 534). Several scholars have observed that separatist sentiment and that of union with Sweden predated 1917. Karen Stanbridge notes, however, that the lack of public opinion hostile to Finland suggests that protests, which took place in the post-war period, need be understood within the context of an Europe characterized by a vast cycle of agitation accompanied by the emergence of the principle of self-determination, the so-called 'self-determination master frame' (Stanbridge 2002: 535).

On 3 February 1918, an Åland delegation arrived in Stockholm to deliver to the Swedish king Gustav V, a petition signed by 7135 islanders bearing the date of 31 December 1917, requesting annexation to Sweden (Gregory 1923: 67). The islanders presented two unofficial petitions – the first of December 1917, when Finland became independent and then of June 1919 – in which most islanders declared themselves in favour of reunion (Daftary 2000: 19). The islanders feared that Finland's independence and the possibility of a socialist government could jeopardize the Swedish language and culture of the archipelago.

This concern was not shared by most Finnish Swedish-speakers who lived on the mainland (Rotkirch 1986: 358), having vastly different expectations: rather than aspire to reunion with Sweden, they sought to acquire power within a Finnish majority state (Stanbridge 2002: 544). At the end of the civil war, most of the population of the archipelago indicated intent to become incorporated into Swedish territory. In spring 1919, without consulting the Finnish government, on the occasion of the Paris Peace Conference, the Åland representatives launched an appeal asking that the resolution of the Åland question by referendum be added. Sweden supported their request, putting forward history and language as motivating reasons and declaring that there was no historical foundation for the archipelago to belong to Finland (Jussila, Hentilä and Nevakivi 2004: 135).

The Swedish leaders were convinced that the arguments in favour of self-determination would have a considerable part to play in the peace Conference, believing that if the Åland question should be examined by the allied powers, the islands would certainly return to Swedish sovereignty (Stanbridge 2002: 536). On 12 February 1919, in another meeting with the representatives at the Paris Peace Conference, the islanders reaffirmed that the separatist movement drew inspiration from Wilson's Fourteen Points (Stanbridge 2002: 536). During the first phase of negotiations, the great powers showed themselves well-disposed towards the Åland separatists. Francesco Tommasini, who declared a thorough knowledge of the matter, was particularly sensitive to the islanders' cause, seeing numerous similarities with the irredentist lands.

> The Swedish claims to the Åland islands are based on such solid historical and ethnographic grounds that is seems impossible that Italy, which has based all its war policy on the same foundation, could refuse at least a show of platonic sympathy; such a show, could be accompanied by a reserve justified by the desire to proceed with caution with the allies and for the necessity to resolve the Åland question so as not to step on the toes of Finland, and in the interests of a good relationship between Finland and Sweden. Such an approach does not seem to me to present any difficulties and would make a good impression here where public opinion is favourable to annexation. I know the Åland question in detail, having spoken at length with Mannerheim and all the prominent Swedish figures and would deem it opportune that V. E, before taking any position on the matter, permit me to brief him.
> (*I documenti diplomatici italiani* 1919: 404)

The portrayal of the Åland question in the press reflected the allies' prevalent trend of wanting to hold up the case of the islanders as a defence of the principle of moral, if not political, self-determination (Stanbridge 2002: 539).

The Paris Peace Conference deemed it necessary to submit the Åland question to examination by the League of Nations. On 6 May 1920, the Finnish parliament intended to meet the islanders' demands, proposing a law giving Åland its own regional Council and special rights in consideration of their special status (Jussila, Hentilä and Nevakivi 2004: 135). This 'home rule act' conceded to Åland displeased the irredentist leaders who, referring to the principle of self-determination, turned to the Swedish government, to the king of Sweden, and to international representatives at Stockholm, to express again their desire to reunite with the Swedish motherland (Stanbridge 2002: 542). Besides recognition of a regional Council with legislative powers, the law on self-government reserved competence on some matters to the national assembly in Helsinki. Once freedom of movement, choice of residence and private and patrimonial rights remained under the control of the central state, such a status would not, in any case, have conferred to Ålanders the option of putting a stop to Finnish immigration (Williams 2009: 98).

After rejecting the proposal, the Åland leaders announced their intention to convene a national assembly of the archipelago to take an official position on separation from Finland. Swedish officials supported *in toto* the islanders' requests, exploiting the provocative separatist declarations to induce the representatives of the Allied Powers to intervene resolutely. On 19 June 1920, the Åland question was brought before the League of Nations as a question of international relations. After consulting the representatives of Finland, Sweden and Åland, and having reached a consensus a commission of enquiry composed of three international jurists was set up to look into the matter (Gregory 1923: 64). The members of the commission were called upon to produce as quickly as possible a verdict on the matter of international obligations concerning demilitarization and to evaluate, with reference to paragraph 8 of article 15 of the Convention, if the Åland case came under Finnish jurisdiction or if it was necessary to fall back on international law. The commission verified above all that the question was not strictly within Finnish competence and that the peace treaty of 30 March 1856, was still valid regarding the demilitarization status of the archipelago (Gregory 1923: 64).

According to the commission, the 1856 Convention should remain in force to safeguard 'European interests' (Rotkirch 1986: 366). To justify the decision of assigning the League of Nations the task of giving a definitive verdict, the commission of jurists pointed out that the matter had been raised before Finland became an independent state. As such, the matter could not be treated as a Finnish 'internal matter' (Rotkirch 1986: 366-7). Finland accepted that the League of Nations should rule on the issue (Gregory 1923: 64). On 20 September 1920, the commission drafted a report in which the League of Nations declared itself competent to intervene (Rotkirch 1986: 367). After resolving the legal questions, the knotty political issues remained. For this, the League of Nations set up a commission of experts to examine the question to give useful indications on how to maintain peace in this area. The commission backed the jurists' opinion regarding the competence of the League of Nations to intervene on the matter. On 5 September 1920, the commission ruled on the merits of the Åland case, declaring on the matter of the right to self-determination that, in the interests of peace, a compromise that gave ample liberty to the minorities would be preferable. On the matter of demilitarization of the archipelago, the commission upheld the validity of the 1856 peace treaty (Brown 1921: 271).

On examining the legal, historical, strategic and geographical aspects and having listened to the Swedish, Finnish and Åland representatives, the commission drafted a report dated 16 April 1921, in which they declared with absolute certainty that Åland belonged to Finland and that as such the request to reunite with Sweden was quite illegitimate (Gregory 1923: 65). The commission judged it appropriate that the Swedish language be protected and that in primary schools and technical Swedish be the sole language of instruction. On 27 June, the League of Nations Council established a series of guarantees protecting the culture of the archipelago, which were incorporated into Finnish law on 11 August 1922, as a guarantee (Daftary 2000: 20). The decision taken by the League of Nations was received with bitterness by the Swedes and for a brief period upset relations, 'otherwise excellent', between Sweden and Finland (Weibull 1996: 124). In international circles, the decision was, on the contrary, greeted favourably for it introduced a peaceful way of regulating conflicts involving national minorities. The first plenary session of the Landsting, the first Åland parliament, took place on 9 June 1922 (Eriksson, Johansson and Sundback 1995: 37).

Julius Sundblom, leader of the irredentist movement, was nominated Speaker of Parliament and concluded his speech by paying tribute to autonomy and peaceful relations with Finland. Certainly, there were occasions on which the islanders held on to and emphasized their distinct character in relation to

Figure 1. The seat of the Ålands Lagting (Parliament of Åland). According to the Act on the Autonomy of Åland (also known as the Autonomy Act), the Ålands Lagting is the elected parliament.
The Parliament of Åland by Magne Kveseth on norden.org via Wikimedia Commons.

the Finnish Swedish-speakers, such as the musical and choral that took place during the 1922 midsummer festival. The islanders sang Ålänningens for the first time (Eriksson, Johansson and Sundback 2006: 91), a song for Åland composed by John Grandell, and refused to conclude with the Finnish anthem 'Maamme'. They waved their blue, yellow, blue flag (Eriksson, Johansson and Sundback 1995: 62). The final verse of Ålänningens eulogized the Swedish language, with no explicit reference to the Swedish spoken in Sweden or Finland (Eriksson, Johansson and Sundback 1995: 62). Nonetheless, all this revealed how the notion of sovereignty was fundamentally linked to that of autonomy, as opposed to annexation, which was a testament to non-sovereignty.

As Barbro Sundback points out, one among a panorama of Åland representatives, the islanders' self-image changed over time. In the popular imagination in the middle of the last century, they saw themselves as victims of a cruel destiny that had put the archipelago in the hands of foreign powers. Gaining autonomy modified this perception, giving the islanders an active role in the battle for island sovereignty, with the effect that the islanders would increasingly trust in their capacity to meet the interests and needs of their population through democratic and peaceful means (Eriksson, Johansson and Sundback 1995: 59).

In the popular imagination, the islanders were a distinct group of people, different from all others, be they Finnish, Swedish, or the Finnish Swedish-speakers (Eriksson, Johansson and Sundback 1995: 72). Identity is not something immutable. Over time, the Ålandic identity has evolved, and today many Ålanders describe themselves as Europeans, Nordic, Finlanders and Ålanders. The peaceful arbitration of the Åland question – made possible by the preeminence given to international law – constituted a precedent of undoubted relevance, representing a new model of solving conflicts on the sovereignty of part of a territory held within a national state. It was, in fact, one of the first disputes between states in the years immediately after the First World War and preceded the establishment of the permanent International Court of Justice.

On 9 June 1982, Mauno Koivisto, the newly elected president of the Finnish Republic, invited as guest of honour to the 70th anniversary celebration of autonomy, placed great value on the close relationship between the Finnish state and the archipelago, based on the principle of consensus in matters of autonomy (Johansson 1984: 38). In 1997, the then-Finnish president Martti Oiva Kalevi Ahtisaari, spoke several times of the political consensus that distinguished relations between the Åland islands and Finland following the Second World War. In a speech, he expressed the hope that Finland would continue to promote the autonomy of Åland on the basis of consensus and mutual respect (Eriksson, Johansson and Sundback 2006: 74). Going back to Pertti Joenniemi's words, which sum up well the situation of Åland as a 'land in-between' (2014: 87), we can say that 'the islands have actually become accustomed to being "partly in, partly out", both regarding Finland and Sweden but also more generally in relation to the standard categories and concepts applied in organizing political space' (Joenniemi 2014: 93)

'Universi mercatores Imperii Romani Gotlandiam frequentantes'. Gotland as a strategic island for the security of the Baltic Sea region

The sea creates daring and freedom loving men,
for the open sea is the home of the brave and free.
This love of the open sea with its fresh life of adventure has in the Gutnish people preserved that
strong love of freedom and independence, which has made the independent Gutnish yeomen, the proud Gutnish Vikings – the free sons of the sea – unwilling to submit to the will of a lord
   Alfred Theodor Snöbohm, Götiska stammer (1871)

Gotland is one of Sweden's twenty-five historical provinces (*landskap*), and constitutes a separate county (*län*). On 1 January 2011 Gotland's county became Region Gotland. This autonomy recognizes the significant role played in the history of the Baltic area by the island of Gotland, which had an important trade function from the time of the Roman Empire. Already by the early Middle Ages, the island enjoyed the status of an autonomous peasant republic with its own provincial code of law known as *Guta Lagh* (Cabouret 1992: 194). In the tenth century Gotland was independent of Sweden, but by the twelfth century it was subject to Sweden as shown by a document in Latin dated to c.1120. The text of the document, commonly called *Florensdokument* in Swedish, as well as enumerating the Swedish bishoprics, lists Guthlandia as one of the *insulae* of Sweden (Peel 2009: VIII). From c. 1100 onwards Gotland was organized into twenty *thing* districts that served as means of organizing both societal relations and the physical space. The all-thing of Gotland, the island's central assembly and supreme legal instance, reveals the existence of an egalitarian society of free farmers on Gotland during the Viking Age and Middle Ages.

The image of Gotland as an egalitarian farming and trading society is mentioned in the *Guta Saga* and *Guta Lagh* (Myrberg 2009: 101–3). The *Guta Saga* (composed in the thirteenth century, the sole surviving manuscript dates from the mid-fourteenth century) is the founding text of the community of Gotland. It describes how the islanders signed a treaty with the Swedish kingdom in the pre-Christian period that proclaimed the independence of the island. The ancient Gotlanders or Gutes (*gutar*) represented themselves as a nation in their own right, with their own specific language that was distinct both from that used by the continental Swedes and that used by the Geats (*götar*), the people inhabiting Götaland, a historic land in the south of Sweden (Edquist 2015: 42). Today, even though the Gotlanders feel deeply Swedish, they tend to underline their regional uniqueness by harking back to the medieval golden age. The *Guta Saga* is divided into three parts: the first (Chapter I) discusses the island's legendary past; the second (Chapters II–III) describes a number of historic events, including the stipulation of the agreement with the Swedish king and the islanders' conversion to Christianity; lastly, the third part (chapter IV) deals with the Gotlanders' obligations towards the Swedish king in the event of war.

The *Guta Lagh*, the law of the Gotlanders, was the fourteenth-century law codex in use on the island. In 1871, local historian Alfred Theodor Snöbohm described pre-Christian Gotland as 'pure democracy in which the people themselves possessed the power and the government, and exercised it' (Edquist 2015: 69). Even though Gotland belonged to the Kingdom of Sweden, Swedish influence was rather limited: 'in the Guta law, the king was not mentioned and he had no rights to any fine, like he had in the rest of Sweden's regional laws [...], which is a very strong indicator that he had no judicial or administrative power on Gotland' (Svedjemo 2014: 190).

The Golden Age of Gotland: Visby, hub of the Baltic

In the medieval communication network on the Baltic Sea, Gotland, rather than being isolated space, was a crossroads of international trade. By the end of the tenth century, Gotland had become a place of passage within the Baltic network of trade relationships (Lindberg 1961: 427–8). In 1161, in Artlenburg, in Lower Saxony, the representatives of Visby signed a treaty with Henry the Lion, the duke of Bavaria and Saxony, which cancelled the trade monopoly previously in existence with the city of Lübeck and making it possible for the rest of the German world to trade at Visby. In fact, it was as a result of this agreement that a large group of German merchants travelled to Visby.

In 1161, the first Hanse trade organization was founded in Visby, taking the name of 'Universi mercatores Imperii Romani Gotlandiam frequentantes' (United Gotland Travellers of the Holy Roman Empire). A document from 1252, a privilege granted by Countess Margaret of Flanders, contains the first mention of a Gotland Travelers Association (North 2015: 55). At that time Visby was a 'dual city'; in other words, it was governed by two councils, one Scandinavian, the other German. It was subsequently run by a single council whose members were chosen from both ethnic groups (Meyer 2013: chap. 1).

The Hanse was a company or commercial corporation that undertook to safeguard common interests. The term designated both the tax that merchants were required to pay in order to become members of a group trading internationally as well as the group itself. Max Weber once noted that the medieval cities belonging to the Hanse League were self-sufficient bodies that, in case of need, could choose to withdraw from international trade due to their reciprocal support within an area that was completely under their control (Gras 2013: chap. VII). The Hanse had no central government, instead governing itself on the basis of a body of laws and custom: 'In its early days, the League aimed to consolidate the legal rights of anchorage, storage, residence, and local immunity, which its members required to conduct their business. It was also concerned to stabilize currency and to facilitate the means of payment' (Davies 1997: 880).

The unique geographical features of Gotland favoured its development in the golden age of the Hanse: 'The history of Hanseatic communications in general, and maritime history in particular, are about connections and communication, tending to ignore the isolation side of the story' (Kreem 2011: 120). During the course of the twelfth century, the Gotlanders, together with merchants from Denmark, Russia and later also Germany, built a trade network between Novgorod, Gotland and Denmark that transformed Visby into a strategic node. The delegates from the different leagues met periodically to establish a common policy. The Gotlanders mainly traded in furs and beeswax, which were not produced on the island but bought in Russia. Although Visby's prominent role in the international trade networks caused it to become a very wealthy centre, it later underwent a gradual decline. Very soon, the league found itself dealing with pirate raids. In that period, there were various contenders seeking to attain hegemony over the Baltic area: the Hanse, the Order of Teutonic Knights and the Kingdom of Denmark. Visby lost its primacy within the Hanse due to an outbreak of plague on the island in 1350 followed by the invasion, in 1361, of the Danish army led by King Valdemar Atterdag. Gotland was plundered and occupied by the Danish troops and subsequently raided by pirates. The island's subsequent exclusion from the trade routes further weakened an economy that was already very fragile.

Gotland goes from Danish to Swedish rule

In 1402, the Gotlanders were forced to lease out their old trading station (*Faktorei*) Gotenhof in Novgorod to the newly emergent city of Reval/Tallinn (Rebas 229). In 1525, Gotland's economy suffered new setbacks when troops from Lübeck pillaged the northern part of the island. From 1398 to 1408, Gotland was occupied by the Teutonic Order before returning under Danish control. In 1411, three years after the island's cession to Denmark, the new sovereign, Eric of Pomerania, began work on Visborg Castle in Visby. After the dissolution of the Kalmar Union, Eric lost the throne of Sweden and Denmark, and withdrew to his island fortress, where he sought to regain his power. About a century later, the island's importance re-emerged. Between 1517 and 1520, it became the base of operations for the fleet of Admiral Søren Norby, which engaged in raids and acts of piracy.

On 18 May 1518, Norby, who was highly esteemed by the King of Denmark Christian II, received the island as his personal fiefdom directly from the sovereign. At that time, the kingdom of Denmark had been engaged in a war against Lübeck and the Kingdom of Sweden; its ultimate victory was due in no small measure to Norby's contribution. He exploited Visby's strategic position to obtain huge military successes, also playing a decisive role in the blockade of Stockholm, which allowed Christian II of Denmark to secure the Swedish throne, albeit for only a brief period. On several occasions between 1524 and 1524, Norby or his men were forced to barricade themselves in the impregnable Visborg fortress (Glete 2013). Gotland remained under Danish control until 1645 when the island was ceded to the Kingdom of Sweden under the Peace of Brömsebro, in the context of the Thirty Years' War. It was briefly reconquered by the Danish (1676–8) before returning under Swedish rule: on that occasion Visborg fortress was almost totally destroyed.

In nineteenth-century historiography, this event was considered totally natural because it meant the recognition of Gotland's natural belonging to Sweden. According to Gotlandic historiography, 1361, the year marking the start of Danish rule of Gotland, was the 'year of misfortune' (Thordeman 1939: 27) because it coincided with the beginning of a political season distinguished by corruption and oppression that would only end with Gotland's return to the motherland.

Few Gotlandic historians recognized the discontent of the Gotlanders. Among them was nineteenth-century historian Theodor Erlandsson, who wrote: 'in the beginning [...] this unification caused a harmful interruption of people's development. Gotlandic civilization had never ever been Swedish, but had been independent from the start. Therefore, there was also long a general dissatisfaction with the new order' (Edquist 2015: 84). In 1908, Erlandsson was among the founders of the Bunge Museet, an outdoor ethnographic museum which shows how the Gotlandic peasants of the past lived. 'In Gotland tradition sets up a rural mindscape: "tradition is all over the countryside, every parish, every family, every group can have its own tradition"' (Ronström 2005: 9). Bunge Museet is Gotland's version of Sweden's national ethnographic museum in Stockholm, Skansen.

Here, '"tradition" is produced, in a poetics that centers on the local and regional, "the folk" and "the peasantry" of the 17th to the 19th centuries' (Ronström 2005: 5). The Swedes wasted no time in developing a strategy to improve the island's agricultural productivity, which was lower than that in the other areas in the kingdom. In the eighteenth century, there were only 195 km^2 of arable land, half of which always lay fallow as part of the practice of crop rotation.

From 1766 to 1788, Gotland was governed by Carl Otto von Segebaden, who ushered in a period of social renewal and economic development for the island. Von Segebaden introduced agrarian reform, new crops and oversaw the construction of a modern road network. His efforts were much appreciated and he was considered a hero. He was even compared to Gustav I Vasa, the founding father of Sweden. Jonh Nihlén described Segebaden as 'Gotland's "father of the nation"' (Edquist 2015: 87). The nineteenth century saw the launch of policies for wide-scale land reclamation and the reorganization of land ownership: in 1820, a drainage programme was carried out followed by extensive deforestation that produced approximately 470 km^2 of additional arable land. Wheat crops went from around 10,000 tonnes in 1805 to 50,000 tonnes just a century later. Thanks to the exploitation of natural resources in the nineteenth century, Gotland experienced sharp demographic growth.

Between 1800 and 1880, the population grew from 31,000 to 55,000. Nevertheless, in the 1880s, following a series of poor harvests, there was an increase in emigration: 6,000 people (10 per cent of Gotlanders) emigrated to the Swedish continent or to the United States. There was also demographic movement within families who moved from rural areas to towns, especially to Visby. In 1900, the urban population was 8,400 people compared to 4,600 in 1850. Moreover, growing industrialization in the early 1900s led to an increase in income levels and in purchasing power. The creation of a railway network helped to start up a previously marginal economic machine, revealing the importance of Gotland's agricultural production for Stockholm. The industrial revolution that took place on the island led to the birth of food processing industries and a timber industry. Gotland was able to supply timber for the coal mines in Great Britain and the Ruhr (Zucchetto and Jansson 1985: 24–5).

The strategic and military importance of Gotland

During the 1808–9 Russian-Swedish War, Sweden lost Finland and on 22 April 1808, Russian troops under Admiral Nikolay Bodisko occupied Gotland. However, the Russian presence lasted only three weeks (Mikaberidze 2005: 42).

During the Crimean War (1853–6), the combined British and French fleet used Fårö Bay as a temporary base with around 200 warships and 238 other craft docking in this natural port. Sweden introduced conscription on the island, creating an infantry regiment in 1887: slowly but inexorably, the military presence on the island increased.

At the beginning of the twentieth century, the Swedish government bought up land in Fårösund, on northern Gotland, and in 1938 a coastal artillery division, KA 3, was set up. Because of a national defence resolution in 1936, the coastal artillery defence on Gotland was enlarged with 'permanent defense establishments' in Fårösund (Feldmann 2010: 28). During the two world wars, Gotland was fortified but remained otherwise untouched by wartime events. There were a number of incidents in Swedish waters including the destruction of part of the Russian navy by the German ship SMS Albatross in 1915 and the sinking by a Russian submarine of the Swedish passenger ship S/S Hanse, which was heading for Visby from the mainland in 1944. At the end of the Second World War, the island temporarily housed around 10,000 refugees from the Baltic States, who had fled from the advancing Soviet troops (Wedin 2017: 140–1).

During the Cold War, the military presence was stepped up and two field artillery regiments were stationed on Gotland. The Gotland Brigade comprised three mechanized battalions, a company of assault vehicles and one of anti-tank artillery. In addition there was a coastal artillery regiment, an anti-aircraft artillery regiment, and two further mechanized regiments. This military presence on the island, concentrated in a few thousand kilometres, reveals Sweden's high level of alert, 'especially if we consider the tendentially neutral position of Sweden' (Congregalli 2018). Following the dissolution of the Soviet Union, the regiments stationed in Gotland were gradually demobilized, until 2005 when the demobilization process was completed. It was then that the island became a very popular summer tourist resort.

Russia's invasion of Crimea in 2014 was obviously a cause of concern for the NATO countries lying within Russia's orbit: Estonia, Latvia and Lithuania introduced compulsory military service and launched a series of measures to train civilians in use of weapons and guerrilla techniques in the event of a Russian invasion. In March 2015, Russia's military performed large-scale war games in the waters south and north of Sweden and Finland's coastlines. Some 30,000 Russian soldiers rehearsed a military takeover and seizure of Gotland, Bornholm, Åland islands and northern Norway. We cannot ignore the fact that Gotland is Sweden's strategically located island province because it is roughly

90 kilometres off mainland Sweden, 130 kilometres from Latvia and only 248 kilometres from the Russian exclave of Kaliningrad.

From 2015 onwards, Sweden began to take steps to begin remilitarizing Gotland, given its leading strategic role in the Baltic area:

> Maintaining Gotland in Swedish hands is vital to the protection of the mainland as well as ensuring the island cannot be used by a potential occupier to extort concessions from Sweden. Retaining Stockholm's control over Gotland is also necessary to allow the North Atlantic Treaty Organization (NATO) unfettered access to Estonia, Latvia and Lithuania with reinforcements via the Baltic. Were Moscow to take control of Gotland Island, the Baltic Sea would be transformed into a Russian inland sea, severely limiting the aerial and sea-based activities of the region's other littoral countries. As a result, the Baltic States would be cut off.
> (Elfving 2017)

In 2016, the Swedish government allocated more budgetary resources to national defence by hosting NATO-led military exercises on its territory. The Swedish Defence Commission notes that

> The security situation in Europe has deteriorated over time, due to Russia's actions… an armed attack on Sweden cannot be excluded, nor can the use of military measures against Sweden, or threats thereof. The Swedish total defence will be developed and designed to ensure that Sweden is prepared in order to meet an armed attack against Sweden, including other acts of war on Swedish territory.
> (Bergman Rosamond and Kronsell 2020: 8)

Furthermore, in October 2016, Sweden objected to the use of the Gotland port of Slite for the construction of the Nord Stream 2 gas pipeline, due to concerns about the defence of Gotland (Gotkowska and Szymański 2016). In December 2017, Sweden established a unit of 350 soldiers based on Gotland (The Associated Press 2020).

This renewed military presence on the island stems from fears of an eventual Russian occupation of Gotland: 'if we have a conflict concerning the Baltic countries, that there would be a need for Russia to occupy Gotland and use it as a base for preventing support from Nato' (Schofield 2016).

Gotland: historic heritage and tourist brand

The collective imaginary is dominated by the idea that Gotland experienced a golden age in the medieval period and the tourist industry focuses a lot of its energies on promoting initiatives intended to evoke the island's medieval past. Nowadays there are two dominant narratives on Gotland: the medieval one and the folklore one: 'Heritage and cultural identity are important for the region's economic prosperity' (Edquist 2015: 113). An article published in 1940 in *Sapere*, Italy's oldest scientific journal, points out that although Visby was no longer strategically important as a 'maritime city', it still had 'traces belonging to the most important Swedish trade centre of the Middle Ages' (Podestà 1940). The article mentioned the 'ruins of magnificent churches, eleven of which still standing, giving the city a character that can only be found travelling much further south in Europe' (Podestà 1940). This Italian scholar imagined that Gotland's historic heritage caused it to resemble certain Mediterranean islands, thereby, in a certain sense, enhancing the Baltic Sea: 'One could almost believe that a classic Mediterranean island has been transported, as if by magic, to the distant Baltic' (Podestà 1940).

In 1874, Per Arvid Säve and other local intellectuals established Gotlands Fornvänner (The Friends of Gotland's Antiquities), an association that aimed to promote the island's medieval and prehistoric heritage. The following year, the association founded a museum known as Gotlands Fornsal (the Hall of Gotland's Antiquities) followed, in 1929, by the influential annual journal *Gotländskt Arkiv* (Holmén and Edquist 2012: 75). Gotlands Fornvänner looked at Gotland's

Figure 2. A view of the Medieval Week in Visby in 2011.
Medieval week, Östergravar, Visby, Gotland by Helen Simonsson on flickr.

cultural history 'rooted in a Romantic notion of the countryside and its people' (Edquist 2015: 49). Every year since 1984, Gotland hosts a medieval week with various events that have proved very popular among tourists.

Although the original idea was inspired by a wish that took shape during the 1980s to connect Swedes again to their local heritage, the medieval week has become a '"paradise for all who like jousting, markets, church concerts, street theatre, fire shows, storytelling, walks, lectures and more" with more than 500 events in one week, attracting 40000 visitors' (Schaub 2020: 31). The construction of Gotland's medieval imaginary is a project that has been pursued coherently for a long time: 'The dominant topic in the island's regional history writing, from the nineteenth century and well into our own age, is the stress on the perceived peaceful, prosperous and independent "peasant republic" of the early Middle Ages' (Holmén and Edquist 2012: 77).

Gotland has referred extensively to its heritage of history and identity as one of the main arguments in favour of a claim for greater powers of self-government although this did not give rise to a strategy of regional self-government (Olsson and Aström 2004: 349). Visby has become both a symbolic gateway to the outside world and 'a linguistic archaism, a true endemism expressing a kind of insular withdrawal' (Cabouret 1992: 195). This vocation is confirmed by the fact that in 1995 Visby was inscribed on the World Heritage List. 'The Committee decided to inscribe this site on the basis of criteria (iv) and (v) considering its outstanding universal value, representing a unique example of a north European medieval walled trading town which preserves with remarkable completeness a townscape and assemblage of high-quality ancient buildings that illustrate graphically the form and function of this type of significant human settlement' (Malmros and Hallberg 2012: 53). This recognition followed in the wake of a series of measures introduced by the Swedish government to promote Visby's cultural and architectural heritage. In 1973, a special committee drew up a report with the title *Visby – Staden Inom Murarna* (Visby – the Town within the Walls), on the basis of which 'the whole town was declared to be an area of historic and cultural value to which special consideration must be given' (Malmros and Hallberg 2012: 54).

In the mid-1980s the municipality of Gotland, the County Administrative Board and the Regional Museum decided to cooperate for the nomination of Visby to the World Heritage List. On 18 August 1987 Visby was recognized by the Swedish National Heritage Board as an area of 'national interest'. In the 1990s the government provided financial support for the restoration of private-owned properties. 'The County Administration classified almost 260 buildings as historic buildings protected under the Heritage Conservation Act. Every property under legal protection was fully documented and was provided with an individual maintenance plan' (Malmros and Hallberg 2012: 54). This important milestone achieved by Visby highlights that the city has become a 'strategic resource for the development of the island of Gotland' (Malmros and Hallberg 2012: 55). For this reason, it is essential to develop a shared strategy for the conservation and protection of its cultural heritage involving the Regional Museum, house owners, private businesses and the public sector and organizations.

Gotland's history comprises two representations or creations of the insular imaginary: the first is based in the Middle Ages and revolves around the concept of *Gesellschaft*, because it is distinguished by individualistic social relations based on exchanges; the second is associated with the period from the eighteenth to the twentieth century and celebrates *Gemeinschaft*, or the inclusive farming community (Edquist 2015: 89). Gotland is the perfect place for producing 'mindscapes of the past' (Ronström 2005: 6). 'To travel to an island is to travel backwards in time, which is why islanders often are described as especially "old-time" and authentic' (Ronström 2005: 5–6). As outlined by Samuel Edquist, the Gotlandic regional identity serves 'as complement' to Swedish national identity (2015: 125). To borrow Michael Billig's (1995) celebrated expression, if we accept that Swedish identity is a 'banal nationalism' (1995) based on ideological forms practiced every day, like the display of the national flag or performance of the national anthem, we might equally suggest that the Gotlandic identity is a 'banal regionalism': 'it is seldom aggressive or overtly xenophobic, but nevertheless it is a doctrine about *us* being something different from the others' (Edquist 2015: 126). In Gotland, this 'banal regionalism' is closely tied to the island's branding, which 'is about producing local distinctiveness' (Ronström 2008: 17). As observed by Owe Ronström 'visibility can be sold, and attention can be converted into hard currency or cultural capital at festivals, "culture weeks" and other types of "foreign exchange offices" in the cultural experience market' (2008: 17). In other words, 'local distinctiveness [is] a key to local and regional development, and a way for peripheries to move closer to the centers' (Ronström 2008: 17).

The island's branding serves to attract tourists, as revealed by the success of the medieval week, which brings large numbers of visitors to the island every year. Nevertheless 'among islanders, especially from the countryside, it is not uncommon to mutter over the annual invasion of medievalists. There is even a mock-resistance movement among the most daring refuseniks, jokingly called "Våga vägra medeltiden" [Dare to refuse the Middle Ages]' (Ronström 2005: 12).

John R. Gillis's remarks about Pacific islanders apply equally well to the Gotlanders: 'islanders today often find themselves promoting the image of remoteness as vital to the tourist trade, while struggling against the notions of backwardness and inferiority that this image brings with it' (2001). The sensation of living in isolation that brings with it nostalgia for a glorious past is expressed very well by a popular song in Gotland:

> Gotland is a large island with too few people. An island on the fringes, out of the way. 100 kilometers of water lie between Gotland and the Swedish mainland, over 200 between the island and the Baltic coast. The Baltic, which once made Gotland one of northern Europe's most important centres, today makes Gotlanders isolated and different. Transport is long and dear, direct communication difficult. Everything must be planned, nobody can drop by. [...] Gotland – a beautiful isle with character and distinctiveness, that attracts and maintains. A delimited, surveyable unit. A land of its own with a history and culture its own. To that must be added the remains of a mystical and original fellowship that now, alas, is almost lost to us.
>
> (Lundberg, Malm and Ronström 2003: 102–3)

Saaremaa and Hiiumaa: A border zone between West and East

On a meadow like that we celebrate tonight
Where dusk and dawn meet
Everyone has been busy
During this day filled with work and joy
Oh, chat and coo smartly,
Young soldier with a golden star
These nights are so light and short
It's impossible to catch the flaxen-haired girl

Song 'Saaremaa waltz' (1949)

Saaremaa (2673 km^2) and Hiiumaa (989 km^2) are among the largest islands in the Baltic Sea. Saaremaa is an Estonian county (maakond). In addition to the main island of Saaremaa, Saare County comprises the islands of Muhu an Ruhnu in the Bay of Riga. Muhu is linked to Saaremaa by a causeway, only completed after a lengthy process of construction. The decision to build the causeway dated to 1852 but forty-four years were to pass before it was opened to traffic. The causeway was inaugurated on 27 July 1896 in the presence of the widow of Mihail Alekseyevich Zinoviev, the civilian governor of Livonia, who had died the previous year, and of his successor, governor Vladimir Dmitrievich Surovtsev. The causeway was renamed 'Sinowjew' in honour of Zinoviev (Saaremaa Turism 2021: 13).

The language spoken by most of Saarema's inhabitants is Estonian; however, until the Second World War, it was not unusual to find locals who understood and spoke German, the language spoken by the land-owning aristocracy and by the merchants in the city's most important town, Arensburg (present-day Kuressaare) (Edquist and Holmén 2015: 12). *Saaremaa waltz* is a popular tune written for an afterparty of a working campaign in a kolkhoz in the late 1940s, evoking the landscape imagery of Saaremaa (Sooväli 2004: 13). It is a very popular tune in both Estonia and Finland, where it became famous when the celebrated Estonian baritone Georg Ots performed a Finnish version of the song during his tour of the country. Thanks also to the popularity of this song, numerous Finnish tourists chose Saaremaa as their holiday destination in the 1990s, giving a huge boost to the development of the local tourism industry. If we are looking for the geographical centre of the Saaremaa and Hiiumaa islands for Europe or even for the whole world we will find it right here. The islanders, who are known for their strong sense of irony, like to say: 'the center is here! If you don't believe that, measure it up – it is all the same distance in every direction!' (Raukas 2009: 4–5). Their belief that they were situated in a strategic position at the centre of the world is due to the islands' geographic proximity to the important maritime routes in the Gulf of Riga. They were also located on the 0 meridian in the Russian empire until Greenwich was adopted internationally. For this reason, over the centuries, both islands attracted the attention of political and trading interests of the surrounding area: Danes, Germanic orders of knights, Swedes, Russians, Germans and Soviets, who were all keen to affirm their hegemony in the Baltic region. The islands are therefore at the 'center of the world' – of the Baltic world at least – while, at the same time, they appear to be suspended in an indefinite temporal location. In fact, using a striking phrase, tourists travelling to Saaremaa from the mainland are said to be heading for: 'an island where time rests' (Raadik Cottrell and Cottrell 2020: 274).

From Teutonic Order to Swedish rule

The island economy has always been based on maritime trade and fishing. In the words of French geographer Georges Chabot,

> Among the young Baltic states, Estonia seems to be perfectly suited to maritime activities: 1160 km of mainly rocky, jagged coastline, 800 islands, several of which are as large as a French department; two inlets – the Gulf of Finland and Gulf of Riga; a magnificent position in the centre of the eastern Baltic with its many nations: Sweden, Finland, Russia, Lithuania, Germany, Poland.
>
> (1935: 203)

Before Christianization (800–1200 AD), life on Saaremaa thrived: the island's inhabitants had relationships with Vikings based on the exchange of goods.

Vikings travelling from Gotland to Russia would stop off in Saaremaa where they would prolong their stay (Sooväli 2004: 55). In 1220 the Swedish King John I and his bishops launched a programme to Christianize the western part of Estonia. This area also came under the hegemony of the Teutonic Knights: in 1227, Saaremaa ended up under the control of the Order (Sooväli 2004: 56). Most of the island became part of the Bishopric of Ösel-Wiek, whose centre was Haapsalu on the mainland. The bishop had a castle built in the town of Kuressaare as the symbol of his domination of Saaremaa and named it Arensburg (Eagle Castle) (Cabouret 1994: 326).

In 1560 the Bishopric of Ösel-Wiek was sold by the last bishop Johannes V von Münchhausen to King Frederick II of Denmark. Saaremaa became part of Danish Estonia. According to the nineteenth-century Baltic German pastor Martin Körber, Saaremaa experienced a generally positive period of its history during the reign of Frederick II (Edquist and Holmén 2015: 276). This view, shared by nineteenth-century German historiography, is at odds with the studies carried out by Estonian historians who have raised the issue of the condition of the peasants. It is their opinion that the legal status of peasants actually worsened during the period of Danish domination (Edquist and Holmén 2015: 277).

From 1573 to 1645, the entire island was under Danish possession (Raukas 2009: 71). In 1645, Saaremaa was ceded from Denmark to Sweden by the Treaty of Brömsebro. Saaremaa became part of the Swedish domain in the period in which the Swedish Crown launched the Reduction, a measure that established the return of the fiefs that had been granted to nobles in the first half of the seventeenth century. In actual fact, according to the Estonian historian Elena Öpik, 'Saaremaa was exempt from the Reduction in 1680 because of its special status as Queen Christina's fiefdom. Christina wanted a reduction to improve her own financial status, but it started late, and it is unclear whether it even managed to cover its administrative costs'(Edquist and Holmén 2015: 278).

There is a consensus among historians that Saaremaa experienced progress in both the fields of literature and education under Swedish rule (Edquist and Holmén 2015: 279). The first document referring to the Swedish community of Hiiumaa dates from 1470 'when the Master of the Teutonic Order released them from the duty of daily labor in exchange for an annual fee of twenty Riga mark per district'(Wawrzeniuk and Malitska 2014: 27–8). By virtue of the dispensations granted by the Master of the Teutonic Order, the Hiiumaa Swedes were free to earn a living as fishermen or farmers, to cultivate the land and sell its produce. This Swedish community lived mainly in the northern part of the island and represented around a seventh of the total population of Hiiumaa (Wawrzeniuk and Malitska 2014: 28). In 1563, when the rule of the Teutonic Order came to an end, Hiiumaa was annexed by Sweden, remaining under its authority until 1710. Initially, Swedish peasants continued to enjoy the privileges that they had been granted under feudal law; nonetheless between 1590 and 1630, the Hiiumaa Swedes came under the rule of feudal landlords who had no intention of respecting the privileges enjoyed by these peasants. According to Janne Holmén 'the Swedish period seems less happy in history writing from Hiiumaa than is the case on Saaremaa. While on Saaremaa the central theme of the narrative is the struggle between the Crown and the nobility, on Hiiumaa it is the conflict between nobility and peasants that is the focus' (Edquist and Holmén 2015: 281).

In 1620 Count Jakob De la Gardie was given Hiiumaa as an enfeoffment. Four years later, King Gustavus II Adolphus sold him the island to keep in perpetuity as a fief. On the death of Count Jakob De la Gardie, the island was inherited by his son Axel-Julius De la Gardie who in 1659 forbade the Hiiumaa Swedes to trade freely with lime and cattle (Wawrzeniuk and Malitska 2014: 28).

From Russian domination (1721) to independence (1917)

At the end of the Great Northern War (1700-21), the long struggle for dominance over the Baltic Sea stemming out of the hegemony acquired by Sweden over the preceding decades was brought to an end when Estonia, including Saaremaa and Hiiumaa, was formally ceded by Sweden to Russia by the Treaty of Nystad. According to Janne Holmén, 'to Soviet era history writers, the Russian period was problematic: from a Marxist standpoint, the feudal system of the time had to be condemned, but on the other hand criticism of Russia could be interpreted as covert criticism of the Soviet Union, which was of course unthinkable' (Edquist and Holmén 2015: 283). Both islands were part of the Russian empire. However, under Russian administration, the two islands were separated because Hiiumaa remained under Estonian rule while Saaremaa, along with the rest of Livonia, was ceded to the Russian Empire, becoming part of the Governorate of Livonia. Despite their geographic vicinity, this administration weakened the ties between the two islands: moreover, Saaremaa's contacts were directed south while Hiiumaa was oriented eastwards. This division was one of the factors hindering the formation of any common 'island identity' connecting the Estonian islands (Edquist and Holmén 2015: 263-4). Saaremaa's maritime vocation is confirmed by the presence of prominent navigators, including explorer Fabian Gottlieb von Bellingshausen (1778-1852) famed for circumnavigating the globe in 1803 and participating in an expedition to Antarctica, during the course of which he discovered the Traversay Islands (1819), Peter I Island (August 1820) and Alexander I Land (Migliorini 1930).

In 1846-7, in the hope of improving their conditions in the Russian Empire, 30 per cent of the population of Saaremaa (around 14,000 people) decided to convert from Lutheranism to the Orthodox religion (Sooväli 2004: 56-7). Hiiumaa was inhabited by a greater number of Swedish peasants than Saaremaa: this was also due to the fact that the island had remained under Swedish rule for a longer period of time, from 1563 to 1710 (Edquist and Holmén 2015: 13). In 1721 the Hiiumaa Swedes requested that Peter I confirm their old privileges. Nevertheless, they obtained no response and for this reason, they submitted a request for this issue to be considered by the Restitution Commission founded by Catherine I. This attempt was also unsuccessful because the commission played for time, claiming that it needed to consult a descendant of Axel-Julius De la Gardie. In fact, while respecting the personal freedom of the Hiiumaa Swedes, Russia claimed that it was necessary to give them the same fiscal status as the Estonians.

In 1740 the Estonian peasants were declared the personal property of their landlords and in 1755, the Russian Crown returned the estates on Hiiumaa to the family of De La Gardie-Stenbock. In the summer of 1779, the Hiiumaa Swedes sought to reach an agreement with Count Karl Magnus Stenbock with the aim of obtaining complete freedom. The Swedish peasants on Hiiumaa were given the right to stay on their farms until March 1781 (Wawrzeniuk and Malitska 2014: 29). At that time, Grigorij Aleksandrovič Potëmkin, military man, diplomat and governor-general of New Russia, Azov and Astrakhan as well as lover of Catherine II, had been assigned the task of taking charge of the colonization of the Azov and Black Sea territories. He interceded with the queen to ensure that she emitted a decree which would give the Hiiumaa Swedes the chance to move to New Russia. As a result, on 8 March 1781, a decree was passed that laid down the terms of the resettlement of the peasants of the manor of Körgessaare (Hohenholm) to New Russia province:

> They must leave his lands. We are ruling to resettle these Swedish peasants, in total around 1000 persons female and male, to New Russia province in order to accept them as state peasants of the local establishment.[…] Prince Potemkin, the governor-general of New Russia, Azov and Astrakhan, will be responsible for the fulfillment of the resettlement, for setting and allotting favorable state lands, for settling them and for their supplying.
>
> (Wawrzeniuk and Malitska 2014: 30)

In the spring of 1782, the Swedish peasants on Hiiumaa were forced to emigrate from Hiiumaa (Dagö in Swedish and German) to the steppes, in Ukraine. They established their own village Gammalsvenskby on the Crimean peninsula, about fifty kilometers from the centre of Kherson Oblast in Ukraine of today. The village founded became known as 'Gammalsvenskby' (from the Russian 'Staroshvedskoe', literally meaning 'Old Swedish Village') (Wawrzeniuk and Malitska 2014: 13). This community existed in a sort of physical and mental isolation, struggling to open up to the outside world: the customs, island traditions, songs, riddles and proverbs traditionally used in Hiiumaa were preserved at least up to the First World War (Wawrzeniuk 2014: 95). In a letter dated 1849 addressed to the school inspector Carl Russwurm, three representatives of the villagers pointed out that there were fifty-two families of 'pure Swedes' (rena swänskar) in Gammalsvenskby (Wawrzeniuk 2014: 94). As outlined by Piotr Wawrzeniuk 'the Swedish identity of the former islanders was also preserved by their attachment to a particular form of Lutheranism, the archaic Swedish language of the sacred texts they carried with them to southern Russia and collective memory that encompassed the rights and privileges as free yeomen under the rule of the Teutonic Order and Sweden' (2014: 97). The Swedish community in Gammalsvenskby survived until 1929 when many of its members began to move to Sweden and the community gradually disappeared. Most of the few remaining Dagö Swedes left the island in 1941 (Wawrzeniuk and Malitska 2014: 15) and the Swedes in Reigi and Kärdla quickly Estonianized. The Estonian Swedes remained on the Pakri Islands, Ruhnu and Osmussaar (Tallinna Rootsi-Mihkli kogudus).

Independent islands

Until 1917 Estonia was part of the Russian Empire. In October 1917, Saaremaa and Hiiumaa were conquered by the Imperial German Army. The local population tried to resist but could do little to stop the German troops who were far greater in number. According to the Estonian historian Evald Blumfeldt, who was writing in 1934, the German army was allowed to sack the island for three days. The German authorities placed constraints on the islanders' personal freedoms and made it compulsory to teach German in the local schools. Blumfeldt also wrote that 'the attempts by the local Germans to take Saaremaa into the German Empire as an independent principality came to an end when the German troops left the Baltic after the German Revolution in November 1918' (Edquist and Holmén 2015: 287). On 24 February 1918, Estonia declared independence.

After the outbreak of the German Revolution in November 1918, the Germans decided to hand over power to the provisional Estonian government, which mobilized its troops to stem the advance of the Bolshevik forces. Representatives of the draftees called on the people to revolt. On 16 February 1919, in the village of Kuivastu on the island of Muhu, three government officials carrying out this mobilization were killed by the locals, triggering an uprising and the formation of a peasant army of over 1,000 men (The free dictionary by Farlex). The aim was to '"overthrow the power of the landowners" on the island, divide the land between people and not go to war' (Estonica. Encyclopedia about Estonia 1919). More than ten landowners were killed and the rebels demanded the takeover of manors. Given that the rebels claimed to be acting on behalf of the local government, many gave them support.

The republic of Estonia was so new at this time that they did not have any loyalty to it. The local Defence League unit proved incapable of combating the rebels effectively; this led to a 242-strong death squad led by Lieutenant Jaan Klaar, commander of the gunship Lembit, landing on Muhu on 18 February. The death toll was high with 185 people losing their lives in the clashes (Estonica. Encyclopedia about Estonia). The Saaremaa uprising in 1919 is described as 'ülestous' (revolution, uprising) in Soviet Age publications and as 'mäss' (rebellion, mutiny) in most other Estonian texts. Although there is a lack of consensus among Soviet historians regarding the precise reasons for this revolt, an increase in taxes along with the draft and requisitions were all unpopular measures that would have contributed to provoking the Saaremaa uprising (Edquist and Holmén 2015: 288). Following the signing of the Treaty of Tartu on 2 February 1920, after difficult negotiations, Soviet Russia recognized the independence of the Republic of Estonia (Republic of Estonia. Ministry of Foreign Affairs 2020). It was then that 'Estonian academic history became a Volksgeschichte, a history with a romantic approach whose focus was on writing the history of the dominant group, not a Landesgeschichte describing the people living in the area' (Edquist and Holmén 2015: 246).

Saaremaa during the age of silence

After obtaining independence, Estonia was forced to live with the constant threat of Communist subversion that led its government to assume an authoritarian stance. In 1934, the Prime Minister Konstantin Pätsand Commander-in-Chief Johan Laidoner violated the constitution by establishing an authoritarian regime. In 1938, Päts became President of the Republic of Estonia. This marked the beginning of the so-called 'age of silence', a form of right-wing presidential authoritarianism that lasted until 1939. Until the Estonian Land Reform of 1919–20, fishermen, who were also farmers, fished in the coastal waters near the shore and were required to pay a tax to the wealthy landowners who owned the properties adjoining the sea. Competition from Russian fishermen in the Estonian coastal waters declined between 1890 and 1905.

After 1920, the right to fish at sea was exempted from taxes. In the 1930s, Saaremaa was one of Estonia's most backward regions in terms of agricultural development. The percentage of arable land was rather low and not very productive according to a 1934 publication entitled *Saaremaa* written by the historian Blumfeldt, the geologist Artur Luha and the geographer Tammekann (Sooväli 2004: 74). A counterpart to this description of the island's physical geography can be found in a portrait of its human geography with very different tones. Republished in 1963 as *Saaremaa raamat*, it offers a very flattering depiction of the islanders' distinguishing characteristics: they were described as having an attractive appearance, above average intelligence, stronger and taller than other Estonians while the women are mentioned for their beauty and skill in carrying out agricultural work (Edquist and Holmén 2015: 256).

On the eve of the Second World War, the islands were fully integrated into the Estonian state, or at least this is the impression that Tallin wished to convey. Konstantin Päts' official visit to Saaremaa (20–1 August 1939), on the occasion of the celebrations for the twentieth anniversary of the birth of the Saaremaa Defence League, seems to bear this out (Loel 2008). Päts was received with full honours by the locals who greeted him with jubilation, songs and floral tributes (Eesti Kulturfilm). No less than 10,000 people were waiting to meet the President of the Republic on his arrival in Kuressaare. Describing the atmosphere on Saaremaa, the newspaper *Pärnumaa Teataja* wrote: 'the Saars are considered reserved and modest by nature, people who keep their feelings hidden.' At the reception for the President of the Republic we saw that great events and profound impressions are capable of breaking through their outer shell of reserve.

The arrival of the Head of State was met with enthusiastic, tumultuous applause. 'And when the President of the Republic spoke of the conquests of the islanders, emphasizing our willingness to defend our homeland, many people were moved to tears' (Loel 2008). Although just a few days later, on 23 August, Estonia's fate was sealed by the Molotov–Ribbentrop Pact, nothing in the newspapers suggested what events lay in wait for the country. However, it is undeniable that Päts did allude to hard times on the horizon even as he sought to reassure the population, claiming that

> Crossing the Estonian border is no easy matter […] we will not allow anyone to cross the borders of our country and to impose their violence […] if this should happen, the entire nation will rise up as one to defend what is right and the flags that are waving here and throughout our country will be the flags beneath which our young adult men and women will gather as a united front against the enemy.
>
> (Loel 2008)

The first Soviet occupation

The traditional image of Estonian national identity is based on an ideal of landscape exemplified, for example, by Angla tuulikud (Angla Windmills), an area comprising windmills as well as a pond with ducks, rabbits, a group of old tractors and a thresher, agricultural equipment and goat pens. Tourist operators act as merchants of memory (Le Goff 1988) exploiting natural and cultural elements to sell the emotion of nostalgia in the context of our consumer society (Sooväli 2004: 105). But the image of Saaremaa appears in a very different light when seen from the Soviet perspective: in this case, 'the imagery of Soviet Saaremaa opposed nature with the power of man. Urbanization carried out in the countryside, mechanization of agriculture, industrialization and transformation of Kingissepa into a modern Kuressaare signified the right to the well being of the Soviet man even in the isolated periphery' (Sooväli 2004: 105). As outlined by Joni Virkkunen the Estonian imaginary evoked by the phrase, 'My home is tiny as a birds nest's alike" is a direct contrast to a Russian song 'Great and spacious is the country where my home is', which encapsulates the idea underpinning Russian spatial identity (Virkkunen 1999: 83).

On 24 September 1939, the Russian Minister of Foreign Affairs Vyacheslav Mikhailovich Molotov, established a military base agreement between Estonia and the Soviet Union that would allow the Soviet Union to establish military bases on Saaremaa, Hiiumaa and in the mainland around Paldiski. In 1939, Soviet military bases were set up in western Estonia. By June 1940, all Swedes had been evacuated from Osmussaare, the Pakri islands and Naissaare (Tallinna Rootsi-Mihkli kogudus). In August 1940 Estonia, like Latvia and Lithuania, was occupied and incorporated into the Soviet Union as the Estonian Soviet Socialist Republic. It has been estimated that between fifty and eighty thousand people – that is, between 8 per cent and 10 per cent of the total population of Estonia – were deported from their places of origin. The aim pursued by Stalin was to 'weaken the existing non-state activism, to promote the Soviet territorial ideology and to speed up both the social reconstruction and nationalization of the post-war Soviet state' (Virkkunen 1999: 84). Those deported were replaced by Russian workers devoted to the Soviet cause who came from areas neighbouring Estonia.

The official Soviet-Estonian history writing stressed the importance of the arrival of these workers in the process of construction of socialism in Estonia: 'during the years of building socialism, the specific weight of other nationalities increased within the Estonian working class, but the identical interests and goals and common work linked the settlers into a single Soviet Estonian working class ... Political educational work was used in trying to help workers to free themselves from the influence of the bourgeoisie-nationalist propaganda' (Virkkunen 1999: 84). As outlined by Lars Rönnberg, the Soviet occupation had dramatic consequences for the Estonian Swedes: the islands were turned into military bases, their homes were seized, farms were destroyed, and their contacts with their relatives in Sweden were broken off.

The arrival of the Soviets marked a drastic curtailing of Swedish culture, which had, until that time, been safeguarded and promoted: 'there were Swedish Schools, we had our own newspaper, there were certain parts of Estonia, some of the islands, which were more or less only Swedish-speaking, so there was a majority in certain areas in Estonia. And with a population of about ten thousand Swedes it was one of the larger minorities in Estonia' (McAlinden 2007). The international community did not approve of the annexation of the Baltic Republics to the Soviet Union and, on 23 July 1940, the American Secretary of State Benjamin Sumner Welles refused to recognize its legitimacy. The *Congressional Record: Proceedings and Debates of the 81st Congress, Volume 95, Part 1*, states:

> During these past few days the devious processes where under the political independence and territorial integrity of the three small Baltic Republics – Estonia, Latvia, and Lithuania – were to be deliberately annihilated by one of their more powerful neighbors, have been rapidly drawing to their conclusion. [...] The policy of this Government is universally known. The people of the United States are opposed to predatory activities no matter whether they are carried on by the use of force or by the threat of force. They are likewise opposed to any form of intervention on the part of one State, however powerful, in the domestic concerns of any other sovereign state, however weak.
>
> (Office of the Historian)

Summer War in Saaremaa (1941)

The Molotov–Rippentrop Pact was terminated following Hitler's decision to launch Operation Barbarossa in June 1941. In 1941, Saaremaa was occupied by Nazi Germany: it was followed by the establishment of the *Reichskommisariat Ostland*, a strategic outpost that allowed Nazi Germany to put in place countermeasures against the Soviets. The non-Soviet historiography tends to emphasize that the German soldiers were initially perceived by the islanders as liberators who could contribute to the return of the Estonian republic. However, this initial perception soon made way for the realization that the Germans were occupation forces just like the previous invaders (Edquist and Holmén 2015: 296). In Saaremaa, before the arrival of the German army, there was no guerrilla organization comparable to the Metsavennad operating in continental Estonia. The Metsavennad (Forest Brothers) (Mertelsmann 2016: 164), who took their name from the places – woods and forests – where they met – were nationalist elements who engaged in actions of sabotage and guerrilla activity against the Soviet government.

In the spring of 1941, a secret society named SSR (Great Finland) was formed in Torgu. Led by Henno Tammart, a school teacher and former scout leader from Saaremaa, the society proved to be very short lived and was disbanded in the summer of 1941 after the arrest and deportation of its leader (Ojalo). Before the arrival of the German troops, there were isolated groups of individuals who engaged in counter-propaganda, which mainly involved diffusing messages received by radio or appealing to islanders not to sign up. There were various interconnected reasons for the lack of activism relating to the relatively large numbers of people from Saaremaa who were deported and arrested; the island's isolation from the continent that resulted in a lack of awareness of the overall situation; the efficiency of military surveillance as well as the huge numbers of Red Army soldiers; and, last but not least, the absence of large forested areas. All of these conditions combined to make it hard, if not impossible, for the Metsavennad to carry out its clandestine activities.

Following Germany's invasion of the Soviet Union on 22 June 1941, around 10,000 Forest Brothers formed organizations called Omakaitse (Home Guard) to oppose the forces of the NKVD, destruction battalions and the 8th Army (Major General Ljubovtsev). The movement of the Forest Brothers became a mass movement in summer of 1941 in the wake of the intensification of the repressive policies of the Soviet Union and the start of mass deportations in June 1941 (Estonian World 2021). It was then that the Red Army's destruction battalions were created with the aim of combatting the Forest Brothers. These battalions used 'scorched earth tactics', which involved destroying crops and cattle, as well as industrial equipment. They sacked and burned farms believed to have links with the Forest Brothers. Courts martial were set up and sentenced to death anyone suspected of being a member of the Forest Brothers movement or of having provided them with support (Estonica. Encyclopedia about Estonia 1941).

Vassili Riis, the head of the NKVD on Saaremaa, wrote in his autobiographical book *Kolmandat teed ei ole* (There is no third road, 1960) that the Destruction Battalion had succeeded in eliminating the 'bandits' in time, before they could organize themselves (Edquist and Holmén 2015: 294). The population of Kuressaare was immediately banned from participating in any kind of meeting on the street, in parks or squares. Already in the first week of the war, orders were given to seize cars, motorbikes, bicycles and radios. The worries of the local population grew to the point that on 28 June, the commander of the local garrison, General Yeliseyev, ordered the militia to seize all firearms within forty-eight hours along with other weapons (Ojalo). The Forest Brothers fought against the destruction battalions and anyone they held responsible for having provided the Soviets with assistance in organizing the deportations. Between 7 and 9 July, the German 18th Army crossed the southern border of Estonia where they worked in cooperation with the Forest Brothers. In the summer of 1941, a small group of men was formed (about a 100 altogether), known as the Valjala forest guerrillas. Although they did not engage in active guerrilla activities, they launched an operation that managed to oppose the seizure of the wheat harvest from the farms near the forest. One of the guerrilla units in the forest near Leisi had a radio, a vital piece of equipment for the transmission and reception of information, one of the few to have escaped confiscation by the occupying troops. In early July 1941, a secret Estonian militia group was formed in Kuressaare – led by Johan Raudseppa – managing to gain control of important institutions like the militia, the post office and the prison. The militia kept abreast of developments in the conflict thanks to a radio concealed near the post office (Ojalo 2019).

After the arrival of the German army on 19 September, a militia group formed in Leisi earlier that month held a meeting that established the Leisi Parish Security Committee, which had the task of recruiting loyal men trained in maintaining order (Ojalo). On 9 September 1941, the Germans launched Operation Beowulf (Unternehmen Beowulf), carried out by the German 61st Infantry Division with the support of the naval units of the Kriegsmarine and the Finnish Merivoimat, which was intended to occupy Saaremaa, Hiiumaa, Muhu and Vormsi. After the fall of Tallinn and the forced withdrawal of most Soviet naval vessels to the bay of Kronstadt, 'the only remaining positions of the Baltic Fleet outside the Gulf of Finland were the coastal artillery positions in Moonsund archipelago (Saaremaa, Hiiumaa, Worms and Muhu)' (Åselius 2005: 230). 23,700 men of the Red Army's 3rd Rifle Brigade were garrisoned on Saaremaa and Hiiumaa, which were in such a strategic position that the Germans planned to take them over by early September 1941 (Askey 2014: 329). The Wehrmacht achieved its objectives, destroying the large Soviet garrison on the island, and completing the operation by 22 October.

From the second Soviet occupation to independence

The German troops were defeated in October–November 1944 by the Red Army in the course of the Moonsund Landing Operation. Kurresaare fell to the Soviets on 20 October 1944. Saaremaa was under Soviet control on 23 November 1944 (Feldgrau). The Soviet Union regained the territories belonging to the *Reichskommisariat Ostland*: this occupation could be interpreted as being legitimate because it came under the terms established by the Molotov–Ribbentrop Pact, whose validity stemmed from its ratification in peace times.

The Soviets presented the annexation of these territories to the Soviet Union as the mere restoration of the status quo prior to the German occupation. According to Soviet propaganda, the Estonians, Latvians and Lithuanians voluntarily chose to become part of Soviet Russia. The Estonian nationalists, however, considered the 1920 Treaty of Tartu as tangible proof of the illegitimacy of the Molotov–Ribbentrop Pact and of the forced incorporation of Estonia to the Soviet Union. In 1944, Estonia was renamed the Estonian Soviet Socialist Republic. The Soviet occupation marked the start of a complex programme

Figure 3. Signs of the Soviet presence are still present in Saaremaa. Soviet WWII memorial, Tehumardi, Saaremaa, Estonia. 27 July 2007 by Mark A. Wilson on Wikimedia Commons.

of repression: a network of informers was created with the aim of identifying individuals who might betray the Socialist cause, i.e. people in contact with the western powers or opponents of the regime. This system of control of the population was unable to prevent the rise of revolutionary movements, first and foremost, the Metsavennad, which had the support of both British and American intelligence and carried out its clandestine activities in Estonia as well as in Latvia and Lithuania. Resistance groups were harshly repressed in the wake of the pervasive action of KGB agents.

After 1945, following the Soviet occupation and the introduction of the socialist regime, fishing cooperatives were set up; as late as May 1985, a fishing kolkhoz called 'Saare Kalur' was established on Saaremaa along with a smaller cooperative called 'Hiiu Kalur' on Hiiumaa (Cabouret 1994: 319–20). In the early 1950s there was a process of collectivization that saw the creation of around 150 kolkhoz on Saaremaa as well as on the island of Muhu. This involved the construction of large areas of housing in Orissaare, Salme and Kuressaare. The latter experienced a dramatic transformation from a popular harbour and health resort to an industrial hub (Sooväli 2004: 57). There was also a widespread trend that saw people moving from the coastal areas to the towns (Sooväli 2004: 61). Since 1946 Saaremaa was declared a restricted zone. This meant that until 1989, foreigners and most mainland Estonians were forbidden to visit the island. In the wake of the second Soviet occupation, Estonia, like the other socialist republics belonging to the Soviet Union, was kept in complete isolation. The Soviets built military outposts on Estonian beaches to prevent local inhabitants from fleeing to Finland. Referring to the 'pirate spirit' of the islanders, the head of the Mihkli open-air museum Tormis Jakovlev, noted that 'the beaches functioned as a window and a link to the west in the Soviet age, when the authorities tried to limit other contacts with the outside world' (Edquist and Holmén 2015: 262). The Soviets also interrupted all contacts with the West by installing radio and television antennas that only transmitted information approved by Moscow Opposition to the Soviet Union became covert, going underground, as revealed by the message written on a ballot paper in the 1947 election for the Supreme Soviet of the Estonian SSR in Saaremaa: 'I tighten my belt and do not elect tormentor'. This opposition movement was considerably less combative and radical than that of the Metsavennad (Virkkunen 1999: 86). From the 1950s to the late 1980s, these highly restrictive measures combined with the creation of military bases had a disastrous impact on the island's economy and negative influence on maritime trade.

The combined effect of the Nazi and Soviet occupations, emigration to the West and deportations to Siberia resulted in Saaremaa's population falling from 58,000 in 1922 to 28,000 in 1959. In fact, deportations were an extremely important factor: between 1940 and 1953, no less than 8,588 people were deported from Saaremaa, a far greater number compared to other areas in Estonia. Most families emigrated to the West, mainly to Sweden and Finland, especially in 1944 (Sooväli 2004: 61). Even though the relationship between the Soviet occupiers and inhabitants of Saaremaa gradually developed into one of peaceful coexistence, if we are to believe the words spoken by the then deputy mayor of Kuressaare, Jaan Lember, some months before Estonia declared independence: 'They [the border guards] are a sign of Soviet power. [...] But as long as this power does exist, let them stand there. They don't bother us, they're polite, they immediately understand where they've landed. ... These fellows adopt our culture. They learn how to say "hello" in Estonian, "goodbye", "thank you"' (Feldmann 1990). On 20 August 1991, Estonian independence was regained with the collapse of the Soviet Union: new perspectives would soon open up for both Saaremaa and Hiiumaa.

Ruhnu, 'Pearl of the Gulf of Riga': The island disputed between Estonia and Latvia

*Man learns more about
himself at sea than he does on land, as the
sea is more changeable than man. Land provides
a sense of safety. Land offers protection
from the whims of the sea*

Documentary *Ruhnu* 1965

A 'Swedish' island?

Ruhnu Island is situated in the middle of the Gulf of Riga, 19 miles from the Latvian Courland Peninsula, 29 miles from the Estonian Kihnu Island and 35 miles from the Estonian town of Kuressaare on Saaremaa Island. Ruhnu (Runö in Swedish) has belonged to the Saare administrative region since 1986. Until 1944 Ruhnu was inhabited by Estonian Swedes, a Swedophone minority living in the north-western part of Estonia and on the islands. The Estonian Swedes call themselves Aibofolke, 'island folk' (Tallinna Rootsi-Mihkli kogudus). There are almost none left nowadays.

The island's history is distinguished by the Swedishness of the population and Sweden's influence on political and administrative matters. A letter sent by the Bishop of Courland to the governor of Ruhnu in 1341 confirms the recognition of the islanders' right to reside on their land and manage their property under Swedish law.

Following the dissolution of the Livonian Order (an order belonging to the Teutonic Knights), the island, which had been part of the Livonian Confederation, became part of the dominion of the Duchy of Courland (Lott 2018: 85), a vassal state of the Grand Duchy of Lithuania. From 1621 to 1708, Ruhnu became part of the Kingdom of Sweden, which recognized the unique status of the islanders: unlike other Estonian Swedes, Ruhnu's inhabitants retained significant decision-making powers and considerable autonomy, especially with regard to inheritance laws. On Ruhnu, land and property were passed down to the next generation. Given Ruhnu's strategic role, Sweden sought to ensure the loyalty of its population. In 1688, Karl XI signed a royal decree limiting the number of births as well as the construction of new homes on the island. This decision was motivated by the lack of timber leading to a need to apply quotas to wood, which was needed as fuel for the lighthouse. Ruhnu's population never exceeded 400 inhabitants: this was possible thanks to the control exercised by the community itself as well as by the Loandskape, the local parliament, in which all confirmed men had voting rights (Rudling 2006).

In 1721, the island became part of the Russian Empire's Governorate of Livonia, which controlled the island until 1915, when it was occupied by Germany. The Russians granted considerable autonomy to the island, 'which operated as a mini-republic, with its own *thing*, or parliament, and legal order' (Rudling 2006). The young men on the island were exempt from military service because the community decided to use the surplus wheat produced in order to obtain this privilege. As outlined by Anders Rudling 'the social control was strong, and the community farmed and toiled very much like a communist society. As there were no taxes, there was a system in which the inhabitants took turns in doing day labour for the community. A German visitor in 1846 described how the Runö Swedes differed sharply from the Latvians, in that they lacked the timidity and submissiveness of the Latvians, who feared the "zehniga Wahzescha" or "the noble Germans"' (2006). In the summer of 1866, the majority of the Estonian Swedes on Ruhnu sought conversion from Lutheranism to Russian Orthodoxy. The inhabitant used the threat of conversion to leverage concessions from the Lutheran consistory. In fact, after their requests were met, they did not follow through on their initial threat (Tøllefsen and White 2021). In a letter from Bishop Donat (Babinskii-Sokolov) of Riga to Prince Sergei Shakhovskoi, governor of Estland, dated 18 August 1886, we learn that in 1866, the Ruhnu-Swedes, numbering 600, drove their pastor from the island and turned to the bishop to accept them into the Orthodox Church. However, their attempt to convert to the Orthodox religion was unsuccessful due to the difficulties involved in bringing Swedish-speaking clergy to the island:

> Exhausted by the struggle to defend Orthodoxy on the mainland and given the lack of people knowing Swedish to take the positions of priest, psalmist and teacher, the bishop, with the special advice of the regional governor, sent a priest and an official to convince the residents of Ruhnu to remain in their previous faith until a later time when people would be prepared to occupy the clerical positions. Indeed, the seminary pupil Orlov was instructed to learn Swedish in order to take the position of priest on Ruhnu. Orlov studied Swedish and translated the liturgy into it, but the residents of Ruhnu did not further renew their desire to become Orthodox and remain until this time bad Lutherans.
>
> (Baltic Orthodoxy)

Apple of discord between Estonia and Latvia

When Estonia and Latvia became independent at the end of the war, they both made territorial claims to Ruhnu. The shift from tsarist Russia to an independent Estonian republic affected the legal status of the Swedish-speaking minority in Ruhnu. As outlined by Glenn Eric Kranking, 'the mainland border largely followed ethnic divisions, and since Runö was isolated in the Bay of Riga and inhabited entirely by Swedes, there was no clear ethnic or geographic dividing line. Estonia and Latvia left the decision to the islanders, which led to negotiations and expeditions by both sides' (Kranking 2009: 97). The Ruhnu-Swedes played an important role in the international relations between Estonia and Latvia. Major disputes were had with Estonia particularly about the town of Valka and the Ruhnu Island. The Estonian Swedes had the position of Minority Secretary with the Government, and their own representation in the Riigikogu (the unicameral parliament of Estonia) (Tallinna Rootsi-Mihkli kogudus).

In the declaration of independence dated 24 February 1918, Estonia claimed that 'the Republic of Estonia includes within its borders Pärnu County along with the Baltic Sea Islands – Saare-, Hiiu- and Muhumaa and others which are traditionally inhabited by the Estonian nation in the great majority' (Lott 2018: 85). However, if we examine the 1922 census, we can see that this declaration did not tally with reality: Estonians were not a majority in Ruhnu. The population of Ruhnu Island was composed of 252 Swedes, 10 Estonians (3, 7 per cent) and 2 Germans (Lott 2018: 85). Despite this, on 17 January 1919, the Estonian Provisional Government decided to declare Ruhnu Island part of Estonia. However, the islanders were left completely in the dark about this declaration, which initially remained purely symbolic, because in the winter months there were no links between the island and the mainland, making it impossible for Ruhnu's inhabitants to receive this vital piece of news.

On 23 May 1919, money was allocated to 'buy seal blubber from Ruhnu island' (Üldentsüklopeedia 2013). While on the island, the Estonian government representatives behaved exactly like *conquistadores* in the New World: 'the visit was in some ways quite similar to colonist expeditions to the natives of the New World. The ship had "barter currency" loaded onto it in Tallinn, including salt, petroleum, flour, leatherware, guns and ammunition, and alcohol (even though Ruhnu locals were known for their teetotalism)' (Ķibilds 2018). On 14 June 1919, an Estonian delegation arrived in Ruhnu. The Ruhnu-Swedes saw these negotiations as an opportunity to obtain further guarantees – stipulations, rights and privileges not available to other parts of Aiboland (the historically Swedish-speaking areas and towns of northern and western Estonia) – including access to state-held land. They therefore reached an agreement with the Estonian authorities who gave permission to Ruhnu men to fulfill their military service obligations on the island, rather than face deployment in other parts of Estonia (Kranking 2009: 98).

Estonia then established its Ruhnu Island Commission, which soon left for the island. First, the Commission stopped off Kuressaare where its members consulted experts in order to 'obtain useful tips about the customs and traditions of the islanders so that the expedition would be an unqualified success' (Üldentsüklopeedia 2013). After reaching Ruhnu, the Commission spoke to the islanders in Swedish, underlining that the Estonian government intended to protect the interests of the entire population. Trade agreements were set up: the islanders sold seal blubber and received cash and exchange goods (salt, wheat flour, petroleum, guns, cartridges, but also spirits and wine. In Section 2 of 'The Provisional Order of Government for the Republic of Estonia' it listed land areas that fall within those boundaries, among them the Estonian islands 'Saaremaa, Hiiumaa, Muhumaa, Ruhnu, Kihnu, Vormsi, Osmussaar, Pakri Islands, Naissaar, Aegna, Prangli Islands, Suur [Tütarsaar] and Väike Tütarsaar' (Lott 2018: 85). However, Latvia refused to give up, presenting 'the Memorandum on Latvia', on the occasion of the 1919 Paris Peace Conference, which declared Ruhnu Island part of Latvia on the basis of the historical inclusion of Ruhnu into the Courland Duchy, as well as by the fact that the lighthouse and radio station located on the island were important for navigation to/from Riga (Lott 2018: 86).

Again on 15 July 1921, the Latvian minister of foreign affairs sent a letter to his Estonian counterpart in which he explained the reasons behind Latvian claims on Ruhnu. He wrote: 'taking into consideration these geographical, economic and historical observations, my Government cannot renounce Runö Island and in the final delimitation of the maritime boundary between our States, the island of Runö must be attributed to Latvia' (Lott 2018: 87). The Estonian reply was not long in coming: the government reiterated Estonia's right to sovereignty over Ruhnu, specifying that this question was not a subject matter of the Estonian-Latvian boundary commission and was only to be discussed between the two States via diplomatic channels. In fact, Ruhnu was not, at the time, on the agenda of the Latvian Provisional Government: Estonia, having now won its freedom, was mainly concerned with protecting its borders, while Latvia had an unstable government. Moreover, it had a debt of gratitude with Estonia, for having come to its aid during the decisive battle in the Latvian War of Independence fought near Cēsis in June 1919 (Ķibilds 2018). Estonia agreed to help on the promise of

Ulmanis's government to relinquish the town of Valka. They were even ready to give up Ruhnu in return but the Prime Minister of Latvia Kārlis Augusts Vilhelms Ulmanis did not keep his promise (Public broadcasting of Latvia 2020).

The widespread food shortages on the island were an occasion to strengthen ties with Sweden: in 1919, the government in Stockholm sent the island a series of supplies including sugar, tobacco, flour, petroleum and mittens (Kranking 2009: 98). Although the war was over, there were fears among Ruhnu's inhabitants that their freedom of movement might be restricted and that they would end up remaining on the island in a situation of poverty. Nikolai Blees, the Estonian secretary for the Swedish minority, reassured the population, underlining that compulsory residence on Ruhnu was no longer in force (Kranking 2009: 98–9). In a letter to the Swedish King, dated 18 October 1920, the Ruhnu-Swedes petitioned for the protection of Sweden:

> The residents of the island of Runö in the Bay of Riga, driven by their longtime desire, wish to be reunited with the motherland, Sweden... For hundreds of years, Runö has been home to an entirely Swedish population... Even if other countries claim us, we have always felt ourselves to be Swedes in both heart and soul, and have never chosen to be anything other than Swedes. We have held onto our Swedish language and our Lutheran faith, and our yearning has always been, and our heart's desire to belong, to Sweden... Our wish is to be neither Estonian nor Latvian subjects but rather Swedish. And now if Runö is as they say a no-man's-land, we feel it is the most appropriate time to express our desire... We are Swedes. That is what we want to be, and nothing more.
>
> (Kranking 2009: 99)

Ruhnu's Swedish community soon found reason for complaint with regard to the Estonian authorities. Despite the guarantees that they had been given, it was demanded that the island's young men would serve time in the Estonian army. The population also protested at the high taxes and the fact that they were not allowed to chop wood for their own use from the state forest. In 1921, the islanders turned to the Swedish government, asking for the island to be annexed to the Kingdom of Sweden. In the summer of 1921, the Estonian Prime Minister Konstantin Päts (Eesti Vabariigi President) visited the island and embarked upon negotiations with Hans Steffens, the head of the local community, to discuss the island's status as part of Estonia. All these negotiations came to naught because Sweden did not wish to follow up these irredentist claims by the islanders, holding this to be an internal matter for Estonia to deal with (Alenius 2006).

In 1922, in an attempt to meet the islanders' requests, it was established that Ruhnu's conscripts could serve time in the island's lighthouse.

In August 1923, the minister of the interior Karl Einbund visited Ruhnu. It was on this occasion that a definitive decision was made regarding the status of local conscripts: the government confirmed the proposal of the ministry of interior to arrange the Ruhnu island's military obligation service in a way that during the war the mobilization-aged could perform the defence, communications or other service on the home Island. They also confirmed, according to the local customary law, the islanders' right to take heating material from the island's forest for free (Üldentsüklopeedia 2013). As pointed out by Alexander Lott, Sweden was in favour of Estonian sovereignty over Ruhnu given that there was a very large Swedish-speaking community in north-west Estonia (2018: 88). As far as the Estonian Swedes were concerned, they were aware of the fact that 'if they'd join Latvia, where Swedes had never lived in such numbers, the Ruhnu locals would have lost their ties to their minority and their ethnic homeland' (Ķibilds 2018). However, Latvia did not withdraw its claim to the island.

In October 1923, Anton Jürgenstein, the Estonian member of the Parliament and the representative of the Coast Guard, attempted to evaluate a potential cession of Ruhnu Island in exchange for 30–40 farmsteads situated in the frontier area of Võru County. However, this attempt failed due to the opposition of foreign minister Friedrich Akel, who affirmed that the Ruhnu islanders wished to keep their status quo unchanged (Lott 2018: 88–9). On 25 October 1923, a bilateral Estonian-Latvian conference was held in Tallinn: on that occasion, the Latvian government expressed willingness to recognize Estonian sovereignty over Ruhnu in exchange for monetary compensation, but met with Estonia's refusal. Thus, the supplementary Convention that was concluded between Estonia and Latvia in Tallinn on 1 November 1923 does not make any reference to the status of Ruhnu. From then on, Latvia made no further claims on the island in any subsequent bilateral meetings, but only recognized Ruhnu Island as part of Estonia under the Maritime Boundary Treaty in 1996 (Lott 2018: 89). According to Article 7(1) of the United Nations Convention on the Law of the Sea (hereinafter LOSC) Ruhnu Island should be part of a fringe of islands near Estonian coast in order to draw a straight baseline to and from the islands (Lott 2018: 89). In the space of just a few years, Ruhnu became a tourist destination for Latvians. In 1939, Ulmanis himself launched the first tourist ship 'Banga' for its maiden voyage to Ruhnu (Ķibilds 2018).

The rediscovery of Swedish language and culture

At the end of the First World War, the inhabitants of Ruhnu had attempted to return under Swedish sovereignty. This sense of identification with Sweden had been building up over a long period of time: in the early 1900s, a movement of rediscovery of the Swedish language and cultural heritage started to take shape in the Estonian territories inhabited by Swedophones. In 1909, the Swedish Education Society in Estonia (SOV – Svenska Odlingens Vänner) was set up with the aim of contributing to the preservation and promotion of the Swedish language and culture. In 1917, the Swedish elite orbiting around the SOV had founded its own political party– the Swedish People's Party (Svenska Folkpartiet), whose press organ was, from 1918 onwards, the newspaper *Kustbon* (Tallinna Rootsi-Mihkli kogudus). The first issue of *Kustbon* explained the newspaper's purpose in the following terms:

> The Swedish tribe [folksstammen] here has in particular many interests to exercise and protect now. In the struggle for existence, solidarity is the greatest necessity. Kustbon is published to further this objective. It is to be a harbinger for compatriots out here – to remind us of our obligations, promote our political and civic rights, and according to our capacity contribute to the greater public good and our individual needs.
>
> (Kranking 2009: 81)

In 1921, as we have seen, the Swedish foreign minister rejected the islanders' irredentist claims, at the same time, reiterating that Sweden would always seek to protect Ruhnu in diplomatic relations with Estonia given that 'the Runö-Swedes were "of pure Swedish race" and had previously belonged to the Kingdom of Sweden' (Kranking 2009: 100). As outlined by Jörgen Hedman and Lars Åhlander, the Ruhnu-Swedes perceived themselves to be a people distinct from other Estonian Swedes (Rudling 2006). In the early 1920s, Ruhnu and its pre-modern society became the object of attention of numerous ethnography and biologists who flocked to the island to record 'their folk songs and measuring and categorizing their race, determining in the scientific language of the day that "language and race far from completely correspond to each other... the Runö population constitutes a mixed product of the Nordic and Eastern Baltic race"' (Rudling 2006). They saw the island as a unique hotbed in which Swedish culture had developed. In fact, they believed that Ruhnu, Estonia's most isolated island in the Bay of Riga, had been less affected by the influence of the Baltic Germans, Estonians or Russians. Scholars in Sweden romanticized Ruhnu to the point of affirming that it was possible to carry out more in-depth analyses of Swedish culture and language by examining the island and its inhabitants thoroughly (Kranking 2009: 125).

Visitors to the island reported having had the impression of observing 'an outdoor museum'; its culture was described as 'det svenskaste av allt svenskt' (more Swedish than the Swedish) (Rudling 2006). This rhetoric emphasizing the specificity of Ruhnu and of the Ruhnu-Swedes was long-lived and can be found – basically unchanged – in the declarations made in 2007 by the President of the Svenska Odlingens Vänner, Lars Rönnberg, who, when asked 'what makes the Estonian Swedes so unique anyway?', replied 'there are Swedes in Finland, there are Swedes in Sweden and there are Swedes in Estonia. And the Swedes in Estonia were fairly isolated so the language and the culture has preserved much of what it was from several years ago. So they are the true Swedes? More or less the true Swedes, yes' (McAlinden 2007).

The island from the 1930s to Soviet rule

In the 1930s, the local representatives of the Swedophone community of Ruhnu were involved in promoting Swedish identification among the Ruhnu-Swedes. Their initiatives were partly hindered by the stance assumed by the Estonian central authorities.

Figure 4. Ruhnu women in folk costumes in 1937.
Rahvariietes Ruhnu naised 1937. Aastal by an unknown author on Wikimedia Commons.

In 1936, Ruhnu's Pastor Carl Gustaf Grönberg, aware of the importance of education in safeguarding Swedish culture and language, wrote to the Estonia Committee, 'the question is about the best method to protect Swedishness on the island and raise the people culturally… If the school is to fulfill its role in the service of Swedishness and cultural work in a sufficient manner, it needs its own building' (Kranking 2009: 180). Moreover, Grönberg was also worried about the demographic drop due to the exodus of the younger generations, above all, of women who were leaving the island to become housekeepers in Sweden. The pastor therefore called for a two-year limit on visa permits for these girls, requiring them to return to Ruhnu at the end of that time (Kranking 2009: 185).

Following the coup by Konstantin Päts and the outlawing of political parties, the *Kustbon* newspaper was forced to cease publication in 1935. The following year Nikolai Blees founded *Nya Kustbon*, as an independent venture. That same year, SOV managed to obtain permission from the new government to relaunch the publication of *Kustbon* under an agreement that required them to refrain from touching upon political issues. Blees could not accept these conditions and continued to publish *Nya Kustbon*, competing with *Kustbon* and SOV. However, Blees' editorial experience proved short lived and was interrupted at the end of 1936 when his funding ran dry. *Kustbon* was published until 1940 when the war made it impossible to continue printing the newspaper. The Communist Party of Läänemaa Province in Estonia published the Swedish-language newspaper *Sovjet-Estland* although only a few issues were printed between 1940 and 1941 before it was forced to shut down due to the arrival of the German troops in the area (Newspaper Index).

During the Second World War, Ruhnu was occupied by the Soviet Union (1940–1) and then by Nazi Germany (1941–4). During the early stage of the Nazi advance in the Baltic, the Runhu-Swedes struck back against the Soviets. Those days are evoked by a contemporary witness, Tomas Lorenz, who described their dissatisfaction with the Soviets in the following terms:

> It is mentioned in history books that the Runö residents had their own little revolution, in 1941, in the middle of the summer. When we heard that the Germans were on their way, we imprisoned the Russian garrison, pushing them back to the mainland. But the week after, a much larger Russian force came to the shore of Runö and imprisoned the Runö residents that led that revolution and five of our leaders faced a firing squad.
>
> (Kranking 2009: 250–1)

In November 1943, just under a hundred islanders moved to Sweden. In August 1944, shortly before the Soviet troops occupied the island again, the entire population of the island with the exception of two families, boarded a ship for Sweden. The islanders who emigrated to Sweden established the Forening Runobornas association to preserve the history and culture of the Ruhnu-Swedes. During the Soviet occupation and afterwards, the island was repopulated with people from Estonia as well as serving as a base for a small garrison of Soviet soldiers. Between 1945 and 1948, Ruhnu experienced an influx of people from the nearby island of Kihnu (Üldentsüklopeedia 2014). Although the economy was essentially based on fishing and sealing,[1] the agricultural activity on the island grew considerably following the creation of an independent collective farm (kolkhoz) (1949–70). On 26 September 1950, Ruhnu Commune became a village soviet and was attached to the Pärnu District (raion). This administrative division existed until November 1986.

In 1951, the collective fishery Kommunismi Majak (Lighthouse of Communism) was set up, leading to relative prosperity by leaving sufficient initiative to private enterprise. In 1958, an electric power plant driven by a diesel engine was constructed on Ruhnu; in the mid-1960s, improvements were carried out in the agricultural sector, a road was built, and work began on the construction of a port. 1965 was a symbolic year for the island because it marked the first games between the neighbouring islands of Kihnu and Ruhnu, an event with a huge following all over Estonia that was held annually until 1971.

1965 was also the year in which Andres Sööt made his ten-minute documentary *Ruhnu* (1965). *Ruhnu* was the first Soviet Estonian documentary released after the Second World War that romanticized Estonian nationalism. It features idealized characters and landscapes: the island is a kind of hotbed where the Estonian national discourse could be expressed and developed. A particularly significant shot in the documentary zooms on an iron cross commemorating a Russian lighthouse keeper who had died in 1890: 'The "good old Swedish era" had ended, to be replaced by the reign of the Russian Tsar. Static images in the shot convey the passage of time' (Västrik 2015: 14). The film has a romantic vision of the island, this small piece of land that became the object of outside attention, discovery and ultimately conquest. In one excerpt we hear a voice-overasking: 'what compelled the ancient fishermen of Gotland to come to the

---

[1] The Latvian name, Roņu sala literally means 'Seal Island'. Since medieval times, its inhabitants were Swedish seal hunters. The seal blubber was turned into oil used for lamps. They made a living by selling seal oil in the nearby ports, mainly Riga.

barren Baltic Sea?'. The reply is supplied by another voice-oversaying: 'the need to find a piece of land, an island of one's own; and once found, to conquer the sea' (Västrik 2015: 14).

Ruhnu's development and attractiveness took a hard hit when a violent storm on 2 November 1969 destroyed the port and led to the liquidation of the local collective fishery as of 2 September 1970. The population fell sharply, dropping from 222 in 1966 to 98 in 1972. The fishing industry collapsed following the departure of the working-age population. By 1980, there were only forty-three inhabitants on the island, most of whom were pensioners or employees. Seen through Latvian eyes, Ruhnu's history appears rather different to the one described in the Soviet era film. Regret at Latvia's failure to annex the island emerges very powerfully from a documentary produced by the Public Broadcasting of Latvia in 2020. The intro to the documentary points out that in geographical terms, the island is closest to Latvia and this undeniable fact would have been a motive for bringing Ruhnu within Latvia's orbit:

> The island of Ruhnu could have been Latvia's one sea island, if only… If only what? By looking at the map it seems logical: the closest mainland point to Ruhnu is Cape Kolka in Latvia, just 36 Km away. Riga is the nearest state capital at 110 Km, while Tallinn is twice as far away. The closest port is Latvia's Roja, just 45 Km.
>
> (Public broadcasting of Latvia 2020)

The filmmaker also points out how, on numerous occasions, the Estonian government had revealed its lack of interest in the island's fate: 'meanwhile, the Estonians never cared much for Ruhnu. They neither built anything of importance on the island nor rushed to live there. In the 1930s, only 5 of the 280 inhabitants were Estonian' (Public broadcasting of Latvia 2020). In the final scenes of the film, the speaker asks, 'perhaps Ruhnu is the reason for Latvian inferiority complex, our belief that Estonians are always overtaking us?'. They also underline that Estonia would have had 'bigger cities, larger ports, convenient geography, and more land, even without Ruhnu' (Public broadcasting of Latvia 2020).

4

Autonomy and independence in insular Mediterranean areas

We will go on to focus on case studies in the western and central Mediterranean region. The common thread running through the history of Sicily, Malta, Sardinia and Corsica are the narratives produced by insular political actors, which are distinguished by self-victimizing representations based on a periphery/island centre/continent dialectic. We will outline the political demands of autonomist/independentist groups and the rhetoric produced by these actors, which is based on the paradigm of insularity. In the Mediterranean area, we observe a dynamic based on the dual concept of island/mainland in which the insular regions, institutionally dependent upon a centre situated on the mainland, feel penalized by their belonging to/dependence upon a national context often perceived as hostile.

The *corda seria*: The tireless dialectic of the Sicilian elites

One can safely say that insecurity is the primary component of Sicilian history,
and it affects the behaviour, the way of being, the take on life [...]
inability to establish relationships outside of the private sphere,
violence, pessimism, fatalism [...] At a certain point,
insecurity and fear have reverted to the illusion that such insularity
[...] is a privilege [when it actually engenders]
a sort of alienation and madness, which, in terms
of psychology and customs,
elis attitudes of presumptuousness,
haughtiness, and arrogance.
Leonardo Sciascia, La corda pazza (1970)

'Poor island, treated as conquered territory! Poor islanders, treated as savages, who must first be civilised. And the *Continentals* had descended upon them to civilise them' (Pirandello [1913] 1918: 92): these words spoken by one of the characters in Luigi Pirandello's novel *The Old and the Young* skilfully evoke the Sicilian imaginary. 1861 was a watershed year in Sicily's history. Until then, the island had been under Bourbon rule but following the Expedition of the Thousand, it became part of the newly formed Kingdom of Italy. In fact, the unification process of the Italian territory began here on Sicilian soil, accompanied by shouts of 'Viva l'Italia e Vittorio Emanuele II!' (Long live Italy and Victor Emmanuel II!). The Italian State then found itself having to dialogue with an extremely heterogeneous Sicilian elite.

The crucial nature of this date – 1861 – is further confirmed by the fact that unification was followed by the birth of the 'Sicilian question', which exploded violently on two occasions: in September 1866, the very 'year of misfortunes' in which Giovanni Verga ([1881] 1972) would set the story of his Malavoglia family, there was a popular uprising against the Italian State known as the Seven and a Half Days Revolt, and in 1874 'when political Sicily anticipated the parliamentary end of the Right' (Giarrizzo 1987: XLV). 1866 was 'the epilogue to the Garibaldian revolution of 1860–62' with 1874 marking the moment in which 'the Sicilian question became the first act of the southern question – and not merely in terms of public and private inquiries' (Giarrizzo 1987: XLV).

In the late eighteenth century, the alienability of fiefs had helped to blur the boundaries of the island's ruling class and thus 'the Sicilian nobility turning up at the unitary assignation was an open elite' (Di Gregorio 1994: 106). During the long nineteenth century, there was no distinction between the roles of big landowners and entrepreneurs with small to medium landholdings: 'the landowner, whether aristocratic or not, would act like an entrepreneur or like landed gentry in relation to market fluctuations and the opportunities offered by the land, according to a model described as one of "mixed farming"' (Di Gregorio 1994: 107). The demands of the island's elites were finally recognized in 1946, when a special statute was granted against the background of a country that had just emerged from the ruins of the Second World War.

Sicilianismo: the history of a concept

Sicily's insular specificity is a literary topos rooted in a chronotopical dimension in the sense described by the philosopher Mikhail Mikhailovich Bakhtin, that is, the fusion of time and space in the imaginary of someone living in a given place (Salsano 2019: 137–45). Three expressions have been coined in order to describe the uniqueness of that 'way of being Sicilian' referred to by the writer Leonardo Sciascia: *sicilianità*, *sicilitudine* and *sicilianismo*, which, despite their differences, all share the recognition of the unique state of inhabiting an island. Insularity is the condition that ensures that there are the grounds for all three terms to have substance.

Figure 5. The Strait of Messina marks the territorial discontinuity between the mainland and Sicily.
Villa San Giovanni and the Strait of Messina by Scott Barron on Flickr.

Sicilianità (Sicilianity or Sicilian-ness) is an original, anthropological fact that reflects modes of behaviour typical of Sicilians and evokes the island's practices and customs. Given these premises, 'sicilianity' may tip over into a picturesque characterization of the way of being an islander.

Sicilitudine (Sicilianitude), a term coined by the painter Crescenzio Cane and subsequently reused by Sciascia, refers to an intellectual condition of isolation, exclusion, insecurity and subalternity. This concept refers back to the ambiguous attitude of not wishing or being able to flee from the island. 'Which is the ambiguity of not being able to place oneself frontally against and within the Sicilian context [...] It is the ambiguity of Ovid's *nec tecum nec sine te vivere possum*' (Papa 1996: 585). According to Sciascia, this feeling of isolation creates an identity crisis in Sicilians who adopt forms of diffidence with regard to those outside their family circle, perceiving them as invaders or usurpers. They subsequently develop a tendency to victimhood and fatalism along with the illusion that their Sicilian origins represent a privilege (Biazzo Curry 2001: 141). *Sicilitudine* is a concept rooted in its time: an idea in line with the 1960s deriving from négritude, emphasizing the tendency of many Sicilian intellectuals to identify with the least of the earth (Orioles 2010: 227–34). Revealing a certain assonance with *sicilitudine* is the term coined in 1980 by Lucio Zinna, the poet from Palermo, and also taken up by a prominent Italian author, in this case, Gesualdo Bufalino: *isolitudine*. This word evoking a tendency to isolation is 'almost a subterranean thread (or rather a submarine thread), linking the idea of life on the island with that of being radically alone in the world' (Papa 1996: 585). *Isolitudine* is also experienced by those emigrating, not just by those remaining on the island: while the superficial, picturesque structures of *sicilianità* are easily put aside, it is harder to oppose the emotional, intellectual condition associated with *isolitudine*. Bufalino describes this neologism in the following manner: 'Island and solitude at once. This is what we Sicilians are dominated by: on the one hand, we feel reassured by the sea, which envelopes us with its maternal embrace, on the other we feel cut off from what excludes us. Overcome by a feeling that is both one of claustrophilia and claustrophobia' (1996).

Lastly, the term *sicilianismo* expresses an attitude that is both political, bordering on regionalism, and intellectual in its insistence upon the specificity of the island, which requires the adoption of political measures tending to recognize its insularity. Sicily, by virtue of having provided itself with a chronotopic dimension fuelled by an insularist rhetoric, is an island that has also aroused the curiosity of non-islanders, drawn by its *sicilianità* but also by its *sicilitudine* and *isolitudine*.

Landing in Palermo in 1787, Johann Wolfgang von Goethe, one of the many illustrious European Grand Tour travellers, felt that in Sicily he had found 'the key to all' and that 'Italy without Sicily leaves no image on the soul' ([1816] 2013: 280). The Sicily of the 'Grand Tour' was a land of profound contradictions, where a sensational natural environment and profoundly stratified culture contrasted with the ruins of the present. Between the 1800s and 1900s, as foreign travellers admired the Greek and Mediterranean character of Sicily, one particular aspect of *sicilitudine* began to take hold in the collective imaginary. This was the image of a 'closed' island seeking to preserve its original characteristics, dating back to the period when Sicily was inhabited by Sicels and Sicani, and attained the height of expression in the Norman period (Barone 2020). The political culture that ensued laid claim to Sicily's specific insularity, *sicilianismo*. An expression of the feudal aristocracy, *sicilianismo* came about in opposition to the attempts by the Bourbon monarchy to modernize the economic and social structures of the Kingdom of the Two Sicilies.

The contrast between the Neapolitan monarchy, which sought to implement cautious reforms, and the Sicilian nobility, which was interested in conserving its privileged status, emerged on repeated occasions. The aristocracy also revealed its ability to ride the wave of the independence revolts of 1820 (which were limited to western Sicily and part of central Sicily) and 1848. Some decades later there was renewed resistance to the introduction of measures dismantling feudal privileges, again distinguished by the traits of 'sicilianist' rhetoric – this time directed against the Savoy unitary state (Barone 2020). Post-unitary *sicilianismo* drew upon the familiar anti-Bourbon themes with the addition of a new aspect, that of anti-unitary Meridionalism, which drew upon a narrative influenced by victimhood: despite Sicily's human and material resources, it would always be kept in a state of subjection. Those responsible for administering the island – whether Bourbons or Savoys – continued to advance the interests of the central State at the expense of the Sicilian masses.

This insularist rhetoric featured the same fatalism and 'insularity of mind' referred to by Giuseppe Tomasi di Lampedusa, the result of centuries-old policies experienced as damaging the real interests of the people. The words of this Sicilian writer evoke the image of Sicily outlined by the insularist elites: the locals perceive the ruins of antiquity, the splendid monumentality – present in the cities as much as in the villages – as indecipherable phantoms that reveal the passage of the successive governments and that have marked their presence with self-referential works. The specifically sicilianist insularist paradigm is based on the idea that the governments that administered the island, acting as tax collectors, revealed their most boorish character, ending up by influencing the very nature of the Sicilians themselves: 'all these things have formed our character, which is thus conditioned by events outside our control as well as by a terrifying insularity of mind' (Tomasi di Lampedusa ([1958] 1961: 182).

This lasting strand of *sicilianismo* runs through Sicilian history beginning with Michele Amari's interpretation of it in *La guerra del vespro siciliano* (1851) and developing further in the studies carried out by Massimo Ganci. In 1933 – at the height of the Fascist era – economist Giuseppe Frisella-Vella, a professor at the University of Palermo, published *Gli orizzonti scientifici della 'cosiddetta' questione meridionale* in which he drew upon all the arguments of 'quintessential *sicilianismo*', based on the idea of a Sicily that was a cradle of civilization (Marino 1971), showing how the island had established an inexhaustible relationship with the Mediterranean area (Butera 1998: 185–91). Nonetheless, between the two world wars, an anti-regionalist historiographic trend emerged in the wake of the reflections made by Benedetto Croce in his *History of the Kingdom of Naples* (1923): this strand emphasized the role that Bourbon reformism and the liberalism of the intellectual bourgeoisie played in the Italian unification process, also drawing attention to its distance from the island's baronage, interested in protecting its feudal privileges and responsible for the island's backwardness. This Crocian interpretation was taken up by Ernesto Pontieri whose *Il tramonto del baronaggio* (1943) highlights the reforming activities of the viceroy Domenico Caracciolo, pointing out that their failure was due to the weakness of the 'civil class' (ceto civile) and the powerful opposition to any proposed innovation from the feudal aristocracy (Barone 2003: 173). Rosario Romeo's *Il Risorgimento in Sicilia* (1950) kept faith with Croce, opposing the sicilianist vision by means of which he had sought to define the Sicilian 'civil class' that had actively participated in the 1860 Risorgimento events (Barone 2003: 173).

The post-war period (1950s onwards) saw the emergence of a historiography with Marxist leanings – specifically Gramscian leanings – focusing on aspects connected to social conflict, to political and union movements, and inter-class relationships: historians like Paolo Alatri (1954), Salvatore Francesco Romano and Francesco Renda sidelined the sicilianist idea of Sicily as a nation, instead shining the spotlight on the southern Sicilian peasant movement. Working together with workers from northern Italy, these Sicilian peasants strove to promote social progress, using their struggle and issuing demands to oppose the alliance between northern industrialists and large southern landowners responsible for the backwardness of the island and giving rise to the 'southern question' (Barone 2020). Nonetheless, these Marxist scholars, including Renda and Ganci, were also the interpreters of acute forms of a modern *sicilianismo*: a left-wing version that we could define as a regional Labour version. This Gramscian interpretation also made it possible to discover, alongside the island's atavistic backwardness, the extraordinary driving force of the subaltern classes, which were capable of mobilizing against the feudal system that the baronage sought to preserve at any cost.

The sicilianist historiographical approach dominated the post-war period until the 1960s, even in summaries (Barone 2003: 172) as shown by *Storia della Sicilia* by Francesco De Stefano (1948), *Storia della Sicilia post-unificazione* in three volumes by Francesco Brancato, Salvatore Francesco Romano and Giovanni Raffiotta (1956–9), or De Stefano and Francesco L. Oddo's *Storia della Sicilia dal 1860 al 1910* (1963). The sicilianist ideology found new alliances: in fact, 1970 saw the publication of *Storia della Sicilia medievale e moderna* by Denis Mack Smith.[1] This work – printed in several editions due to its enormous success – has an oversimplified vision based on a preconceived belief in the permanence of the original character of the 'Sicilian people', which was held responsible for the ills afflicting the island's society and politics. The historian Giuseppe Giarrizzo criticized Mack Smith but ended up clashing with Sciascia, who accused him of attacking the British historian for personal and academic reasons (Iachello 2018: 614–17). In actual fact, Giarrizzo wished to underline that his was a political judgement: by dwelling on the commonplaces pertaining to the periods of Arab, Norman, and, finally, Spanish domination and to the specificity of the Sicilian character, this 'threadbare *sicilianismo*' ran the risk of impoverishing the ethical and civil value of the historic interpretation (Iachello 2018: 617). In an interview given by Leonardo Sciascia in 1971, when he was a guest on a programme called 'La cultura in Italia', he reflected on the obvious lag in the reconstruction of Sicilian cultural history by historical research. He mentioned a number of themes that had effectively been disregarded by historians, such as Sicily's cultural relations with Spain, the history of the Inquisition in Sicily, and the history of piracy ('an element of key importance in defining this sense of insecurity'). Sciascia also criticized Sicilian intellectuals for their failure to study various cultural aspects of the island in sufficient depth: 'the history of Sicilian culture is the history of the island's striving for independence and autonomy. But when we ended up with autonomy we had only an idea not a proper grounding, hence the flaws of this institution' (Sciascia 1971).

[1] Originally published as *A History of Sicily* in 1968 as two volumes (*Medieval Sicily 800–1713* and *Modern Sicily after 1713*).

According to Barone, 1975 was a watershed moment in the methodological approach of scholars of Sicilian history. An important work published in that period is the 1977 *Potere e società in Sicilia nella crisi dello Stato liberale* whose authors 'proposed a new reading of some of the modernization processes of the economy and of the political system between the age of Giolitti and Fascism, reshaping the Gramscian concept of "agrarian bloc" in an ideological form' (Barone 2003: 176). This new interpretation, anticipated by Barone's criticism of Ganci's sicilianist positions (Barone 1978: 309–30), emerged on the occasion of the conference held in October 1981 under the title of *La modernizzazione difficile. Città e campagna dall'età giolittiana al fascismo*. Giarrizzo invited historians to equip themselves with interpretative tools that would eschew a vision of Sicily, and of the Mezzogiorno, in general, as being condemned to immobilism (Avagliano et al. 1983: 23). As pointed out by Barone,

> The term 'modernizzazione' (modernization), accompanied by the adjective "difficile" (difficult) contained clear ambiguities [...] Yet this ambiguity could be exploited by the desire to leave behind the sandbars of the old Meridionalism, to avoid reproposing the eternal immobility of the Mezzogiorno crushed by latifundia, lacking a middle class and cities, crowded only by a rural populace condemned to desperate Jacqueries, definitively without hope and without 'history'.
>
> (Barone 2003: 177)

The publication of *Sicilia* in 1987 – edited by Maurice Aymard and Giuseppe Giarrizzo, and belonging to an Einaudi series devoted to regional history – showed that this deleterious vision based on the atavistic immobilism of the island's history had finally been left behind. This milestone work deconstructed both the sicilianist myth and the Gramscian vision centred on ruralist Meridionalism, drawing a more complex picture connecting the socio-economic processes with the supralocal political dimension in a dynamic of conflict for power (Barone 2020). The prejudices rooted in the dualist metaphor of North against South – progress against backwardness – were finally demolished by a solid group of historians and social scientists who, in 1987, founded the magazine *Meridiana. Rivista di storia e scienze sociali* and the Istituto meridionale di storia e scienze sociali (IMES). As Salvatore Lupo has noted, although Rosario Romeo and Gastone Manacorda had very different ideological stances – the former was liberal, the latter was Gramscian – they both agreed in their definition of the Mezzogiorno, which 'should be considered as a fragment of modernity, just like any other place in this world. What must be tackled is the way in which it was modernized – *hic Rhodus hic salta*' (Lupo 2015: XII). This changed perspective even took the history of the Mafia into account: the studies carried out by Salvatore Lupo (1993) and by Rosario Mangiameli (2000) recast the theory suggesting that the origins of the phenomenon of the Mafia lay in the presumed immobilism of Sicilian society in order to reveal that, on the contrary, they needed to be traced back to the 'traumatic fractures that broke the order of the ancien régime in the course of the nineteenth century, inserting Sicily into the mechanisms of the commercial and industrial revolution' (Barone 2003: 180) As Lupo and Mangiameli have pointed out, 'the historic reality lies at a considerable distance from the stereotype. The mafia of the latifundia, generally portrayed as unchanging, has its own history, which reflects the evolution of landownership and of the agricultural industry, which experienced profound crises and transformations between the 19th and 20th century' (1990: 24).

From the late 1980s onwards, the historiographic interpretation accredited at scientific and academic level revealed the historical inconsistency of the suggestion that Sicily's mental and cultural isolation stemmed from its insular geographical condition. As proof, it showed how the island had participated fully in transnational history and that it had been fully integrated in international cultural, commercial, and intellectual networks from antiquity onwards. The physical isolation resulting from its insularity stemmed from a literary narrative depicting the island as a monad invaded by foreigners; however, this vision did not correspond to the centuries-old history of a dynamic and multicultural Sicily.

Autonomism and independentism in Sicily in the first half of the nineteenth century

During the Napoleonic period, Sicily became a 'constitutional laboratory', a testing ground for extremely advanced experiences (Ricotti 2005: 394). On 19 July 1812, the Sicilian parliament met to approve the new constitution, which had a strong British influence. Based on a liberal model aimed at administrative decentralization, it was clearly opposed to Napoleonic centralism. Unlike the coeval Cadiz Constitution with its strong focus on the recognition of legislative power, the Sicilian constitution was moderate and inclined to compromise (Grimaldi 2017: 210). From the very beginning of Sicily's modern history, we encounter characteristics that would prove lasting; firstly, the logic of compromise between the elite and the centre, at that time represented by the king.

The Sicilian constitutional experience did not really lead to a political and social upheaval, given that it adopted a dualistic system based on the dynastic legitimization of the king and on that of the Sicilian parliament, the expression of the insular nobility. In the way it was developed, the 1812 constitution involved just two actors: the sovereign and the aristocracy (Giarrizzo 1968: 53–66). The circle of Sicilian nobility expanded during the eighteenth century when a minor nobility flanked the ancient nobility. This happened because it was possible for anyone with the economic means to do so to purchase an estate, *conditio sine qua non* in order to obtain a noble title (Di Gregorio 1994: 87). The seditious laws of feudalism of 1812 abolished the feudal institution in Sicily by interrupting this process of expansion of the ranks of the aristocracy; by now, however, the class of 'minor nobility' sought to consolidate its position, sometimes backing and sometimes distancing itself from the nobility with a more ancient lineage. The Restoration saw the progressive entry of the bourgeoisie into the Sicilian political arena. Favouring its rise was the development of trade networks, linked above all to the export of agricultural produce and sulphur; the intellectual circles, which included exiles and conspirators, used the same routes used by these flows to diffuse ideas like democracy and constitutionalism (Isabella and Zanou 2016).

In the first half of the nineteenth century, especially in the 1830s, there was a surge in cultural associations, in Catania and Palermo, which did not just emerge as literary cliques but also as meeting places for political discussions: Sicily and the Mezzogiorno, and not just northern Italy, experienced an elite sociality in this period (Signorelli 2015). The Sicilians revolted in 1820, in 1837, and in 1848 (Basile 2015: 52–66). The reintroduction of the Cadiz Constitution (1812) in Spain in March 1820 also had consequences in the Kingdom of the Two Sicilies because it induced the Neapolitan Carbonari to organize themselves and demand a constitution. The aim of the Carbonari uprisings was obtained and, on 7 July 1820, King Ferdinand I was forced to extend the Spanish Constitution. When the news reached Palermo, a rather violent popular revolt broke out that saw the popular masses taking to the streets together with the artisan corporations, with the support – at least initially – of the nobility. Very soon *sicilianismo* split into two currents: while the city corporations called loudly for the introduction of the Cadiz constitution, the island's notabilate, faithful to its conservative spirit, sought the restoration of the oligarchic constitution granted to Sicily in 1812. In the end, the artisan and popular factions prevailed through violence, with a number of notables being killed in the process (Villari 1975: 55). It became necessary to form a *giunta* or provisional government at Palermo to restore order and prevent the situation from deteriorating further.

The 1820 insurrection against the Bourbon government ended up being channelled into a demand for autonomy by the Sicilian nobilitate. The Palermo insurgents drew up a manifesto – signed by Count Giovanni Aceto Cattani, Carbonaro, member of the 1812 parliament, and a fervent supporter of the liberal reform of the Constitution – in response to the proclamation of the Prince Vicar General. The manifesto called for negotiations to bring about the granting of independence as well as the adoption of the Spanish constitution in order to suppress the unrest. Sicily's request did not regard 'her separation as a country but as a government' (Basile 2015: 54). Subsequently, on 26 July 1820, the Provisional Government sent its representatives to other towns in Sicily with the aim of identifying deputies capable of working in a collaborative, unitary spirit with the Bourbon government in order to form an elected Chamber and reach a shared decision with regard to the statute that was to be accorded to the island. However, there were still too many tensions between the various towns and cities for their collaboration in a joint project to be feasible. For this reason the conciliation proposal submitted to the Palermo delegation by the Neapolitan government in August 1820 proved impossible to implement: in fact, it provided that if there were unanimous consensus among the Sicilian towns and cities, Sicily would be granted autonomy, that is, its own parliament and administration, on condition of swearing loyalty to the king and of having a joint army and diplomatic corps with Naples (Grimaldi 2016: 1–6). When the news got out that the conciliation proposal had not been accepted by the majority of Sicilian towns and would therefore not be implemented, riots broke out on the streets of Palermo.

On 5 October 1820, the Palermo delegation signed a convention with the aim of re-establishing order and of allowing the Neapolitan troops to enter the city. Article 2 of the Convention read as follows: 'The majority of the votes of Sicilians lawfully convened will establish the unity or separation of the national representation of the Kingdom of the Two Sicilies' (Grimaldi 2018: 228). The project failed, the Provisional Government was dissolved, and officials were ordered to swear an oath of loyalty to the kingdom. Neither one of these documents – the Manifesto of Count Aceto or the Convention – contained any revolutionary motions that might be interpreted as an attempt to subvert the established order or, even less, to seek an overall transformation of Sicily's economic and social structures. The aim of the authors of the convention was to obtain greater bargaining and decision-making powers with regard to the state authority represented by the king. Although they made explicit reference to past Sicilian independence, the motions of the insurgents were not an expression of separatist demands: their instances should be contextualized as belonging to the context of a request for autonomy and administrative decentralization rather than as independentist or separatist demands.

The island's elites did not seek a separation from the Bourbon kingdom but the maintenance of the constitutional system that had remained in force until 1815, when, by the decree of 8 December 1820, Ferdinand IV became Ferdinand I, King of the Kingdom of the Two Sicilies, thereby ending Sicily's centuries-old sovereignty. In this sense, the idea of a 'Sicilian nation' was connected to the restoration of the system of privileges that had benefited the baronage in the past; in fact, Palermo's aristocracy had experienced the negative effects of the suppression of the free port in Palermo and the loss of the monopoly of its courts (Basile 2015: 55). These clauses represented Sicily's statute of autonomy and were endorsed by Article 17 of the 1812 Constitution, which established the independence of the Kingdom of Sicily even in the event of the Bourbons regaining the throne of Naples (Basile 2015: 54). Count Aceto Cattani was strongly in favour of establishing a 'liberal brotherhood' with the Neapolitans with the aim of helping to maintain Sicily's economic, political and social interests (Basile 2015: 57) and was certainly not motivated by anti-Neapolitan tendencies: Sicily's union with Naples did not imply an acknowledgement of Naples' domination of the island rather than the need to confirm a separation between two systems in the same state. The federation formed by these two systems would guarantee them reciprocal protection from any attempts to alter this equilibrium coming from outside. However, the situation was far from resolved.

1848 in Sicily

It was no coincidence, therefore, that the 1848 Springtime of the Peoples began in the Sicilian capital. On 12 January 1848, the people of Palermo rose up against the Bourbon government: the heterogeneous group of rebels demanded political reforms, a constitutional charter, and greater social justice. Ferdinand II decided to grant Sicily a Constitution, which was due to come into force on 10 February. The Charter, drawn up on a representative and censitary basis, presupposed the recognition of the authority of the monarchy, which, in turn, undertook to guarantee Sicily a degree of political autonomy. The popular insurrection was followed by the prompt mobilization of the nobilitate, aware that it would not be expedient to react passively to advancing events. The circumstances required them to respond as a ruling class capable of handling a situation that could have resulted in unexpected outcomes, of maintaining and consolidating their authority, and of winning back the spaces and positions of power lost in the post-Napoleonic period (La Manna 2020: 688).

The expression 'Sicilian nation' diverged from the idea of 'sovereign nation' typical of Napoleonic state constitutionalism; the island agreed to share sovereignty with the king, even though there were continuing aspects of hostility towards the Neapolitan government (Basile 2017: 198). The 1848 revolts also saw federalist tendencies emerging: Michele Amari (Romeo 1961: 637–54), one of the leading exponents of this current, identified the 1812 Sicilian Constitution as a constitutional model that, with the necessary adjustments for the new political context, might be valid for the entire Mediterranean basin. The exponents of liberal Catholicism, in particular, saw federalism as a feasible solution because, while recognizing Bourbon sovereignty, it would also have allowed a certain degree of autonomy (Basile 2017: 202–10). This constitution was founded on a concept of autonomy and conceived in the wider context of an Italian federation rather than in anti-Neapolitan terms.

Michele Amari's Risorgimento ideas were based on a re-reading of the island's history through a sicilianist lens. In his celebrated book, *Storia dei musulmani di Sicilia* (1854), Amari suggested that the Muslims were responsible for forging the Sicilian identity and autonomist spirit. According to Amari, the Islamic influence diverged radically from Byzantine despotism, distinguishing itself for its democratic exercise of power and the rejection of every form of social hierarchy. The arrival of the Muslims marked the start of an enlightened period that saw the end of the latifundia, which only made a reappearance following the Norman conquest of the island (Arcifa 2020). There was no mention of the concept of 'Sicilian nation', which became the focus of insularist rhetoric in the post-unitary period, as we have seen, and of the sicilianist journalism that sought to corroborate a victim mentality based on the 'betrayed Risorgimento'.

From Unification to the *Fasci dei lavoratori*

The Liberal Right was in power continuously from 1861 to 1876, when the then premier Marco Minghetti, after having announced in a parliamentary session that he had balanced the State budget, faced internal opposition from those against a state takeover of the railways. The members of the Liberal Right hostile to Minghetti's statism voted together with the Left, causing the government to fall. The so-called 'parliamentary crisis' of 1876 brought to power a moderate left-wing government without an election and with an investiture by King Victor Emmanuel. It was led by Agostino Depretis, proponent of 'trasformismo' (transformism), which would become a feature of Italian politics and involved forming parliamentary majorities in relation to specific programmes, thereby overcoming the traditional distinction between left-wing and right-wing. The 1876 parliamentary crisis had its roots in the electoral defeat of the Historic Right in Sicily two years earlier. The resignation of Minghetti and the birth of the Depretis government were therefore a direct consequence of events on the island, where the vote had clearly caused the prime minister to lose his majority in Parliament (Renda 1987: 159–62). Until then, right-wing governments had adopted a policy of granting jobs and honours to Sicily's lower middle class and middle class, with the aim of channelling them into the government party.

It was precisely in this 'centralization weakened by a policy of ante-litteram favours' that the Sicilian ruling class 'found an effective surrogate for the autonomy to which they had mainly aspired due to their ambitions of local predominance' (Adorni 1994: 339). In the wake of the parliamentary crisis, the agrarian bloc used Sicilianist rhetoric as a 'defensive ideology' aimed at 'preserving its autonomous bargaining capacity in the regard of the State' (Adorni 1994: 339). In 1876, the Liberal Leopoldo Franchetti, who had anxiously watched the Left come to power, and Sidney Sonnino, a Meridionalist, also from the moderate right, went on an unofficial trip to Sicily to study the island's economic and social conditions. In 1877, they published the results of their inquiry in two volumes entitled *La Sicilia nel 1876*: in it, Franchetti and Sonnino portrayed a Sicily beset by misery where an ineffective or absent State had been replaced by the power of the Mafia (Franchetti [1876] 2011: 36). Franchetti and Sonnino's inquiry, *Lettere meridionali* (1878) by Pasquale Villari, and Giuseppe Zanardelli's account of his 1902 trip to the south of Italy (he was the first head of government of unified Italy to visit the South), followed by Giustino Fortunato's studies launched the trend of studies into Meridionalism. This term referred to the entire area of historic, economic, and social studies into the problems that had emerged after Italian unification due to the inclusion of southern Italy in the institutional context of the Kingdom of Italy.

Following the parliamentary crisis and the rise of *trasformismo* tactics in politics, there was a profound crisis in terms of political representation and government. Towards the end of the nineteenth century, peasant revolts sprang up all over the island, protesting against *gabelloti* (bailiffs) and *mezzadri* (sharecroppers) who managed the estates for the absentee landlords and were considered the expression of oppression. 'They shouted, "*Morte ai cappeddi*", or death to those wearing hats (as opposed to the humble *coppola* worn by peasants and miners)' (Licata 1965: 164). These protests, which had previously failed to produce any results because they were not organized, were channelled into the Fasci dei lavoratori (Workers Leagues), the organized political expression of a popular mass movement that emerged between June 1892 and December 1893. The experience of the Fasci was the 'first political expression of the process of social mobility' because 'the explosion of the movement took place [...] at the height of a progressive transformation of channels of hegemony and of a request for status by emerging groups' (Lupo and Mangiameli 1983: 230). In this way, as Eric Hobsbawm has pointed out, a primitive, spontaneous movement could produce a movement with a clearly defined programme and modern ideology (1963: 93–107).

In 1894, the movement was suppressed by Prime Minister Francesco Crispi who set up military tribunals and dissolved the socialist workers' party. Francesco Crispi, like Antonio Starabba di Rudinì, both Sicilian premiers, was subjected to relentless, intense pressure by the Sicilian elites as well as by ordinary tradesmen who drew the government's attention to the problems affecting the island, appealing to their Sicilian origins. The birth of the Fasci dei lavoratori created huge problems for the mechanisms of power and for the system of relations built up by Crispi and Rudinì during their term of office (Adorni 1994: 334–8). In the early 1900s, the Sicilian ruling class sought to regain its hegemonic role; the Florio shipping company (Cancila 2008), sulphur producers and citrus fruit producers created an alliance among the bourgeoisie 'with an essentially conservative ideology, that of *Sicilianismo*' (Barone 1987: 300): in actual fact, they 'disguised themselves by means of "Sicilian interests," embracing regionalism and anti-Giolittism' (Lupo 1981: 31–2).

From the post–First World War period to the Liberation of Italy

In the period after the First World War, relations between landowners and the 'northern capital' were highly conflictual, 'with the capital making real threats against ground rent' (Lupo 1981: 18). Following the advent of Fascism, Sicilian society experienced a kind of 'suspension' of its balance of power. During the Fascist period, the sicilianist current promoting, in literary circles, the idea of the rebirth of Sicily founded on its glorious past was replaced by a militant *sicilianismo* in direct opposition to fascist centralization (Lupo 1977). In the 1930s, the sicilianist discourse matured and developed in particular in the intellectual circles operating within *Problemi siciliani. Rivista mensile della rinascita mediterranea*, the review directed by Filippo Lo Vetere and Giuseppe Frisella-Vella (Lupo 1981: 146). Two independentist groups emerged: one was based in Palermo and led by Lucio Tasca, member of the landowning class; the other a more progressive movement with populist tendencies led by Antonio Canepa, the 'guerrilla-professor' (Ganci [1978] 1986: 184–6). This young intellectual with anarcho-socialist leanings was active in the Resistance, working with the British Secret Service in the 1940s, while always seeking to advance the cause of Sicilian independence (Cimino 1988: 133–41).

In 1941, using the pseudonym Mario Turri, Canepa signed the manifesto *La Sicilia ai Siciliani*, which would become the cornerstone of sicilianist anti-fascism (Gaja 1962: 368–81). In the early 1940s, Sicily saw the emergence of a number of separatist groups, from the landowning bloc, from various sectors of the pre-fascist nobilitate and from the urban petty and middle bourgeoisie. On 5 August 1941, Mussolini, mistrustful of the loyalty of his Sicilian officials, issued a telegram to all the ministers in the Kingdom that read: 'all officials born on the island are shortly to be dismissed from the Sicilian offices' (Trizzino 1945: 15). All of these independentist groups were channelled into a single movement thanks to the efforts of Sicilian noble Andrea Finocchiaro Aprile, who, in 1943, founded the Movimento per l'Indipendenza della Sicilia (Movement for the Independence of Sicily or MIS) (Paci and Pietrancosta 2010: 7–13); MIS also had an armed wing, Esercito Volontario per l'Indipendenza Siciliana (Voluntary Army for Sicilian Independence or EVIS) that was led by Antonio Canepa. As noted by Andrea Miccichè, 'the heterogeneous composition of the Movement and the alternance of levels and positions, which saw agrarian conservatism flanked by democratic tendencies, markedly republican positions alongside pro-monarchist confluences, nobilitate and interclass radicalism, resulted in a fluctuating political line. At times, these oscillations also concerned the independentist objectives, sometimes favouring federalist or even autonomist tendencies' (2019: 2). Creating a favourable context for this project was the Allied invasion of Sicily, codenamed Operation Husky, which was launched in July 1943.

While Americans of Sicilian descent 're-discovered' 'Sicily through the eyes of the many colourful immigrants from the island' (Mangiameli 2020), the Independentists dreamt of separating from Italy. In the wake of the Allied landing, a manifesto welcoming the liberators circulated in Palermo; signed by the committee for Sicilian independence, it mentioned that 'a number of men of proven loyalty and experience have joined together to make the necessary arrangements and to request the cooperation of the great nations united for the purpose of the constitution of the new State of Sicily, the formation of a provisional government, and the admission of a Sicilian delegation to the future peace conference' (Marino 1979: 19). Finocchiaro Aprile did everything in his power to build relationships with the Allies, convinced that the Sicilian question would only be resolved in the context of the international relationships that would come into being once the war was over (Marino 1979: 19–21). Moreover, the administrators and officials appointed by the allies considered the alliance of intents with separatism an occasion for a repositioning (Mangiameli 1987: 559). The constitutional project put forward by Finocchiaro Aprile, which was a kind of compromise between British parliamentarism and American presidentialism, was an expression of the Independentists' desire to reduce Sicily to a status of 'gilded vassalage' that would have seen the new Sicilian State 'administering an "indépendance octroyée" with all the necessary guarantees for the respect of "democratic" principles' (Marino 1979: 21). Finocchiaro Aprile began by trying to gain the support of the Allied Military Government of Occupied Territories (AMGOT); when this failed he sought a dialogue with the national political movements welcoming a federal union between a Sicilian State and the rest of the peninsula. Given the role being assumed by the MIS, the parties of the Comitato di Liberazione Nazionale (National Liberation Committee or CLN), which were undergoing a phase of internal reorganization, were forced to enter into a dialogue with this new actor.

One of Finocchiaro Aprile's main interlocutors was Randolfo Pacciardi, the leading exponent of the Republican party (Ganci 1986: 244), which supported the federal cause. On 28 July 1945, *Sicilia repubblicana*, the party organ of the Sicilian Republican Party, published an article with the title 'Autonomia-Separatismo' that underlined the existence of an indissoluble link between autonomies and national unity. To prove that the two could coexist, the author quoted federalist Giuseppe Ferrari who wrote – still in the nineteenth century – 'there was a widespread misbelief that federation meant division, disassociation, separation; but the word federation comes from "foedus", which means pact, *union*, reciprocal *link*, and the link of the federations is flexible and powerful' (Partito repubblicano siciliano 1945). The Republican newspaper claimed that it wished to reflect the will of the 'Sicilian People' which 'actually wanted, (whatever the beliefs of so-called liberation committees or separatist leaders, both of whom are *false* interpreters of the island's will) the Federal Republic in which Sicily must have, and will have, its historic parliament, its own budget, and its *own constitution*. A national constituent, therefore, but also a regional constituent' (*Partito repubblicano siciliano* 1945). Given the impossibility of reaching an agreement with the Republican Party, on the eve of the institutional referendum calling upon Italians to vote for either a republican or monarchist state, Finocchiaro Aprile, supported by the independentist component on the right of the MIS, took a monarchist position, supporting Humbert of Savoy as King of Sicily (Ganci 1986: 244). The first issue of *Trinacria*, the official organ of the MIS, which was published on 20 July 1946, contained an article titled 'La beffa dell'autonomia' (the Insult of Autonomy), condemning autonomy because it could only lead to an 'insult' to the 'Sicilian people' (MIS 1946).

The fall of Fascism and the separatist proclamations made by Finocchiaro Aprile led to the political bargaining table the question of the recognition of the autonomy that would be brought about in 1946 with the approval of the island's special statute. As later pointed out by the Sicilian Nino Novacco, Secretary-General of SVIMEZ (Association for the Development of Industry in the South), 'autonomy was the national price paid for the short but powerful virulence of the *"separatismo"* proposed by Andrea Finocchiaro Aprile, and by the powerful landowning interests, as well as due to a mistaken *sicilianismo* asking for "reparations" and historic compensations' (2005: 558). The populist Finocchiaro Aprile, who was demanding secession from the national State, was prosecuted for being an instrument of the Mafia, landowners and latifundists.

The recognition of autonomy represents a watershed moment in the island's history: it was then that the island's elites adapted their sicilianist rhetoric to the *Realpolitik* of a State seeking to adopt a stance in discontinuity with fascist state centralism. However, independentist ambitions made way for a consolidation of the newly acquired autonomy; it was now a question of negotiating with the post-war national parties, from a position of autonomism, in order to establish Sicily's role in the Italian Republic. From the Bourbon administration to the birth of the Republican State, the Sicilian ruling class revealed its aspirations towards autonomy, considered as a constant dialectic between the island elites and the central State (whatever this was). These elites used a sicilianist version of the insular rhetoric to acquire consensus within the island's society. As pointed out by Rosario Mangiameli: 'by calling for the unity of island interests and putting themselves forward as the representatives of the entire Sicilian people with regard to the State, they would safeguard their own position as the ruling class' (1980: 93).

Sicilianismo has a complex history that does not descend exclusively from the presumed capacity of the ruling class to recycle itself. Although it is undeniable that *trasformismo* played a major role in Sicily's history, the political debate as well as the ideological reading of *The Leopard* exaggerated its scope. *The Leopard* is set in Sicily in 1860, where change is represented by the red shirts worn by the Garibaldini: we see *trasformismo* take effect as the ruling classes side with Garibaldi, jumping on his bandwagon. But we should remember that this is a twentieth-century interpretation proposed by Tomasi di Lampedusa who, in 1958, was well aware of the decline of his social class, the aristocracy, undermined first by fascism and then by the war and the post-war peasant movement.

Sicilianismo was an instrument at the service of anyone who wished to use it. In the twentieth century, it was used with profoundly ideological implications, from the right through to the left, entering the context of the mass society, which offered such fertile terrain for the growth of ideologies. For example, at the suggestion of Palmiro Togliatti, secretary of the Italian Communist Party, the Sicilian Communists adopted a specific markedly sicilianist language to acquire credibility in the eyes of the people: although they were part of an internationalist movement, that was not deeply rooted at the local level, it was necessary to create the conditions for their actions to be fully shared, and they did so by using this approach (Togliatti 1965). As Miccichè points out in reference to the separatist period, 'the autonomist choice of the leading national parties is part and parcel of that claiming of rights that denounces the misgovernment of the island in the past, using arguments not dissimilar from separatism, also deriving this from the *sicilianismo* that seems to be dominating the public discourse in these years' (Miccichè 2019: 3). Twentieth-century regionalism is now distinguished by a more pronounced *sicilianismo* than regionalism in Risorgimento times. This typically sicilianist approach to 'reparations' emerges from the words of Girolamo Li Causi, secretary of the Sicilian Communist Party, who, while criticizing the separatists for having followed a line of political opportunism to defend their privileges, acknowledged that they had affirmed 'the right and vital need that underpins the reparations for the wrongs done to the Mezzogiorno' (Miccichè 2019: 13).

The sicilianist open elite used insularist rhetoric both to legitimize its position at grassroots level as well as with regard to the centre. Moreover, it showed that it was ready to reformulate its insularist discourses in response to the opportunities offered by times of crisis (during the nineteenth-century revolts, on the occasion of Italian Unification, in the wake of the Allied landings), framing its demands in a context that could be national or even European so as to safeguard its continuous exercise of power; while maintaining the capacity, when the time was ripe, to mediate between instinct and social conventions, the famous *corda seria* – or 'serious cord' – first evoked by Pirandello.[2] An instrument close at hand for anyone wishing to reach out, support for the hegemony of the ruling class and typical characteristic of Sicily's politico-cultural tradition, *sicilianismo*

---

[2] In Pirandello's play, *Cap and Bells*, he refers to the three cords responsible for our social interaction: the serious, the civil and the crazy.

was a language aimed at reinforcing its bargaining power with regard to external political interlocutors. In the first lines of the introduction to the volume *La Sicilia*, Giuseppe Giarrizzo made an opportune and extremely pressing affirmation: 'the Sicilian culture' – he wrote – 'delights in that diversity: whether strong or weak, it does not indulge in criticisms or analyses, preferring to oppose myth with myth, model with model. And yet that myth is part of Sicily's history: and the historian who is called upon to liquidate it with criticisms every time it distorts "the facts" or stains "the cause" must defend its presence and its role in his account; he may recognize it as a character yet may not make it the heart of a model' (1987: XIX). Leonardo Sciascia traced back to the mythical dimension all of the elements nurturing *sicilianismo* including *sicilianità*, melancholy, isolation, which ended up representing an excuse:

> That's what we Sicilians are like. That's the way we are and the way we will always be [...] these are myths and these are undoubtedly excuses [...] and at that point *sicilianità* is an absolutely negative fact because if we scratch the concept of *sicilianità* as it was commonly diffused [...] this *sicilianità* is nothing but the mafia [...] another form of self-repression.
>
> (1971)

The 'besieged citadel': Maltese nationalism between British imperialism and Italian irredentism

Purely political motives are not enough to change the physiognomy of a people recognized as Italian by the imperial authorities themselves, at a time when they had no concerns about Italy and freely acknowledged that we are Italian

Enrico Mizzi, *La Massoneria Inglese e l'Italianità di Malta* (1934)

From the Order of Malta to the French occupation

By virtue of its strategic and geopolitical relevance, the Maltese archipelago has always been considered to be the heart of the Mediterranean in the collective imagination. A key moment in Maltese history took place in 1522 when the island of Rhodes, a Christian outpost governed by the Knights Hospitaller (also known as Order of St John), fell into Ottoman hands. In 1530, Emperor Charles V, who had inherited the crown of Aragon and the Kingdom of Sicily, granted the Maltese archipelago to the Order, which had by now been left without headquarters for eight years. The Knights Hospitaller imposed their foreign rule upon the island, stripping the Maltese aristocracy of rights recognized by the Aragonese sovereigns including ancient privileges of autonomy linked to the municipal regulations represented by the two Università (municipalities) in Malta and Gozo. Following the arrival of the Knights, the Università lost their autonomy and were subjected to the control of the Order (Ferlazzo Ciano 2018: 24–5). As demesne land, Malta enjoyed a relative degree of autonomy within the Crown of Sicily. In addition to the Università, there was also a Consiglio Popolare (town council) made up of nobles with a power of veto over decrees proposed by the Sicilian king regarding the archipelago's legal system.

The sovereignty of the Order led to the gradual erosion of the power of the Consiglio Popolare, ending with its suppression in 1777 (Ferlazzo Ciano 2018: 48). The Knights changed their name to the Order of Malta. Right from their arrival, they took steps to fortify the island, exploiting its favourable physical features like the deep, narrow inlets surrounding the bay known as Porto Grande (Grand Harbour or Dockyard Creek in later English maps) (Frasca 2004: 45). In 1565, the Order managed to resist an Ottoman siege lasting over four months, later known as the Great Siege: this event, still celebrated as a national holiday

Figure 6. A panoramic view of the fortifications which were built to make Valletta an invincible capital city for the Order of St John.
Le bastion Saint-Salvator de La Valette (Malte) by Jean-Pierre Dalbéra on Flickr.

on 8 September, is known as il-Vitorja (the Victory) and il-Bambina (the Virgin Mary). This holiday marks four events that are particularly important to the Maltese: the end of the Great Siege of 1565, the conclusion of the Napoleonic occupation of 1800, the Italian Armistice with the Allies and the Feast of the Virgin Mary. In 1566, in the wake of the Great Siege, work began on the construction of the new capital of Valletta, a guarded fortified city.

This transformed Malta into a military bulwark and impregnable archipelago, defined 'Italy's antemurale'. The Order was constantly engaged in wars against the Ottomans and in fighting off the threat posed by the piracy of the Barbary states on the north African coast. For almost three centuries, the Maltese archipelago was the seat of the maritime military power charged with defending Christian Europe from the Ottoman threat. The Maltese gradually ended up being excluded from the exercise of power and the Grand Master came increasingly to resemble an absolute sovereign. There was a widespread popular discontent that resulted in numerous rebellions – including the 'Rising of the Priests' of 1775, led by the priest Gaetano Mannarino – all of which were harshly suppressed. However, thanks to its strategic geographical position, Malta was coveted by foreign powers. Sovereignty over Malta would have reinforced the French geopolitical position in the eastern Mediterranean in the wake of the

Treaty of Campoformio (1797) decreeing the hegemony of Napoleonic France over the Ionian islands.

On 9 June 1798, Napoleon Bonaparte appeared off the coast of Malta on board a convoy from Toulon heading for Egypt and requested a laissez passer from Grand Master Ferdinand von Hompesch zu Bolheim that would allow the French fleet to enter the port under the pretext of taking on water supplies. His request was not granted because it would have violated the Order's status of neutrality and, moreover, under the 1798 treaty, only four vessels at a time were allowed access. Napoleon's reaction was not long in coming: the following evening (10 June), 15000 French soldiers disembarked on the island and took possession of Malta. On 12 June, an agreement was drawn up whereby the Order of the Knights transferred to Napoleon Malta, Gozo and Comino, renouncing all its rights to sovereignty and to the possessions that it had held for 268 years. In exchange for signing the Act of Capitulation, the Grand Master was awarded a pension and indemnity. Although the Kingdom of Naples had maintained a position of neutrality with regard to France from 1796 onwards, the Napoleonic occupation of the island led the Bourbon monarchy to enter into an alliance with Great Britain. On 18 June, before leaving for Alexandria, Napoleon left a French garrison on the island under the command of General Claude-Henri de Belgrand Vaubois, who was appointed governor of Malta. Claude-Henri de Belgrand Vaubois informed the Kingdom of Naples of France's intention to maintain neutrality, thereby maintaining commercial relations between Malta and Sicily. In fact, Ferdinand IV of Naples (also known as Ferdinand III of Sicily) established a number of measures aimed at restricting France's military operations.

A cordon sanitaire was placed around the islands, ostensibly to prevent the diffusion in Sicily of diseases from the Maghreb countries. However, it was actually a pretext for a naval blockade interrupting the trade flow between Sicily and Malta, thereby leading to a shortage of food supplies. The French army wasted no time in replacing the ancient institutions of the Order, sacking churches and attempting to sell seized church property. This provoked a popular revolt on 2 September led by 10,000 Maltese irregular soldiers under the command of Emmanuele Vitale and Canon Francesco Saverio Caruana. The rebels did not have enough ammunition for an assault and provisions were beginning to dwindle so they sent a delegation to Naples on 6 September to ask Ferdinand IV to support the Maltese cause. On 19 September, while awaiting the arrival of British ships to the archipelago, six Portuguese warships came to the aid of the rebels. In the meantime, the Maltese speronare ships were given permission to land in Sicily for food supplies (Ferlazzo Ciano 2018: 35–8). At the end of September, a convoy of British ships under the command of Sir James Saumarez arrived off the Maltese coast. The battered convoy, which was on its return from its victory against the French in the Battle of the Nile (1–3 August 1798), needed to carry out repairs but found a very tense situation due to the clashes between the Maltese and the French occupying forces.

After meeting the representatives of the Maltese, Saumarez took on the role of mediator, offering a truce to General Claude-Henri de Belgrand Vaubois on their behalf, but did not receive the hoped-for response. Before setting off for Gibraltar, Saumarez offered the Maltese irregulars military aid. On 19 September a squadron of six Portuguese warships arrived at the island to create a naval blockade that would prevent the French from getting supplies to Valletta. This fleet was joined by three British ships under Captain Alexander Ball and at the orders of Admiral Horatio Nelson. Captain Ball was appointed military governor, an office that allowed him to intervene with the Maltese and later win the trust of the rebels. Right from the start of the insurrection, the rebels had set up a civil government, the National Assembly, dominated by Francesco Saverio Caruana, who would be appointed bishop in 1831 (Ferlazzo Ciano 2018: 38). From the beginning of 1799, the lack of food supplies shaped the unfolding of events: Nelson was unable to pursue the blockade with his forces. He had unsuccessfully sought help from Ferdinand IV of Naples, who had fled from the French advance on Nelson's flag ship, taking shelter in Sicily. On 7 February 1799, three deputies from the Maltese National Assembly travelled to Palermo and appealed to Ferdinand IV of Naples to allow Great Britain to provide protection should the sovereign not consent to send help in the next three months. Nelson, William Hamilton, the British Ambassador at the Bourbon Court, and his wife Emma, a friend of Maria Carolina and Nelson's lover, all exerted pressure on Queen Maria Carolina of Naples, with the result that Ferdinand IV of Naples finally decided to send help and provisions to the island. Subsequently, Captain Alexander Ball was named commander of the Maltese forces and Civil Commissioner of the island, governing in the name and on behalf of Ferdinand IV of Naples (Frasca 2004: 52).

On 11 February 1799, Ball invited a number of National Assembly representatives, including Caruana, to his residence in Palazzo Sant'Antonio, in Birchircara, to discuss a constitutional project. At the end of the meeting, which was presided over by Ball, it was decided that the National Assembly would be transformed into a Congress in which the villages and clergy would be represented with the presence of a vicar of the diocesis. 'In that period Malta underwent a similar experience to Sicily in 1812, following the reforms of its parliamentary institutions by Lord Bentinck [...] in this case, given that the Maltese lacked political experience and someone capable of autonomously supervising the drawing-up of the constitution, Ball acted on their behalf' (Ferlazzo Ciano 2018: 46). As Angelo Grimaldi has pointed out, the British played a key role in the Sicilian Constitution of 1812 by supporting the demands of the Sicilian barons: the Constitution 'responded to the Sicilian aspirations towards independence from the Kingdom of Naples (administrative autonomy), but also to the socio-economic interests of the island's aristocrats and the commercial interests of the English' (2017: 211).

In May 1799, a French fleet under Admiral Etienne Eustache Bruix managed to deliver supplies to Valletta without, however, resolving the lack of provisions crippling the French garrison. In early February 1800, the Neapolitan government joined the blockade. On 5 September, faced with serious food and water shortages, and the spread of disease, General Claude-Henri de Belgrand Vaubois called a meeting of his officers and decided to surrender.

How Malta became British

During the course of the siege, the Maltese had, in fact, offered the sovereignty of the island to Great Britain. In purely formal terms, the island belonged to the Neapolitan Crown: from the Bourbon point of view, the surrender marked the beginning of a British interregnum – at least in theory – that would soon have been followed by the restoration of Bourbon sovereignty in the archipelago. It was against this background that Tsar Paul I of Russia, the former Grand Master of the Order of Malta, sought to reclaim the island for the Order, thereby providing Russia with a naval base in the heart of the Mediterranean. However, in the event, the only flag to be raised over Valletta's fortifications was the British flag and the island passed under the control of Britain. British sovereignty over Malta caused a breakdown in relations between Great Britain and Russia: British vessels were barred from Russian ports; sanctions were introduced along with an embargo on exports of materials for the British shipbuilding industry. In 1801, the position of Grand Master became vacant following the assassination of Tsar Paul I. Pope Pius VII designated Giovanni Battista Tommasi as the Grand Master, thereby delegitimizing Russian aspirations for the archipelago. The attempts made by Alexander I, Paul's successor, to drive the British troops out of Malta were all to no avail.

In 1802, Britain and France signed the Treaty of Amiens that established the provisional British administration on the island as a prelude to the return of the

Order. The Congress had been dissolved under pressure from Ball following the French surrender in September 1800. In the wake of the Treaty, the former members of the Congress drew up a Declaration of the rights of the islands of Malta and Gozo: in it they recognized the sovereignty of the king of the United Kingdom of Great Britain and Ireland, asking for his protection and for the promise not to surrender the archipelago to any other power. Feeling betrayed by Great Britain and fearing the return of the Order, the Maltese sought in vain to restore the Consiglio Popolare (Ferlazzo Ciano 2018: 48–50). The British did not evacuate the island because this would have allowed Malta to return under French influence. During the Napoleonic Wars, Great Britain was able to use the island as a base for its expedition to reconquer the Ionian Islands in 1809, for its contrabanding activities, and in order to send supplies to the Duke of Wellington's troops heading to Spain and Portugal in 1808–1809 (Frasca 2004: 54). After the close of the Napoleonic period and the end of the conflict in Europe, Malta became a Crown Colony. Article 7 of the Treaty of Paris of 30 May 1814 established that the island of Malta and its dependencies 'shall belong in full right and Sovereignty to His Britannic Majesty' (De Bono 1899: 99–100). There was no mention whatsoever of the rights of the Bourbon dynasty regarding the archipelago. Ferdinand IV of Naples lost his sovereignty over the Maltese archipelago but regained full rights over Sicily in 1815. The following year, in 1816, he unified the Kingdom of Naples and Sicily into a new system of monarchy: the Kingdom of the Two Sicilies. This marked the point in which the political links between Sicily and Malta were interrupted: 'by now the only weak link still in place between the two islands was the institution of the *Apostolica legatia*, but on this point every eventual political agreement had to be sought in Rome, with the pope, no longer in Naples, with the king of the Two Sicilies' (Ferlazzo Ciano 2018: 53).

From 1815 to 1964, the year of its independence, Malta was a British colony in the heart of the Mediterranean, subject to the authority of a governor vested with civil and military government who ruled under the local legislation in respect of the British institutions. In 1812, a Royal Commission was set up to develop a system of government for Malta. The first steps taken by the British concerned the Maltese institutional bodies. In 1818, they suppressed the three Università (the municipalities of Valletta, Notabile and Gozo) on the grounds that they were no more than 'Jacobin clubs disguised as charitable institutions' (Ferlazzo Ciano 2018: 54–5). The process of anglicization met with the opposition of the Maltese and it was decided that Italian was to remain as official language. The echoes of the 1830 revolution reached as far as Malta where a generation of liberal lawyers and merchants with a growing political consciousness gathered around Count Camillo Sceberras Testaferrata (Frendo 1989). On 28 June 1831, Sceberras presented a petition requesting a legislative reform, a reduction in taxes, a salary increase for government employees, the improvement of the health system, the establishment of an education system for the poor, but, above all, the establishment of an elected local government, that is, 'a Consiglio di Nativi with a sufficient number of members to be freely elected by means of votes' (Ferlazzo Ciano 2018: 64). The petitioners received no response from the British government so two years later they requested a reply. In an attempt to placate the Maltese, Governor Frederick Cavendish Ponsonby put forward an alternative proposal. After various discussions with the British government, a compromise was reached. On 1 April 1835, the Secretary of State for War and the Colonies, Edward Stanley, passed a law establishing a Council of Government with consultative functions. This body was to be formed by three Maltese nominated by the British institutions and by four representatives of the British government in Malta.

The Maltese Liberals did not welcome the idea of a body completely under British control. Sceberras refused to give up and joined forces with an enterprising young Maltese merchant with Dalmatian origins, Giorgio Mitrovich. He gave Mitrovich permission to go to London and submit the Maltese requests to the British members of parliament, with whom Mitrovich was in good terms. Mitrovich distributed two pamphlets, in English and in Italian (*The claims of the Maltese founded upon the principles of Justice* and *Indirizzo ai Maltesi da parte del loro amico Giorgio Mitrovich che è attualmente a Londra*) to explain to leading figures from the world of politics why the Maltese were calling for their own institutions and to communicate their grievances about the poor administration of Malta. On 8 September 1835, through his friendship with the liberal William Ewart Gladstone, Mitrovich managed to submit a Plan of Reform to the Secretary of State, Charles Grant Glenelg, requesting a major constitutional review of Maltese institutions that would make them more liberal. Lord Glenelg subsequently launched an inquiry into complaints of misgovernment in Malta. On 7 June 1836, a petition was presented at the House of Commons regarding the failure to grant freedom of press and political representation to Malta, which was not passed over in silence thanks to Ewart's involvement. When the Royal Commission landed on the island on 18 October 1836, it was met and accompanied by the Comitato Generale Maltese, a body that had been set up illegally and which hoped to influence the Commission's activities (Ferlazzo Ciano 2018: 67–72). On 16 February 1838, the House of Commons published the report drawn up by the Royal Commission, containing a number of proposals for reform.

Malta: a meeting place for Risorgimento exiles and Maltese elites

These recommendations for reform bore fruit a year later when an ordinance was passed on 15 March 1839, recognizing the freedom of press and abolishing censorship. Under a law of 1756, anyone intending to set up a printing business was required to request a licence, which was inevitably denied (Pulvirenti 2014: 175). Following the abolition of censorship, the British government steered Maltese politics in a more liberal direction and Maltese journalism was born. In the space of just two years, between 1838 and 1839, seventeen newspapers were established; by 1847, just a decade later, they had grown to eighty-nine (Pulvirenti 2014: 178–9). The many newspapers founded in this period (Fiorentini 1982) included two with very different orientations: *Il Portafoglio Maltese*, an expression of Giorgio Mitrovich's liberal and administrative reformism, and the radical *Il Mediterraneo*, founded by Camillo Sceberras (Paci 2012: 15). The exiles from the Italian peninsula, flocking to Malta from 1821 onwards, introduced Risorgimento ideals (Isabella and Zanou 2016): thanks to their contacts with the Maltese liberals, they chose Malta as a temporary shelter where they could formulate their insurrectional plans.

The archipelago, like Gibraltar and the Ionian Islands, was considered a strategic base from which to develop a Mediterranean network of international solidarity (Isabella 2009). But the exiles were more than a fleeting presence: some of them, first and foremost, the Mazzinian Tommaso Zauli Sajani, would make their home in Malta. Zauli Sajani, who moved to the island with his family in 1836, was among the founders of *Il Mediterraneo*, the newspaper that would become the organ of Giovane Italia in Malta. He had considerable sway among the Maltese who were intolerant of British rule, offering them the tools they needed to combat Britain's hegemonic aspirations. These exiles aroused the sympathies of many Maltese. Some of them became involved in journalism, often becoming editors or contributors. Malta's geographic proximity made it the ideal strategic base for the production and diffusion of subversive material intended for the Italian States. Many dedicated themselves to promoting Italian literature studies by founding private schools, academies for poetry and for Dantean criticism. As Bianca Fiorentini has pointed out, 'the writings of the exiles helped to diffuse a general culture on the island, intensifying the national sentiment among the

Maltese [...] the poetic activities of the exiles re-kindled a new spirit of freedom on the island, which contributed to increasing the Reformist tendencies that were already spreading through it' (1966: 32–3).

Among the most celebrated figures to spend time on Malta was Francesco Crispi who, after being arrested and expelled from Piedmont on 10 March 1853, landed in Malta on 26 March 1853, remaining there until December 1854. His decision to go to Malta was also motivated by its geographic closeness to Sicily and by the presence of large community of Sicilian emigrants who were among the protagonists of the events of 1848 (Michel 1948), including Ruggero Settimo, Pasquale Calvi (Facineroso 2013) and Nicola Fabrizi (Pulvirenti 2013). As observed by Chiara Maria Pulvirenti, 'Malta thus became the place of production of symbols and identity rhetoric, which ended up being personified by particularly charismatic figures in the limited space of that place of sanctuary' (2014: 173). Crispi became a friend of conspirator Nicola Fabrizi who was the main 'promoter of Mazzinian ideas' in Malta (Astuto 2009: 19). Towards the end of 1849, Fabrizi formed the Circolo Maltese, a cultural association that became the Associazione Patriottica Maltese, a 'meeting place for exiles and insular elites' (Pulvirenti 2014: 182) and the island's first political organization. While entrepreneurs, university professors and liberal professionals embraced the ideas propagandized by the exiles, most Maltese, influenced by the position of the clergy to liberals, were therefore slightly distrustful of their activities. Francesco Crispi founded and directed an Italian language newspaper called *La Valigia* – later changing its name to *La Staffetta* – first published on 6 February 1854. The newspaper's political leanings attracted the notice of Governor William Reid who expelled the Sicilian politician from the island. Crispi was genuinely interested in the archipelago's affairs: in 1855, he published *Dei diritti della Corona d'Inghilterra sulla Chiesa di Malta* ([1855] 2001) in London, the result of his research in Malta's libraries and archives. He is still remembered in Malta: on 2 June 2001, a plaque was installed on the house where he resided during his Maltese exile, referring to his work, which turned the 'dream of Italian unity' into reality (Ricci 2009: V). That same year, the Istituto Italiano di Cultura in Malta, republished *Dei diritti della Corona d'Inghilterra sulla Chiesa di Malta* with a foreword by Ugo Mifsud Bonnici, President of the Republic of Malta from 1994 to 1999.

The memory of Crispi's stay in Malta is not just linked to his exile but also to the law 'referred to as "legge Crispi", from which some citizens of that State have already benefited to protect their rights with regard to our Country' (Palamenghi Crispi 2009: 379). In 1887, Crispi, who was President of the Chamber of Deputies, passed a law that also applied to 'italiani non regnicoli' – Maltese, Corsicans, people from Trieste, Dalmatians – giving them the right to residence in Italy and to enjoy the same civil rights as 'italiani regnicoli'. The matter of Italian exiles in Malta reveals the contradictions in British politics in the Mediterranean:

> Tending, on the one hand, to export liberalism through the concession of freedom of the press in the territories of the empire and thanks to the use of the refugees to transmit its principles, and forced, on the other, to suffocate the aspirations for political participation and national self-determination diffused by immigrants in its territories, so to avoid disruptive centrifugal forces regarding the motherland.
> (Pulvirenti 2014: 170)

The influence of nearby Italy and contacts established with the Risorgimento exiles had a lasting effect on the linguistic behaviour of the Maltese. During the course of the nineteenth century, identification mechanisms helped to consolidate links with Italy, which increased further through trade contacts with southern Italy. The Italian exiles played an important part in keeping the Italian cultural tradition alive, inspiring Maltese national sentiments. According to Oliver Friggieri, due to its political and geographic limitations, Malta was unable to develop an effective national consciousness without help from outside – represented by the Italian exiles (1995: 1). The echo of Italian events, the idealism and aspirations of the exiles all helped to fuel Maltese aspirations.

Although the first reference to 'Maltese nation' was made in 1796 and is found in the opening words to Mikiel Anton Vassalli's *Lexicon Melitense Latino-Italum* (Frendo 1989: 40). A nationalistic ideological process was not launched in Malta until the arrival on the island of the Risorgimento exiles whose liberal beliefs had a strong influence upon the educated Maltese with whom they came into contact. Not only did the exiles make an important contribution to the Italian Risorgimento movement through their activities in the fields of literature, journalism, politics and education, they also raised awareness of the Maltese Risorgimento given that the archipelago was also subject to foreign rule. It was against this background that Maltese liberalism developed. We should also point out that the exiles were able to influence the Maltese educated classes due to their shared language (Italian). During the 1830s, various attempts were made to request a legislative assembly and Maltese autonomy by means of petitions to the British institutions. However, such requests fell on deaf ears. The 1848 Revolution that took place in nearby Sicily helped awaken the consciences of the Maltese who could no longer agree to being governed by non-representative institutions. Aware of the changes taking place, Governor Richard More O'Ferrall drew up a reform plan beginning with the Council of Government with consultative powers. This resulted in the Letters Patent issued on 11 May 1849, which recognized the Council of Government, a consultative assembly with a minority of members elected by the Maltese population. This body, which was criticized by *Il Mediterraneo*, failed to provide broad political representation and could be suspended by the governor without the need to provide a justification (Ferlazzo Ciano 2018: 82–3). At that time, the Maltese were represented by compliant personalities close to the British government. After the opening of the Suez Canal in 1869, the archipelago's strategic importance to the British navy increased considerably. Until then Malta had had a purely defensive function with regard to French and Russian imperialist aspirations. The opening of the Suez Canal transformed Malta into the nerve centre of British politics in the Mediterranean. In that period, Great Britain had gained control of a series of strategic sites: thanks to its authority over Malta, Gibraltar, Egypt and Cyprus, the British government could protect its routes to India.

The linguistic question in Malta

The matter of language plays an important role in the history of the Maltese archipelago: English, the language of the colonizers, was used alongside Italian and Maltese (a language of Arabic origin), used by most of the population on a daily basis. As the recommendations of the 1836 Royal Commission show, during the initial phase of British rule, no steps were taken to replace Italian with English:

> The English language was relatively unknown in Malta, despite its being a British colony. After analysing the situation, the commissioners concluded that the teaching of Italian and Arabic should continue, as they were more useful for the Maltese public. Commerce in Malta and Italy were intertwined and given the proximity of Malta and Italy, knowledge of the latter's language would surely be more useful than any other language, including the English language.
> (Formosa 2017: 53)

Italian, the island's cultural language, was used in education, in the courts, in public administration, and by the Church. It was the language of the higher social classes, and was used, in particular, by professionals and by the clergy, who also used Maltese language for informal communication.

Over the years, the British realized that if they were to succeed in becoming rooted in the island, they would need to use English and Maltese to counter the hegemonic combination of the Italian language and Catholic religion. It is hardly surprising then that Italian-speaking elites were alarmed by the attempts made by the British authorities to diffuse the use of the English language and by the efforts of British missionaries to spread the Protestant religion. Initially no measures were implemented to hinder the use of the Italian language, which maintained its position of pre-eminence on the island. In 1878, three Royal Commissions of Inquiry paid visits to Malta to investigate the socio-economic conditions on the island (Hull 1993: 25–32). The education report drawn up by Patrick Joseph Keenan, one of the commissioners, who was originally from Ireland, suggested gradually replacing Italian with English. The imperial government agreed to act on the suggestions contained in Keenan's report and, in 1884, it drew up a series of measures to restrict the use of Italian in Malta. In 1899, an ordinance was introduced to stipulate the use of English in court cases involving British subjects and it was feared that English would replace Italian in all legal procedures. The nationalists sought to convince Joseph Chamberlain, Secretary of State for the Colonies, to cancel the implementation of the ordinance, eventually requesting the mediation of the Italian Minister of Foreign Affairs, Marquis Emilio Visconti Venosta, and of Sidney Sonnino. The discussions that took place between the three men in the British Embassy in Rome resulted in a 'favourable solution' involving the suspension of this provision for a period of nine years (Savelli 1943: 438). In the Commons Sitting of January 1902, Joseph Chamberlain announced that in 'deference to Italy', the proclamation of 15 March 1899 regarding the substitution of Italian by English in the Maltese Courts of Law was to be withdrawn (Savelli 1943: 439).

The introduction of English on the island was not coercive: its use by civil servants and merchants resulted from the need to enter into administrative and commercial relations with the British government. English began to gain the favour of the middle class, including young entrepreneurs who had every interest in entering into contracts with the British government, civil servants working for the State and all those hoping to join the civil service, but also among the majority of needy Maltese who needed to learn English in order to request aid. This led to the emergence of an English-speaking petty bourgeoisie as opposed to the Italian-speaking haute bourgeoisie, comprising professionals, professors and lawyers, who sought to defend their positions of power within Maltese society. Keenan's investigation generated a series of disputes that led to the birth of a nationalist movement – initially described as anti-reformist – led by Fortunato

Mizzi. Mizzi had picked up the baton from Ramiro Barbaro, Marquis of San Giorgio, a member of the Council of Government and director of the *Corriere Mercantile Maltese*. Barbaro, champion of radical demands and the generational and ideological link between Camillo Sceberras and Fortunato Mizzi, can be considered to be the first real ideologist of Maltese nationalism (Ferlazzo Ciano 2018: 174–90).

Fortunato Mizzi became the head of the movement, which, in 1887, convinced the British government to reform the 1849 Constitution: although the Crown continued to hold the decision-making power for all matters, elected members were a majority in the Council of Government. They opposed the substitution of Italian by English in debates. From 1883 onwards, Mizzi's pro-Italian party became the promoter of the 'pari passu' compromise, which involved teaching English and Italian at the expense of Maltese. In 1883, Fortunato Mizzi played a key role in founding the newspaper *Malta*. Originally published every fortnight and only later becoming a daily paper, *Malta* became the organ of the nationalist party. The establishment of *Malta* provided a place of aggregation for those who feared that, in the long term, the diffusion of the English language and of Anglicanism rather than Italian and Catholicism would have led to a loss of their culture and therefore of their traditional caste privileges. For this reason, *Malta* always focused on the need to defend the Catholic tradition, and the Italian culture and language. The insular discourses developed by the nationalist elite drew attention to the efforts being made by the British Empire to spiritually uproot the Maltese from their Mediterranean context, imposing upon them a language and culture remote from their insular traditions. The English language and Protestantism were presented as belonging to a cultural and religious heritage alien to the insular heritage. The more educated sectors of Maltese society basically saw Anglicization as a threat not only to their culture but also as a curb to their capacity to exert their influence upon the local population. They feared losing their ascendancy over the rest of the population, which was mainly made up of farmers and artisans. Lawyers, professors and professionals were viewed with respect and reverence by the people who would turn to them – using Italian – if they needed various types of favours, as part of a system of patronage. Although the British held political power, the Italian-speaking elites had a highly elitist cultural power. From the point of view of these elites, the diffusion of English rather than Italian among the lower social classes would have allowed the members of these classes to interact directly with their British rulers, thus eliminating the need for the 'unofficial' mediation of the traditionally privileged classes – and consequently their influence.

Birth and development of Maltese nationalism

The 1880 elections saw the rise of Fortunato Mizzi's Partito Antiriformista, which changed its name to Partitito Nazionalista in 1883. This political organization managed to arouse the national sentiments of the Maltese by appealing to the *Italianità* of the archipelago and attacking the behaviour of the Reformists, accused of working together with the British against Maltese interests. During the First World War, Malta became a strategic base for the British navy, acting 'as a coaling station and shipyard with dry docks for maintenance and repair work' but, most importantly, accommodating and treating the sick (Rudolf 2018: 277). As many as 60,000 sick and injured patients were sent to the island, earning it the epithet of 'Nurse of the Mediterranean' (Rudolf 2018: 277).

At the end of the war, the archipelago experienced an economic recession that exacerbated the situation, fuelling the outbreak of riots. On 7 June 1919, a large crowd of students and workers took to the streets of Valletta to protest against the rise in the price of bread and to request an autonomist constitution: British troops fired into the crowd, killing four. These events became known as Sette Giugno: the nationalist rhetoric turned the murdered civilians into political martyrs and the day became a national holiday. In 1921, in an attempt to calm the waters, the British promulgated the Milner-Amery Constitution, which introduced dyarchy. Self-government was recognized 'in all matters of purely local concern' while the imperial government maintained its authority with regard to 'reserved matters', in other words, defence, foreign affairs and public order (Zanella 1989: 15). Following Mussolini's rise to power, Malta became one of the strategic objectives of fascist Italy (Paci 2015a: 155–67).

The defence of the Italian language was one of the battles that the Maltese nationalists shared with the fascist irredentists. Fortunato Mizzi's son Enrico was now engaged in the cultural struggle for the defence of *Italianità*. He followed in his father's footsteps, declaring his loyalty to the British Crown while continuing to defend the island's cultural and religious traditions. On 7 May 1917, he was imprisoned for subversive activities under martial law. When questioned, during the preliminary phase and hearing following the arrest, Mizzi expressed support for the island's annexation to Italy while also arguing that the Maltese should show their loyalty to the British Crown, given that Malta was under British rule (Savelli 1943: 463). Mizzi was sentenced to a year's imprisonment and the loss of all his civil rights. The sentence also revoked his lawyer's warrant and prevented him from being eligible for election as a representative of the people. Mizzi's statements during the trial did not fall on deaf ears. Over the years, both the nationalist and pro-Strickland press referenced his words, earning him the label of irredentist. On more than one occasion, Mizzi found himself at loggerheads with Gerald Strickland, leader of the Constitutional Party and the main adversary of the pre-eminence of the Italian language and culture on the island. Unlike the previous elections which focused on socio-economic questions, Strickland's party based its 1927 election campaign on ethnic and anti-Italian issues. The failure of various attempts to eliminate the use of the Italian language in institutions and to favour the use of Maltese to the detriment of Italian led the British authorities to support the diffusion of Maltese through arguments based on ethnicity and race. British propaganda sought to prove that the Maltese had Phoenician rather than Latin roots (Vassallo 2012: 111). This kind of argument fired up the Nationalists, who had always defended the *Italianità* and Latin origins of the Maltese people. The theory regarding the Phoenician origins of the Maltese, intended to undermine the foundations of Malta's *Italianità*, angered those claiming that the roots of the Maltese nationality were Latin and Catholic. With the aim of removing all traces of Italian influence in Malta, Strickland renamed a number of Maltese streets that had had Italian names for at least four centuries. At the same time, the Nationalists submitted a proposal to Great Britain that would endow Malta with an autonomy similar to that granted to Canada, South Africa, Australia and New Zealand by means of the Statutes of Westminster in 1933. In other words, they asked for Malta to be granted the status of dominion, which would have safeguarded the Italian language and culture, and the Catholic religion. From their point of view, renouncing Italian culture and language in favour of a 'Maltese language' with Arabic origins would have 'compromised the literary use of Italian', thereby supporting Strickland's case (Savelli 1943: 457).

The 1927 elections resulted in victory for the Constitutional Party, allied to Paul Boffa's Labour Party in the Legislative Assembly. However, the Nationalists obtained the majority in the Senate, where representatives of trade associations sat alongside the clergy. The consensus acquired by Strickland's party in Maltese public opinion, especially among some of the workers, was due to the diffusion of English in schools and the awareness of the ensuing benefits for the popular classes. The first ordinances to be passed by Strickland's constitutional government included provisions replacing the use of Italian with English and Maltese in post offices, names of streets and squares, and even on lottery tickets. It was also established that English would be introduced to courts of law and in notarial deeds.

Around 1930, the simmering political climate reached boiling point for two motives: on the one hand, tensions between the Maltese clergy and Strickland's government due to government attacks on the Catholic religion (Paci 2014c: 551–76), on the other, interference in the island's internal affairs by Italy's fascist government. From the mid-1920s onwards, despite recommending caution in affirming the right of the Italian fascist state to safeguard the Italian language on the island to avoid annoying the British authorities, Mussolini's regime implemented a vast programme of cultural penetration that met with the approval and support of the erudite segment of Maltese society identifying with Enrico Mizzi's nationalist party (Baldoli 2008: 5–20). The use of the Italian language and Italian culture were also defended by anti-fascist Italian exiles on Malta such as Giuseppe Donati and Umberto Calosso, both Italian teachers, who sought to keep the teaching of the Italian language separate from the expansionist aims of fascist Italy, by bringing or attempting to bring Italian–Maltese relations back onto a cultural plane (Peresso 2015). Around 1932, the fascist regime consolidated the means of diffusion of fascism and of cultural penetration by launching a series of initiatives – in Malta as well as back home – in addition to those already in place. Although Malta did not feature among the primary targets of Mussolini's expansion programme, the government in Rome did not give up its hope of annexing Malta, in either the near or distant future (Quartararo 1980: 34). The Nationalist Party obtained the majority of votes in the 1932 elections, and was installed in parliament on 18 October 1932. Enrico Mizzi, now Minister of Education, attempted to obviate the Letters Patent promulgated on 2 May 1932 that limited the teaching of the Italian language to secondary schools and universities and eliminated it in primary schools, where it had previously been taught under the 1921 Constitution. He drew up a programme intended to safeguard the Italian language that involved the creation of free supplementary lessons in primary schools and of advanced courses in Italy for Maltese primary school teachers as well as granting subsidies to private schools teaching Italian. Italian was also to be taught in primary schools outside normal school hours as an optional subject. In the wake of the fiery speeches given by the leading members of the Nationalist Party to mark the 8 September celebrations evoking the Great Siege of 1565, Governor David Graham Campbell issued a proclamation removing the police department from Maltese ministerial control and administration. Another ordinance placed limits on the capacity to act of foreigners. On 2 November 1933, faced with the refusal of the Nationalist Party to accept these restrictions, Ugo Mifsud resigned as the head of the nationalist government, Parliament was dissolved, and the Constitution suspended. The

Governor assumed full legislative and executive powers, and measures were reintroduced to restrict the use of Italian and Italian education and cultural institutions.

The British government passed regulations excluding the Italian language from all public offices, from schools and from universities. On 12 August 1934, the British imperial government promulgated a new Letters Patent eliminating the use of Italian in courts and in all sectors of administration. With the decree of 7 July 1936, the Governor ordered the closure of the Italian Cultural Institute, an important meeting place for the educated class in Maltese society (Paci 2015a: 201). On 2 September, a Constitutional Charter was issued leading to the de facto elimination of any form of local autonomy. In mid-November 1938, a regulation was enacted making it compulsory to use English in university lectures, which were previously held in Italian. Between the end of 1939 and early 1940, further changes were made to the academic statutes, replacing Italian language and banning students from using Italian for their final graduation examinations. Italian became an optional subject and was only permitted in the first two-year period of a literature degree. Italian was no longer to be used for notices in post offices or in government acts, ministerial budgets and notices in the Government Gazette; various Italian street names were replaced with English or Maltese names. Shortly before Italy entered the war in May 1940, the British authorities dismissed all Italian employees working in Malta.

Following Italy's entry into war and the first bombings of the island, the Nationalists remaining in Malta who had actively participated in the fight to defend Malta's *Italianità* were deported to concentration camps in Uganda, where they remained until 1942 (Bondin 1980). Given the geopolitical importance of the island, Great Britain put an end to the Maltese constitutional experience and the island was once again used as a military base. These imperial regulations responded to three different categories of problem: Malta's geographical position and its strategic function within the Mediterranean; the conflicts within Maltese internal politics; and, lastly, the influence of Italian political events on the island's public life. The diplomatic tension between Italy and Great Britain in the Mediterranean basin meant that Malta once again took on the role of military base, meaning that problems relative to the traditions and culture of the people were relegated to the background with respect to strategic and geopolitical matters. The thorny matter of the safeguarding of the Italian language and defence of the Catholic religion had to make way for strategic and geopolitical considerations. Supported by the British government, the anti-Italian policy pursued by Prime Minister Gerald Strickland in Malta succeeded in its aim of weakening the Maltese nationalist party, which was stripped of its press organ, *Malta*, which had been suspended following Mizzi's arrest on 30 May 1940. In June 1940, the newspaper *Malta. Serie romana* was published in Rome on the initiative of a group of young Maltese Nationalists, fervent irredentists, who became members of the Comitato d'Azione Maltese after going to Italy to elude the discriminatory measures of the British government (Fabei 2007).

The Catholic religion was also subjected to attacks similar to those on the Italian language by Strickland's Constitutional Party. Faced with the restiveness of many members of the Maltese clergy, the Holy See sought to calm the waters and prevent matters from deteriorating any further. A conflict with the British Empire would have shaken up the status quo of a profoundly Catholic island where the Church had age-old interests. The insularist discourses tinged with imperialist Fascist rhetoric had ceased to have any appeal for the Maltese people. The heroic resistance of the Maltese to the Axis bombings – recognized by the British Crown by awarding the George Cross to the entire nation – and the many anti-Italian demonstrations were signs of the failure of irredentist propaganda in Malta.

On 21 September 1964, after a rather long phase of political instability, Malta obtained independence from Great Britain, becoming a member of the Commonwealth. The then Prime Minister Aldo Moro delivered a message that was transmitted by the Italian public broadcaster RAI, in which he expressed joy at Malta's independence: 'On behalf of the Italian people, I would like to extend a warm inaugural message to the Maltese people on the occasion of the proclamation of the independence of Malta. Italy, loyal to the principles of her Risorgimento, welcomes with deep feeling and joy the entry of new, free, and independent members into the international community' (1964). Ten years later, on 13 December 1974, the island became a parliamentary republic, deposing the British monarchy with a constitutional vote approved by over two thirds of the parliament and electing the new head of state by means of parliamentary vote. The Constitution promulgated on 21 September 1964 recognized Maltese as the national language and English as the official language. As well as being recognized as a literary and cultural language, Maltese replaced Italian in the Catholic liturgy: 'contrary to what had been claimed throughout the controversy of Italianitá, only "the force of Maltese language could unite the nation once and for all"' (Peresso 2013: 5).

The inescapable choice of the island of 'demoniacal sadness': Sardinian autonomy

Our country has the stuff of a nation,
in the past this stuff never became self-consciousness,
and now that it has,
we conceive it with the mindset of Italians

Camillo Bellieni, *I Sardi di fronte all'Italia* (1920)

In 1920, Camillo Bellieni, one of the key figures of Sardism, coined the expression 'aborted nation' to define Sardinia, highlighting its inability to give rise to a complete state form. Bellieni believed that the island lacked the necessary political, social and cultural conditions for its integration into the central institutional system not to be experienced as a top–down imposition. Although ready to criticize the bureaucratic centralization of the central State, Bellieni was equally ready to reject all separatist hypotheses (Berlinguer and Mattone 1998: XIX).

Sardinia's contemporary history is distinguished by two diverging fronts: on the one hand, the tendency to integrate the island into the central institutional system and, on the other, a wish for autonomy that promoted the local heritage and demanded the right to decentralization. As noted by Luigi Berlinguer and Antonello Mattone, twentieth-century history offers numerous examples of the 'drive towards integration' of this 'aborted nation': the experience of the Brigata Sassari during the First World War, which made it possible to develop 'a new awareness of the "exploitation of the Sardinians" and to give rise to a "new social bloc comprising the intellectual petty bourgeoisie and rural plebes"', the latter forced to experience the trauma of war after the isolation of their villages; the role played by the Sardinian Action Party (PSd'A) in the struggle for a regionalist reform; the contribution made to the national political debate by intellectuals of the calibre of Antonio Gramsci, Camillo Bellieni and Emilio Lussu, to mention only a few; the reflection on the nature of the 1944–8 statute of autonomy; the expectations and pride experienced by Sardinian public opinion following the election of two Sardinian politicians to the presidency of the Republic (Antonio Segni in 1962 and Francesco Cossiga in 1983); and, lastly, the popular feelings stirred up when the Cagliari football team captained by striker Gigi Riva won the 1969–70 football championship (1998: XLII). The myth of victorious Cagliari symbolized the return of an island integrated into continental Italy, self-aware and proud to be a winner.

The verses of Sardinian singer-songwriter Pietro Marras (1982) contain emblematic references to the experience of Sardinian *combattentismo*: 'We will discover how to truly cry / when our dream confirms that the foreigner will no longer pass / When Gigi Riva returns / Come on, come on / we will be fearless / like the Alpini / [...] Together we will shout Italy, Italy / And it will not seem pathetic'. But Sardinia was also defined a 'nation manqué' within the insular narrative: from Sebastiano Satta to Emilio Lussu and right up to Grazia Deledda, Sardinian novelists describe the vicissitudes experienced by their characters – orphans and children of this 'nation manqué' – who move like ghosts, desperately searching for their own origins and identity: 'this is why they live like exiles in their own land, yearning for a space and time that never existed' (Rudas 1999: 280).

Sardism is the distinguishing feature of Sardinian autonomism: it is a 'cross-sectional ideological and political category' embracing a plurality of political visions that have tackled the 'Sardinian question' and asserted Sardinia's right to independence. Describing the cross-sectional nature of this category, Gianfranco Contu sought to define a series of different 'Sardisms': the 'original' Sardism deriving from the veteran movement of the Brigata Sassari; the 'early Sardism' embodied by the Sardinian Action Party of the post–First World War period; the 'emigrant Sardism' that Lussu integrated into the Giustizia e Libertà movement; and, lastly, the 'social-Sardism' of which Lussu was the 'undisputed leader' and which led to the foundation of the Partito Sardo d'Azione Socialista or Sardinian Action Party (1994a: 18).

The 'Sardinian revolution' and three-year revolutionary period (1793–6)

For many years Sardinia was the victim of a Eurocentric stereotype depicting it as a remote place dominated by the vestiges of a primitive past and a natural setting conditioning the daily lives of the men and women living there. In the European imaginary, Sardinia remained a 'small invisible world' until it became a non-secondary element in the international arena in the wake of the war between Savoy and the French revolutionary forces (Salice 2016: 12). British accounts portrayed the island as a place full of prejudices and stereotypes dominated by two actors: on the one hand, the usurping Piedmontese despots and, on the other, the primitive, anarchic Sardinians, who were incapable of living in a civilized world and knew only the language of violence; in the words of a British correspondent (January 1793), 'with chin-length beards, dressed in sheepskin and leather, armed with sabres, guns, pistols, knives, and with muskets and balls' (Salice 2016: 29).

In 1720, the Kingdom of Sardinia, previously under Spanish rule, was brought under the House of Savoy, remaining in its domain until the proclamation of the Kingdom of Italy in 1861. Victor Amadeus II of Savoy found himself dealing with the banditry raging throughout the island and which, despite all attempts to repress it, could rely on the support of the locals. In late September 1792, French revolutionary troops invaded the territories of Savoy and Nice belonging to the Kingdom of Sardinia to oppose Victor Amadeus III, promoter of an anti-French league of Italian States. In late 1792, when the French revolutionary troops disembarked on the island, they encountered the resistance of the Sardinians who proved to be capable of halting their advance. The anti-French resistance movement, which could count upon the guidance and funding of both the nobles of the military Stamenti and the Catholic Church, brought with it a rejection of republican anti-clericalism and of radical anti-feudalism (Salice 2020).

1793 was a watershed in Sardinian history: it was during the so-called 'Sardinian revolution' (1793-6) that the autonomist aspirations of Sardinian took on the form of a popular movement. Sardinian loyalty to the House of Savoy gave the island's ruling class reason to hope that the king might view autonomist instances favourably. The Sardinian elites took advantage of their strengthened position in the wake of the resistance against the French in order to ask the king to restore the privileges that had been gradually eroded by absolutist and reforming policies.

The aim of these requests was to bring about the recognition of the privileges enjoyed by the ancient institution of the Stamenti (1355) - an institution resembling that of the French general estates of Catalan Aragonese origins - last convened in 1698-9 and which represented the three bracci (arms) of the Sardinian Corts (parliament): military, ecclesiastical and civil (or royal) (Birocchi 1992: 94-114). After self-convening, the Stamenti sent six representatives (defined 'prime voci') - two for each arm of the Parliament - to Turin in July-August 1793 where they presented their 'five requests' to Victor Amadeus III. These requests are considered Sardinia's charter of independence (Birocchi 1992). As suggested by the historian Girolamo Sotgiu, the five requests represented the original foundations upon which the island's autonomist instances took shape (Berlinguer and Mattone 1998: XLV): for the first time, a coherent political subject appeared before the authorities to exercise its bargaining powers with the centre (the Kingdom of Savoy).

The aim of presenting these five requests was to define more clearly the extent of the powers exercised by the Savoy dynasty and of those exercised by the institutions of the Kingdom of Sardinia. By the end of the eighteenth century, there was a diffused sentiment – which had spread to even the remotest villages on the island – seeking a redefinition of the spaces of individual autonomy with respect to the sphere of action of the landowners, of the Church, State and Commune (Salice 2011). The king did not exercise direct rule over all lands: in fact, there were royal and feudal domains. Both belonged to the king: the feudal domain was governed directly by the feudal overlord, who could in turn create a 'useful domain' in favour of the community of vassals. As noted by Roberto Ibba, 'after the introduction of the feudal system, extended throughout the island following the definitive institutional affirmation of the Kingdom of Sardinia, the village community obtained full legal recognition and could negotiate for usage rights of agrarian land with the baron to which it was subjected through the relationship of vassalage' (2019: 71). The goal of the Stamenti representatives was not only to obtain recognition of the existence of an organ of representation of the Sardinians – the Parliament – but also to create a regulatory framework that could put autonomy into effect, beginning by assigning the most important posts exclusively to Sardinians. The first of the five requests asked for the right to convene Parliament every ten years, as was customary under Spanish rule and prior to the arrival of the Savoy dynasty. The second called for the restoration of the ancient privileges due to the Kingdom of Sardinia that had been maintained until the arrival of the Savoys: a guarantee that no changes would be made to the feudal system that was the power base of the nobility represented in the military stamento. The third request referred to the need to assign only to Sardinians all civil and military posts on the island – with the exception of the offices of viceroy and bishops. The fourth request concerned the creation of a State Council in Cagliari, comprising mainly Sardinians, which would be consulted on a regular basis by the viceroy. Lastly, the fifth request expressed the desire to establish a Ministry for Sardinian Affairs in Turin. As pointed out by Salice, the five requests sought to strengthen the feudal system, ecclesiastical privileges, civic autonomy and baronial monopolies: 'it was an autonomy of nobles. Not an autonomy with central powers but the duty of the king to issue legislation complying with the constraints imposed by the privileges, regulations, and laws of the kingdom' (2020).

The requests made by the Stamenti representatives were not well-received: Victor Amadeus III, who was busy coordinating the war against France, delegated Count Pietro Giuseppe Graneri, Minister of the Interior, to deal with the Sardinian matter. Graneri in turn ordered the viceroy Vincenzo Balbiano to dissolve the Stamenti without informing the representatives about this decision. For their part, the Stamenti refused to talk to the viceroy because they intended to discuss these matters directly with the king. Fearing that a conspiracy was being hatched in Cagliari, the viceroy gave orders for the arrest of two prominent lawyers, Vincenzo Cabras and Efisio Pintor, who were held to be guilty of plotting against the Piedmontese by virtue of their friendship with Girolamo Pitzolo, one of the Stamenti representatives. Their arrest triggered a popular uprising in Cagliari on 28 April 1794, leading to the flight of the viceroy and assumption of power by the Reale Udienza, the Supreme Court of the Kingdom of Sardinia. This transfer of power, which was, in fact, forced, was made possible by a law dating to 1564, which established that, in the absence of the viceroy, his duties were to be carried out by the Reale Udienza. Although he had intended to amend this ancient custom by appointing a deputy to replace the viceroy, Victor Amadeus III had to bow to events and to political contingencies. In order to strengthen its position of power and ensure the incisiveness of the actions of the local ruling class, the 'patriotic alignment' formed sought to tap into the consensus of what was at that time a 'fledgling "public opinion"' (Mattone and Sanna 2007: 145). In fact, they printed no less than 2000 copies of a pamphlet entitled *Manifesto giustificativo della emozione popolare* dated 28 April 1794, explaining the reasons that had led to the popular uprising against the Piedmontese officials while at the same time insisting upon their loyalty to the Savoy monarchy.

Although built by the literati and representatives of the privileged classes, the independence platform, on which the patriotic movement was based, involved the urban population, above all, which was not unfamiliar with expressions like 'impervious despotism' and the 'perverse illegitimate administration' of the 'agents of the Piedmontese government' (Carta 2000: 124). This led to the emergence of 'a choral emotion (the euphemistic expression frequently used to refer to the insurrection) taking place on 28 April' (Carta 2000: 124). Nevertheless, Girolamo Pitzolo – one of the most influential members of the delegation sent to Turin to present the five requests and welcomed as 'father of the fatherland' upon his return to Cagliari – condemned the 'emotion' of 28 April, asking not only for the reduction of the Sardinian military forces – which he defined as 'national' – but also criticizing the disarming of the royal troops (Mattone and Sanna 2007: 151).

The 1794 Cagliari insurrection had a huge impact upon public opinion of that period, leaving lasting traces in the Sardinian collective imagination: on 14 September 1993, a regional law was passed to establish the *Sa Die de sa Sardinia* (Day of the Sardinian People) to recall and celebrate 28 April, with the involvement of the institutions of the Regione Autonoma della Sardegna

(Autonomous Region of Sardinia) as well as of associations and foundations that have set up a committee to 'promote an awareness of the history and values of independence, especially among the new generations' (Regione Autonoma della Sardegna 1993). *Sa Die de sa Sardinia* was proposed to the public as a moment of 'resistance' against the 'foreigner', of a military insurrection against the 'occupiers', of the liberation from their abuses and tyranny by a 'nation' or 'people' finally in arms. The discourse on the 'Sardinian three-year revolutionary period' also became charged with perspectives that are republican, liberal-democratic or Jacobin, or even autonomist – in a contemporary sense – or independentist' (Salice 2020). In September 1794, the new viceroy Filippo Vivalda disembarked on the island: aware of the difficulties that he would encounter in the exercise of power in the interim before the appointment of the king's delegate in Cagliari, he put four Sardinians in leading positions (Del Piano 1996). Vivalda's aim was to undermine the unity of the patriotic movement, by placing some of its exponents in key roles in the Kingdom of Sardinia with the task of restoring the established order. Pitzolo, who was appointed Intendant-general, sought to reassure landowners with regard to the risk of new civil commotions breaking out while even more conservative positions were adopted by Gavino Paliaccio, marquis of the Planargia, who was nominated general of the army. The exponents of the patriotic movement opposed these appointments, considering them to be unlawful because they were the responsibility of the Reale Udienza. Between 1794 and 1795, Sardinian political life was marked by the opposition between the patriotic side and the 'royalist' side, which defended the ministerial interests of Pitzolo and of the marquis of the Planargia (Mattone and Sanna 2007: 152). Various 'anti-royalist' demonstrations took place, culminating in the popular uprising of 6 July 1795, during the course of which both Pitzolo and Planargia were killed by the mob. The viceroy himself was forced to change tack and to become more accommodating with regard to the Stamenti.

The patriotic side began to experience difficulties due to the different positions emerging in the autonomist movement. The very term 'autonomy' took on very different meanings for the different members of the Sardinian elite. The old aristocracy hoped for a system of government, presided over by the king, that would involve the active participation of the privileged classes and where the taxes paid by the subjects would be established under an agreement between these classes and the sovereign; the middle classes, who had acquired an increasing influence in society, were interested in maintaining the autonomous institutions of the Kingdom of Sardinia even though they were supposed to support the political, social and cultural changes taking place on the island;

the non-aristocratic landowners believed that there was a pressing need to 'reduce the grip of the barons on the land and gradually reform the system of landownership and power on the basis of principles safeguarding the interests of the production world of which they were an expression' (Salice 2016: 21). Lastly, there was a class of professionals, many of whom with titles of nobility, 'an elite sensitive to the values of the century but at the same time still linked to the values inherited from the past, sometimes to the extent of still being integrated with the feudal administrative structures' (Salice 2016: 21). The news of Pitzolo and Planargia's deaths reached Sassari, which opposed the political aims of the patriotic movement, held to be a form of Jacobinism emanating from Cagliari. This gave rise to the so-called 'Sassarese schism': in Sassari – and in the Capo di Sopra district overall – there was a pro-Savoyard orientation in the feudal bloc, which sought to protect its privileges from the dangerous tendencies stemming from Cagliari (Mattone and Sanna 2007: 157).

The situation soon worsened in Capo di Sopra: the countryside had seen the rise of an anti-feudal movement opposed to the payment of duties and clamouring for the abolition of the feudal system, while in the city, the clergy, nobles and civic councillors were determined to maintain the status quo. This feudal bloc, which drew strength from its Savoyard loyalism, hoped to maintain its privileges and repudiate the authority of the viceroy, held to be a tool in the hands of the Stamenti. In February 1796, the Reale Udienza magistrate Giovanni Maria Angioy was sent to Sassari in an attempt to pacify the Capo di Sopra district, torn by the Sassarese schism and anti-feudal turmoil in 1795–6 (Madau Diaz 1979). Angioy, who had been appointed Alternos (deputy of the viceroy), received a warm welcome from the same peasants who had refused to pay their feudal duties to the feudal nobility in Sassari. It seems that the decision to send Angioy to Sassari was motivated by the need to take rein in his revolutionary tendencies: 'Angioy proposed to abolish the feudal system rather than merely adapting it, albeit within the limits of legality and of monarchic governance, leading his former friends to expedite his departure from Cagliari with every means at their disposal' (Carta 2019). In fact, his huge following among the masses and anti-feudal movement made him very dangerous: on 2 June 1796, he set off from Sassari for Cagliari, at the head of an anti-feudal army, meeting with a 'truly triumphant welcome, especially in the villages fighting against the large landowners [...] and accompanied by armed countrymen, whose numbers increased during the course of his journey' (Mattone and Sanna 2007: 169).

At the request of the Stamenti and of the Reale Udienza, following the pronouncement of the Viceroy, Angioy was removed from his office as Alternos.

A price was put on his head forcing him to flee and live in exile. The repression of the Angioyan movement was a victory for the moderates: on 8 June 1796, Victor Amadeus III signed a royal decree establishing the adoption of the Five Requests (Mattone and Sanna 2007: 171). However, these provisions were never enacted, as shown by the assignment of civil posts to Piedmontese officials in 1799 by the new king Charles Emmanuel IV. On 28 August 1799, the Stamenti withdrew the five requests, thereby bringing an end to the 'Sardinian revolution'. In the words of historian Pietro Martini, people looked back on this gesture 'with resentment. Rather than complaining of a loss, they blamed the Stamenti, considering them less the drivers than the supplicants of the ruin of their own work. 28 August 1799 marked the beginning of a political anguish that only ended on 8 February 1848' (1852: 51).

The historical interpretations of the Sardinian revolution have been distinguished by opposing ideological visions: the conservative pro-Savoyard approach drew attention to the weaknesses resulting from the adoption of the principles of the French Revolution (Manno 1842); on the contrary, the liberal perspective exalted the Jacobinist revolutionary aspects, held to be the

Figure 7. The anthem *Su patriotu sardu a sos feudatarios* ('The Sardinian Patriot to the Lords'), is a poetry written by Francesco Ignazio Mannu on the occasion of Sardinian revolution. The mural reproduces an extract from the poetry: 'This – oh people – is the hour to eradicate abuses. Down with all evil customs! Down with dispotic power!'. Murales in Orgosolo by Heather Cowper on Flickr.

first expression of the Italian republican triennial (1796–9) (Sulis [1857] 1987). Recent studies have shown that these opposing interpretations tend to either deny any form of diffusion of illuminist ideas on the island or to overstate the extent to which such theories pervaded political practice. The political formulation proposed by the Sardinian elites remained loyal to the idea of a monarchy moderated by the ancient constitution of the Kingdom of Sardinia and by a community represented by privileged orders and bodies.

The French revolution merely contributed to reigniting the needs advanced by 'jurisdictional particularisms'. The 'nostalgia of the elites for the ancient freedoms now lost' went from an ideal plane to a government action which, when carried out by the radical fringes of the patriotic movement, sought to bring to completion the liberal reform of the ancient Sardinian institutions (Salice 2012: 111). Salice also maintains that the Republicanism of the pro-French minority groups did not play an important role nor was it in a position to influence the balance of power. Even the anti-feudal alliances being set up in villages in northern Sardinia were based on a declaration of complete subjugation to the monarchy: 'because in the world that existed on 28 April, the ideological element of decisive legitimization was unarguably the Monarchy, which was also one of the fundamental laws of the kingdom of Sardinia that the five requests sought to preserve' (Salice 2020). In fact, it was not until he had been given the title of Alternos that Giovanni Maria Angioy was able to lead the anti-feudal peasant movement. Therefore, as Antonello Mattone and Piero Sanna have pointed out, the '"Sardinian revolution" was not a kind of anticipation of the Italian Republican triennial but rather the last significant patriotic revolution of the eighteenth century, which was still indissolubly tied to the social dynamics, to the culture, and to the institutional practices of the ancien régime' (2007: 142–3).

The 'perfect fusion': Sardinia in the first half of the nineteenth century

After the Sardinian revolution, the island's privileged classes merely shifted

> The Monarchy into a political sphere of conservation or, rather, of restoration. These are the elements involved in the drawing up of a new pact between the throne and the aristocracy. A pact repudiating absolutist and illuminist values, the idea of a sole prince at the helm, energetically relaunching the need for the aristocracy to participate in the legislative process and in the government of the kingdom.
>
> (Salice 2020)

The Sardinian elites sought complete inclusion in a context that we might define as one of 'polycentric monarchy', hoping for the integration of the local ruling classes in networks of power, so as to maintain their own privileges, and, in return, helping the sovereign to build up the clientele needed to exercise power in distant territories. In 1802, Charles Emmanuel IV of Savoy abdicated in favour of Victor Emmanuel who decided to appoint Charles Felix viceroy, making him responsible for the administration of Sardinia. Charles Felix governed with a particularly heavy hand, marking the beginning of a reactionary phase that curbed Sardinian institutions.

Referring to the new viceroy, historian Ernesto Pontieri suggests that 'in his mind, all forward movement was grey in colour: whether it was Cagliari's constitutionalism and autonomism, Sassari's secessionism, the anti-feudalism of the countryside or the varying degrees of democratic tendencies leading to Angioyism, he believed that every innovative aspiration was rebelling against the inviolable principle of authority' (1935: 202). The early decades of the nineteenth century saw a process of economic and institutional reforms accompanied by a cultural and political awakening (Atzeni 2015: 49–72). In 1804, the Reale Società Agraria ed Economica Sarda (Royal Agrarian and Economic Society) was established in Cagliari, an initiative revealing the Subalpine government's commitment to reforming agriculture, sheep farming and land ownership, and to reorganizing legislation. The society sought to promote research into new agronomic methods and to diffuse them with the aim of modernizing the agricultural system, thereby leaving behind the old community system.

Nicola Gabriele is among the historians who believe that behind the Reale Società Agraria ed Economica Sarda 'was a more ambitious project, which aimed to create a centre of aggregation favouring the formation of an agrarian bourgeoisie with the closest possible links to the subalpine government' (2003: 503). At the same time, according to this historiographic interpretation, the policy of subversion of feudalism implemented by the Savoy government from 1835 to 1840 had the aim of weakening the island's deeply rooted feudal system, whose 'innate capacity to limit the power of the sovereign' was an obstacle to the control of the territory by the authorities (Gabriele 2003: 504). Some historians including Raffaele Di Tucci (1922) and Maria Luisa Cao (1928) have suggested that it was precisely this Savoyard policy that launched a process of modernization of the island's social and economic structures, laying the foundations for a perfect fusion between Sardinia and the mainland States. According to others like Girolamo Sotgiu (1986), Sardinia's privileged classes supported Savoyard reforms, believing that they would benefit from them. The ex-feudal nobility, in particular, came to the conclusion that they would maintain their privileges thanks to this fusion, given that the conservation of autonomy would not have provided any guarantee that they would maintain their position of advantage (Gabriele 2003: 507).

Leaving aside the different interpretations, we can reasonably maintain that the formulation of the 'perfect fusion', established by King Charles Albert by means of the royal decree of 20 December 1847, would put an end to the legal system of the ancient Kingdom of Sardinia. The fusion was also supported by the commercial and intellectual bourgeoisie, which could benefit from the liberalization of the exportation of oil and wine to extend its capacity to reach new markets and by the Sardinian ruling class, which was able to participate in the Subalpine Parliament in Turin (Zichi 2008: 105–6). Among them were university students, teachers, magistrates, intellectuals with various orientations and ex-feudal nobles: although motivated by their own interests, such individuals were also very idealistic. As noted by Salice, there was a widespread tendency among intellectuals to reinvent the matter of the Montresta Greeks in Sardinia, connecting it to the romantic values of the European Risorgimento and philhellenic sentiments: this reinvention was the 'litmus test for the sensibilities of an elite longing to be (recognized) as European and unreservedly condemning their compatriots who were responding with violence to attempts to reform and regenerate the kingdom promoted on the island by the "illuminated" Savoyard government' (2015a, p. 28).

We find a good dose of philhellenism in Giovanni Siotto-Pintòr's *Storia letteraria di Sardegna* (1843), the handbook of the intellectual class of nineteenth-century Sardinia (Salice 2015b, p. 497). Siotto-Pintòr, a prominent intellectual, royalist and conservative, defended fusion tirelessly because it 'seemed as if it had suddenly ushered in the golden century' (1877: 478). However, thirty years later, he was forced to recognize that it had been a failure: 'we were all mistaken, some more and some less, in conflating politics with the country's economic state [...] and we did not think that while the kingdom of Charles Albert may have taught us to walk swiftly and surely, we could not learn the art of flying in the space of a decade or two' (1877: 476). The liberal Republican Giovanni Battista Tuveri, who had opposed the perfect fusion and was a member of the Subalpine Parliament from the first to the fifth legislature, wrote a polemical article attacking Siotto-Pintòr. The father of Sardinian federalism and promoter of significant territorial decentralization was convinced of the importance of placing the Commune at the heart of the institutional system, within a Republican-Federalist arrangement of the various Italian regions. Without denying the 'instinct of Italian nationality animating the Sardinians', he asked the House of Savoy not to ignore the island's problems and to act in a way that would allow Sardinia to obtain a form of government (Tuveri 1860: 44). In fact, Tuveri maintained,

> We remained Italian, even when we were abandoned to ourselves, even when the rest of Italy served – not always unwillingly – the Germans, the French, and the English: we want to remain Italian. But do we want to endlessly continue exploiting this type of instinct of nationality guiding us so far, do we want to allow desperation to open up a wound in Italy that will struggle to heal?
>
> (1860: 44)

The many faces of 'Sardism' in the unitary State

Following the proclamation of the Kingdom of Italy in 1861 and throughout the second half of the nineteenth century, the Sardinian ruling class became fascinated by the centralized State, given that the federal or autonomist State evoked the composite monarchies of the ancien régime. As far as the Sardinian people were concerned, the State expressed itself through demands for taxation, military service and a bureaucratic, institutional apparatus perceived as a foreign body in the island. Against this background, there was also an increase in banditry, especially in the interior of the island. As a result Agostino Depretis ordered a preliminary parliamentary inquiry into the phenomenon (between 1868 and 1871), which was followed by inquiries led by the Sardinian deputy Francesco Salaris (in 1885), and by Francesco Pais Serra (1894–5). At the conclusion of their investigations, it was decided to implement a series of extraordinary measures. The Sardinian Liberal deputy, Francesco Cocco Ortu, played a key role in the development of the special laws for Sardinia in 1907.

In the early twentieth century, a group of Sardinian writers and intellectuals, including Grazia Deledda, Sebastiano Satta and Francesco Ciusa, promoted a widespread movement of rediscovery of the island's history. It was in this context that the Socialist Attilio Deffenu gave his support to those seeking a solution for the so-called 'Sardinian question'. The aim was to reduce the economic and social inequality between the island and the central State in the framework of the overall commitment to the development of Southern Italy and the islands. In 1914, Deffenu founded the magazine *Sardegna*, which ended up becoming a sounding board for Sardism and a forum excluding the segment of the Sardinian intellectual bourgeoisie focusing on victimhood. This attitude was held to be damaging because it hindered the development of a critical awareness of Sardinia's problems (Paniga 2017: 41–2). According to Deffenu, the island's ruling class was responsible for reinforcing this fatalistic, self-pitying vision. Loyal to his Marxist roots, Deffenu hoped that the focus would be on the capacity to produce wealth within the Sardinian territory rather than on the question of redistributing economic resources (Nasone 2014: 76-7). In May 1918, a few months before the end of the war, as Italy's fate hung in the balance, a pamphlet was published entitled *Per l'autonomia!* by Y. K. The author, Umberto Cao, jurist and leading light of the Sardinian cultural and political scene during the Giolitti era, hoped for the birth of a Sardinian autonomist movement (Atzeni and Del Piano 1993: 35).

After the First World War, the petty bourgeoisie and Sardinian intelligentsia saw autonomist claims and anti-Statist protests as a way of overcoming two contingent facts: the decision to maintain a war-time ban on exports, which had an extremely negative impact on the Sardinian agro-pastoral economy; and the deployment of Brigata Sassari to suppress the strikes that broke out in Turin between 20 and 21 June 1919 (Faucci 1972: 351). A kind of ideal link was created between the actions of Sardinian soldiers and the demand for measures that would to some extent reformulate the special laws of 1907 (Rotondo 2014: 57). The reasons for the overlap between the history of the First World War in Sardinia and that of Brigata Sassari (Fois 2006) are two-fold: first, the heroism of the soldiers and the myth of the combatants, which gave rise to a deluge of celebratory popular poetry nourished by the rhetoric of special envoys from the leading national newspapers (Rotondo 2014: 63). Sassari's war veterans were organized by Lieutenant Camillo Bellieni, disabled veteran who had served in the Brigata Sassari. On 16 March 1919, he founded the weekly magazine *La Voce dei Combattenti*. A whole generation of combatants had made a decisive contribution to the Great War, which Bellieni interpreted as the final phase of the Risorgimento (Cubeddu 1999: 325).

As Liberal, he hoped for federalist reform in Italy and in Europe overall, thanks to which Sardinia would acquire an autonomous statute. On 25 May, 1919, the Sardinian Federation of the ANC (Associazione Nazionale Combattenti) was founded in Nuoro and on 14 September 1919. Its organizational structure was defined in Macomer. Another rather charismatic member of the Federation was the war hero Emilio Lussu, who supported a federal system that would have allowed Sardinia to attain a pronounced form of autonomy, albeit within the context of the Italian institutional framework. The Third Regional Congress of Sardinian Combatants, held on 8-9 August 1920, in Macomer, marked the first appearance of the term federalism in reference to a 'Sardinia that was absolutely autonomous from the Republican state while being an administrative federation'

(Contu 1994b: 9). The Congress of Macomer was influenced by the recent Fiume Endeavour and, in particular, by the interest triggered by the newly founded League of Fiume, whose aim was to create a confederation of 'oppressed peoples', or, in other words, peoples held to be ethnic and linguistic minorities, like the Irish, the Catalans and Maltese (De Felice 1974: 130). This Congress gave rise to the Macomer Charter requesting regional administrative autonomy for Sardinia within a federal republican institutional framework. Camillo Bellieni argued in favour of transforming the movement for Sardinian autonomy into a party because, as he put it, it needed to be a

> Party, not a group, bloc or league because the organization should have the firm outline of a disciplined movement and a historic function not determined by momentary contingencies. It should have a governing council that is respected and obeyed by all the members of the branch, a central committee that will provide specific guidelines for the entire movement on the island.
>
> (Cubeddu 1993: 75)

In the end, on 17 April 1921, the veterans founded a party with the aim of resolving the matter of Sardinian autonomy that became known as Partito Sardo d'Azione or Sardinian Action Party. The demands of this movement concerned economic and social reforms and a more comprehensive reorganization of the state structure, which would lead to the establishment of the regions, thereby countering a centralized arrangement. In order to convince the members of the party to embrace the fascist cause, Mussolini appealed to their anti-Giolittian, anti-parliamentarian tendencies as well as to their wartime experiences. Another effective means of persuasion was the claim that the island risked secession due to some parts of the Sardism movement. This was not the only reason: PSdA members were also induced to 'adhere to fascism before it became a regime, a burgeoning movement with an undeniable desire for renewal' (Del Piano 1995: 45). Deffenu had never shown 'too much enthusiasm' for regional autonomy and autonomy was not a 'fixation' for all PSdA members given that their main goal was to bring about 'Sardinia's rebirth' (Del Piano 1995: 45). In 1922, Mussolini appointed Asclepia Gandolfo as prefect of Cagliari in an attempt to exploit his prestige and influence among veterans, thereby attracting Sardinian former soldiers to the Fascist cause. However, not all members of the Sardinian Action Party became adherents of fascism: during the 5th PSdA Congress held in Macomer on 27 September 1925, the Communist deputy Ruggiero Grieco attempted to read a message from Antonio Gramsci calling upon Sardinian farmers to find a common purpose with the workers: this was effectively a rejection of the pro-fascist political line being espoused by the Sardinian establishment and a proposal for an alliance with the Communist Party. As it turned out, the PSdA stewards prevented Grieco from reading his communication (Contu 1994b: 16).

In the end, the majority of Sardists adhered to fascism – giving rise to sardo-fascism – in the hope of obtaining advantages for the island: the regime rejected every hypothesis for the concession of forms of self-government but in November 1924, the Sardo-Fascist deputies managed to get approval for a bill – the so-called 'legge del miliardo' – earmarking funds for an extraordinary programme of public works on the island. Following the promulgation of the 'Leggi fascistissime', which included legislation outlawing all opposition parties, the PSdA was forced to continue its activities underground. In 1929, Emilio Lussu fled from confinement on Lipari together with Carlo Rosselli and Francesco Nitti, seeking refuge in Paris where he founded the Giustizia e Libertà movement together with a mixed group of anti-fascist exiles. Within the movement, Republican, Federalists, Sardists and Liberal-Democrats all worked together to draw up a political programme for post-fascism Italy (Paci 2011: 104–31). On 27 January 1944, following the fall of Mussolini, who had been voted out of power by the Grand Council on 25 July 1943, and the armistice of 8 September 1943, the Italian High Commission of Sardinia was established under the Head of the Royal Government and given the powers to exercise the functions of central government, provided determined conditions were met. The High Commissioner, General Pietro Pinna di Pozzomaggiore, shared his authority with a council and with a regional council, in which the anti-fascist political parties were all represented. The PSdA came out of hiding and sought to lay the foundations for its re-establishment.

The 7th Congress of the PSdA, held in Oristano in March 1945, was marked by heated discussions when the majority of the party came out in favour of Sardinia's secession from the rest of Italy; a minority, led by Emilio Lussu, rejected all secessionist proposals and expressed a commonality of purpose with the Partito d'Azione, the political party associated with the Giustizia e Libertà movement, underlining the need to adopt a Socialist type of economic model. Another minority tendency, led by Camillo Bellieni, broke away from Lussu and opposed the merger between the PSdA and Partito d'Azione, which now numbered Lussu among its prominent members. In May 1946, Lussu and Mario Berlinguer, Action Party members belonging to the Consulta Nazionale – the legislative assembly set up at the end of the war to provisionally replace parliament until elections could be held – suggested extending to Sardinia the special autonomous statute accorded to Sicily (Contu 1994b: 27). However, their proposal did not meet with the unanimous approval of the other Consulta members who saw it as being imposed from above: the dominant idea was to obtain an autonomous statute from a constituent assembly elected by the people. 'In the end, Sardinia was granted – in extremis – a statute involving far fewer competences than enjoyed by Sicily' (Contu 1994b: 28). Autonomy was recognized on 31 January 1948 and the High Commission governed Sardinia until the election of the first Regional Council on 8 May 1949 (Cardia 1992: 59–85).

The island between two poles: autonomy and integration

Sardinia's twentieth-century history oscillates between two poles: integration with the national State and its opposite, the demand for autonomy. Whenever the Sardinian ruling classes called for autonomism – something that happened on a fairly regular basis – they did so 'to maximize the financial transfers from the State, which were then administered in order to perpetuate that same ruling class' (Cubeddu 1999: 327). The failure of the three-year revolutionary period of 1794–7 was caused by the contradictions expressed by the Sardinian ruling class, the stamenti, while the 'Perfect Fusion' revealed just how strongly the Sardinians desired to be part of the Italian Risorgimento movement. The experience of the Partito Sardo d'Azione, on the other hand, revealed all of the weaknesses implicit in the oscillation between the two poles of integration and opposition to a centralized state. Thus the 1948 Statute came into being with 'weak powers, no structure to apply them with, a number of (declared) enemies, and many forms of opportunism, in every sense' (Cubeddu 1999: 329).

In *The Southern Question*, Gramsci points out that 'the "Mezzogiorno" does not need special laws or any special treatment. It needs a general policy, both external and internal, inspired by respect of the general needs of the country, and not by particular political or regional tendencies' ([1916] 2019: 65). This antonymic opposition typical of Sardinia's history was interrupted by the Sardism expressed by Gramsci – who framed the Sardinian question, along with the wider southern question, within the national question. As an assiduous reader of Gaetano Salvemini, he was aware that the southern question was not a regional but a national matter. Salvemini was the first to realize that the problems of the South were linked to the organization of political power and that this was why the big landowners wished to scuttle and prevent the rise of a modern entrepreneurial class in the south (Lussana 2006: 624–5). For this reason, Gramsci believed that the problems being experienced by his fellow countrymen, by Sardinian peasants and shepherds, were the same problems afflicting the other men and women who were being held back and kept in conditions of poverty and backwardness by the capitalist system. In his opinion, although the histories of the north and south were distinct, 'their class consciousness must be the same. And above all the southern question is a national problem' (Lussana 2006: 632). It is true that Gramsci wrote to his wife, 'If Sardinia is an island [...] every Sardinian is an island in the island' (Lussana 2006: 612) but while acknowledging its undeniable physical and mental isolation, what he really meant was that the island needed to resolve its contradictions – integration and opposition to the central State – by embracing the fight for social emancipation.

An island among many centres: Corsica and the continent

The same Corsicans still bewailing the French conquest of 1768 today,
find themselves forced to accept this and cooperate with it today [...]
now this subjection [...] has somehow left the conquered without a fatherland;
they have become estranged from their old one
without being able to become attached to their new one.
                    Salvatore Viale, *Dell'uso della lingua patria in Corsica* (1858)

Towards the end of the eleventh century, Corsica passed under Pisan control when Pope Gregory VII, in the midst of the investiture struggle with Henry IV, appointed Landulf, bishop of Pisa, as his apostolic legate to Corsica. This same period saw the Republic of Genoa, the traditional rival of the Republic of Pisa, developing a growing geopolitical interest in Corsica and eventually taking control of the island following its victory in the Battle of Meloria (1284). In 1347, a diet of Corsican barons recognized Ligurian sovereignty: under this agreement, a Genoese governor was appointed to administer the island's affairs, to offer protection from Saracen raids, and to maintain limited self-government by the local councils: at the same time, the Corsicans undertook to pay taxes to Genoa. However, Peter IV of Aragon asserted his claim over the island, giving rise to a dispute that only ended in the mid fifteenth century with the victory of the Genoese.

The late 1990s and early 2000s saw the publication of a series of historiographical works by French historians such as Michel Vergé-Franceschi (1996), Antoine-Marie Graziani (1997) and Antoine Laurent Serpentini (2006) whose studies into the Genoese domination of Corsica rejected the stereotypical vision of a backward island, focusing, instead, on aspects revealing a dynamic economic and cultural climate, especially in the Cap Corse.

Such historiographical works have revealed the invalidity of the theories commonly used to describe Corsican history in the modern period. Such theories regard 'the epos of the national independence of the Corsicans; the municipalist claim of an old regime that was ultimately provident and ineffective, if not lenient in the repression by a part of the Italian irredentist, "genoese" current that was extinguished by World War II; the glorification of the merits of incorporation into France by a long hexagonal tradition' (Bitossi 1997: 13).

Between 1396 and 1409, the Republic of Genoa fell into French hands and was placed under the control of a governor appointed by Charles VI of France. This period of French sovereignty was marked by the establishment of the

Casa delle compere e dei banchi di San Giorgio (1407), a consortium of bearers of public debt securities with the function of administering state revenue and taxes as well as of governing the colonial possessions of the Republic of Genoa, including Corsica. Although it had undertaken to maintain local customs, the administration of the Casa di San Giorgio in Corsica launched a campaign against the local barons, forcing them into exile and abolishing all of the island's institutions of self-government. In 1553, after entering into an alliance with Suleiman the Magnificent, the Ottoman sultan, Henry II, king of France, fitted out a Franco-Ottoman fleet and sent it, under the command of the mercenary Sampiero da Bastelica, to invade and occupy Corsica. The threat posed by the Turkish presence in the heart of the Mediterranean elicited an immediate response in the form of joint military intervention by the Genoese and the Habsburg Emperor Charles V. The Genoese Republic, in turn, called upon Philip of Spain and Cosimo I de' Medici to support the troops led by the Genoese admiral Andrea Doria in these battles against the French.

In 1559, after a series of clashes, the two sides signed the Peace of Cateau-Cambrésis, resulting in a series of treaties intended to end the conflict between the Habsburgs and France that saw Corsica returning under the control of the Casa di San Giorgio. In 1562, Sampiero travelled to the court of Suleiman in Constantinople, ostensibly to negotiate a loan. However, the real purpose of his visit was to ask the Sultan to send the Turkish fleet to help the French regain control of Corsica. Although his mission was unsuccessful, the Genoese were convinced that a Turkish fleet would attack the island. Thanks to the benevolence of Catherine de' Medici, Sampiero remained as a guest at the French court for some time. Then in the summer of 1564, he landed in Corsica with a small band of men, justifying his intervention by claiming that Genoa had violated a number of clauses contained in the Treaty of Cateau-Cambrésis. As Antoine-Marie Graziani has pointed out, 'the idea was to transform that "feudal" war into a "national" war, pitting Corsicans against Genoese, even though the conflict was secretly backed by Catherine de' Medici' (2017). In 1567, after obtaining a series of victories, Sampiero was caught in an ambush on his way back home to Bastelica and killed. The figure of Sampiero has been interpreted in many different ways and all too often ideologized: there are those who view him as a forerunner of French Corsica while others have drawn attention to his independent spirit that led him to fight for himself, above all; some have underlined his hostility towards the Genoese domination and there are also those who consider him a precursor of Pasquale Paoli or who have transformed him into a literary myth.

The first phase of the Corsican wars (1729–33)

In the forty-year period between 1729 and 1769, Corsica became a small political hothouse experiencing all the dynamics later affecting other European countries: the crisis of the Ancien Régime, the tax burden, conflicts (between the nobility and the bourgeoisie as well as between the urban middle class and rural classes), jurisdictionalism, or the system of relations between State and Church, economic protectionism and growing popular participation (Dal Passo 2007: I).

After various insurrections triggered and led by Sampiero da Bastelica and by his son Alfonso d'Ornano with the support of France, Corsica experienced a long period of relative stability that ended in 1729. In 1637, the island received the title of kingdom, as a consequence of the recognition of the royal status of the Republic of Genoa. The island's undeniable strategic importance meant that the possession of Corsica played a far from negligible role in the defensive policy of the Genoese republic: Corsica was a 'third southern coast' in addition to the west and east coasts of Liguria (Riviera di Ponente and Riviera di Levante), acting as an 'antemurale' or bulwark in the Ligurian Sea as well as providing a pool for the recruitment of infantry. In military and naval terms, Corsica was a bastion for the protection of Genoa but, at the same time, this third shore was 'undoubtedly the longest, the most exposed, and therefore the hardest to defend' (Beri 2017: 285).

From 1729 onwards, the Republic of Genoa was forced not only to pursue a policy of defence externally but also to ensure controls within the island following the interruption of its 'convergence of interests' with local powers. The consensus and collaboration of the local elites were essential for the defence of Genoa's 'third coast' and 'the Republic, with its modest tax revenue and army could not manage without [this consensus]' (Beri 2017: 296). Thanks to the residual consensus of a part of the local nobility, the Republic was able to stem the emergence of a rebellious faction for over three decades. Subsequently, all attempts to restore order on the island failed and, after 1743, Genoa was forced to call upon troops mobilized by some of the leading members of the loyalist party (Beri 2013b: 174). From 1729 to 1768, Corsica saw a series of intermittent revolts against the Genoese government as well as a phase of civil wars between loyalists and rebels, known as the 'Corsican wars'. But Genoa could not give up its possession of the island and, during the course of the eighteenth century, it did everything in its power to maintain its sovereignty of the island 'even at the price of bleeding the treasury dry, of turning to the Empire and to France, and of accepting the presence of foreign troops in its territory' (Beri 2017: 287). Faced with widespread, growing social unrest, the Republic of Genoa decided to adopt a strategy that would make it even more unpopular in the eyes of the people by banning the possession and carrying of arms in an attempt to limit feuds and vendettas.

In 1715, the loss of revenue from the ban on the use of weapons caused Genoa to introduce the so-called 'Due Seini" tax (named after a ⅓ lira coin known as a *seino*): intended to be a temporary measure, the tax was reconfirmed on several occasions over the years. In the early months of 1730, when the news filtered out that the tax had yet again been extended, a series of revolts broke out in Pieve di Tavagna and in the Castagniccia region that took the form of spontaneous popular uprisings in protest against the tax collection and against the ban on the carrying of arms. The governor of Corsica, General Felice Pinello, asked the Republic of Genoa to send troops to help him quell the insurrections and contacted various exponents of the local nobility – such as Luigi Giafferri – in the hope that they might mediate with the rebels. However, these attempts at pacification foundered and in August 1730, there were more insurrections, initially spontaneous in character, led by various exponents of the island's nobility, assuming an inchoate form of military and civic organization. The Government of Genoa appealed to the Emperor who gave orders for a series of reforms to be drawn up. On 23 and 28 January 1733, the Minor Consiglio approved a series of laws and decrees entitled "Concessioni graziose fatte dalla Serenissima Republic of Genoa a' popoli, e sudditi del Regno di Corsica colla interposizione della cesarea garantia" and "Nuovi ordini, e decreti della Serenissima Republic of Genoa da osservarsi nel Regno di Corsica per il buon regolamento di quell'Isola".

During the period of the War of the Spanish Succession (1700–13) and the ascent to the throne of Philip V, Corsica's strategic importance made it an object of specific interest to France, an enemy of the Empire, of Great Britain and of the United Provinces. In the wake of the treaties of Utrecht and Rastatt (1713–14), which established Austrian influence in the Italian peninsula, France had set aside its ambitions for the island (Dal Passo 2007: 36). In the 1730s, Corsica's role in trade with the East rekindled its appeal for France. Louis XV laid down a precise plan for Corsica that would include a long-term strategy. Initially, French commitment was to consist primarily in sending its military units to the island, in agreement with the Republic of Genoa, acting as mediator between the latter and the rebels while also preventing other powers from staking a claim on the island. It was not until later, as revealed by a dispatch of 26 April signed by the Secretary of State for Foreign Affairs Germain-Louis de Chauvelin and addressed to the plenipotentiary minister in St Petersburg Jacques de Campredon, that France would create the conditions to induce Genoa to 'voluntarily cede' Corsica, with the approval of the Corsican rebels. From the French perspective, this would have protected France from remonstrations by the other powers. The intention was not to annex the island but rather to induce Genoa to 'reach an agreement to draw up a treaty of cession' (Dal Passo 2007: 36).

The first phase of the wars of Corsica drew to a close but, despite various attempts to put down the insurrections – using various means including 'Concessioni graziose' – the Republic of Genoa proved incapable of restoring normality to the unstable situation that had by now developed.

Freeing Corsica: from Theodor von Neuhoff to Pasquale Paoli (1733–55)

The second phase of the Corsican wars was merely the logical continuation of the first wave of insurrections: the rebel leaders travelled to Livorno where they joined other Corsican exiles. This was made possible by the sanction of the Tuscan government and, initially at least, by the fact that Spain had stationed troops in this city. Livorno became the focus of Corsican 'fuoriuscitismo' – or exile movement – as well as the supply base for the rebels. The revolts in the Haute-Corse continued in the wake of the arrest in the summer of 1733 of three prominent Corsicans, including Giacinto Paoli, who was at the forefront of the insurgent leadership (Beri 2011: 29–30). In January 1735, after meeting at Corte, the *consulta* (national assembly) passed a constitution proclaiming Corsica's sovereignty. This first constitutional charter was even cited by Montesquieu, who quoted it in his *Spicilège*.

The 1735 Constitution represented a watershed moment in the history of Corsican independence. It introduced a general diet comprising representatives from each village who had the authority to make decisions regarding all matters, including tax collection. This was a clear sign that the rebel leadership did not intend to seek an agreement with the Republic. Despite this hostile attitude, the new governor Paolo Battista Rivarola implemented a policy of conciliation that attained the desired effect of drawing considerable numbers of the island's nobility into the loyalist camp. In an attempt to thwart the tendencies being set into motion by Rivarola, the rebel leaders turned to Theodore Von Neuhoff, a German adventurer, asking him to intervene in exchange for being elected king of Corsica (Beri 2011: 30–1). After coming into contact with a group of Corsican emigrés in Florence, Theodore von Neuhoff, the son of a Westphalian baron and a woman from the Flemish bourgeoisie, had promised that he would go to Corsica in order to free it from Genoese domination (Michel 1937). After obtaining the military support of the Tunisian bey, von Neuhoff set sail for Aleria in March. On 15 April 1736, the *consulta* met at Ampugnani, electing him king of Corsica. During von Neuhoff's reign, the insurrections spread to the provinces of Pumonte, central Corsica, Balagne, and the south of the island. The new constitution established a diet of twenty-four members, reduced taxation, founded a university, called for the expulsion of the Genoese from the island and limited access to the civil service to Corsicans. However, the reign of the new king was short-lived: after just seven months, the introduction of highly repressive military measures by Rivarola led the sovereign to abandon the island on the pretext of seeking aid. Von Neuhoff sought in vain to return to Corsica in 1738 and 1743, and eventually died impoverished in London. His adventures became so celebrated that Voltaire satirized them in his *Candide*, playfully mocking Theodore in the following lines: "'Gentlemen', said he, 'I cannot claim such noble origin as you. Yet I was once a king like any other. I am Theodore, who was elected King of Corsica. [...] I have had my own coinage, and now I haven't a farthing to my name [...] The five other kings heard this story with gracious compassion. Each of them gave twenty sequins to King Theodore to buy clothes and shirts' ([1759] 1947: 127–8). For different reasons, the various components of Corsican society all saw the revolt against the Republic of Genoa as an occasion to improve their condition. The bourgeoisie engaged in commercial trade with France and Genoa hoped to increase their sphere of influence and avoid the fiscal pressure of the Genoese republic. The popular classes – farmers and shepherds – hoped to escape the coercitive authority of the big landowners and taxation by the Genoese government. Lastly, the nobility hoped to replace the Genoese as holders of political and administrative power (Dal Passo 2007: 453–5).

The early 1730s saw the growth of a dense network of commercial traffic between Corsica and Tuscany in connection with the financial and military needs of the insurrectionists. Livorno, Porto Longone and Portoferraio were all engaged in smuggling contraband to the rebels (Beri 2014: 52). During the course of the conflict, the Casa di San Giorgio had caused the island to become completely dependent upon imports, beginning with salt. The capacity to procure this commodity became the means allowing the rebels to control the territory: the insurrectionist leadership had failed to obtain sufficient stocks of salt, the people would have been forced to turn to the 'coastal strongholds controlled by the Genoese, maintaining commercial links and political subordination to La Dominante' (Beri 2014: 46). Despite the von Neuhoff interim, the war was not over: instead there was a situation of stalemate that saw the insurrectionists failing to conquer the coastal fortresses and Genoa unable to regain sovereignty over the island. This situation would end up being exploited by France, which made no secret of its interest in the island. 1740 marked the start of the War of the Austrian Succession, which broke out when Maria Theresa of Austria came to the throne. The Republic of Genoa – allied with France and Spain against Austria, Great Britain and the Kingdom of Sardinia – found itself crushed by debt and struggling more and more to control the island. It was forced to delegate all of the leading public posts – from defence to the maintenance of public order and food supplies – to the local notables (Beri 2013a: 330). In the summer of 1748, the continuing difficulties forced the Republic of Genoa to once again turn to France for help in administering law and order on the island while waiting for a series of concessions to be granted to the Kingdom of Corsica. Versailles sent 1500 troops under the command of the marquis de Cursay to Bastia. Corsica was placed under joint Franco-Genoese administration and divided into two distinct areas of jurisdiction with reciprocal frictions.

The Corsican events soon went from local phenomenon to becoming known throughout Europe. In his *De l'esprit des lois*, Montesquieu drew attention to the importance of the recognition of 'good civil laws' in allowing the Genoese Republic to maintain its control over the island. He was referring to the amnesty act passed by Genoa on 18 October 1738 in order to remedy a number of unfair laws regarding Corsica in its political and civil legislation (Montesquieu ([1748] 1989: 144). European observers saw events in Corsica as 'a paradigmatic case for European culture regarding opposition to an unfair government violating an existing political pact' (Trampus 2014: 65). Between 1745 and 1748, the administrative and judicial structure established by the Genoese in 1729 ceased to exist. Consequently, the judges of the Republic of Genoa were only allowed to exercise their authority in their cities of residence – Bastia, Ajaccio, Calvi and Bonifacio – while the rest of the island came within the remit of the French institutions, which were not answerable to the Genoese government (Beri 2013a: 320).

Given the many difficulties involved in controlling the territory and the fact that neither France nor Genoa could count on a diffused military presence, they were forced to establish a series of relations at local level. Genoa sought to consolidate its links with members of the local nobility with loyalist sympathies while de Cursay built up relations of trust with the nobles belonging to the insurrectionist movement, turning to the popular militias that had been mobilized on the basis of communities and *pievi*, the administrative units of the island's provinces (Beri 2013a: 321). In that period there were three centres of power. The first two were represented by the rather conflictual Franco-Genoese front while the third, which was not formally recognized, was headed by Giovanni Pietro Gaffori, the charismatic leader of the insurgents who was appointed secretary of state with the title of count during the ephemeral reign of von Neuhoff (Beri 2013a: 319).

Corsican rhetoric places Gaffori alongside Pasquale Paoli as one of the forerunners of the 'Nazione còrsa'. The historian Ersilio Michel, whose remarks were influenced by the historiographic climate of the Fascist period (Paci 2014a: 625–40), sketched a hagiographic profile, referring to Gaffori's heroism, 'especially at the siege of Corte (1746), when he did not hesitate to give the order to bombard the castle even though his young son had been placed on the ramparts by order of the Genoese commander. He even turned to the pen to assert the rights of his compatriots' (1932). Consequently, the island was divided into multiple jurisdictions in conflict with each other. This conjunction of different forms of power formally sharing the same degree of authority developed in a complex territory where the various jurisdictions sought to obtain the consensus of the local nobility by granting them privileges, public offices or military ranks (Beri 2013a: 330).

The unrest emerging within the Franco-Genoese faction and the accompanying growth in the authority of the former rebel front must be viewed in the context of a system of patronage and factionalism that is a common theme running through the Corsican wars in the period from 1729 to 1768 (Graziani 1997: 127–201). 1751 saw the final split from de Cursay: Genoa made an explicit request to France to withdraw its troops and to transform its armed help into financial support. However, this did not lead to the pacification of the island. Giovanni Pietro Gaffori – who had been elected General of the Nation by the Orezza *consulta* (advisory assembly) – led a series of revolts that spread throughout the island, even to regions like Cap Corse and Balagne that had remained loyal to the Republic of Genoa. Governor Gian Giacomo Grimaldi reacted by hiring assassins to kill Gaffori (Beri 2011: 35). Gaffori's death was followed by a period of turbulence that ended with the return of Pasquale Paoli, the son of Giacinto Paoli, who had been in exile in Naples since 1739.

Pasquale Paoli between myth and historiography: 'U Babbu di A Patria' (1755–69)

May 1754 saw the return to Corsica of Pasquale Paoli, officer in the Neapolitan army serving at Porto Longone, on the island of Elba, who was 'convinced of the need to abandon the island's tradition of a supreme collegial body of insurgents'

(Franceschi Leonardi 2014). The *consulta* held at Sant'Antonio di Casabianca on 14–15 July 1755 elected Pasquale Paoli General of the Corsican Nation: the insurgents placed under his command launched a 'war of national independence' not only against the Genoese regular troops but also against the forces mobilized by the loyalist nobility. From 16–18 November 1755, the General Diet of Corte approved the constitution known as the 'Paolist constitution', an extremely interesting document with a preamble mentioning for the first time ever 'the theme of happiness, which was initially a religious and philosophical idea then a political principle, before becoming part of constitutional culture and turning into a right' (Trampus 2008: 183). Corsicans were allowed to elect one delegate per one thousand inhabitants to the General Diet, which held the legislative power, establishing taxation and declaring war. The so-called *consulta*, which were previously undermined by internecine conflict, were transformed into provincial assemblies made up of elected representatives. As pointed out by Fabrizio Dal Passo, 'this civic sense was intended to allow the people to overcome particularism and promote the general interest' (2007: 45).

The constitution adopted at Corte conferred wide-reaching powers upon Paoli. He was both Commander-in-Chief of the army and representative of Corsica abroad. Under Paoli, the administration of justice became known for its severity, which often undermined its legitimacy to the point of earning itself the epithet 'Paolist justice' (Dal Passo 2007: 45). This Constitution was distinguished by an underlying ambiguity: on the one hand, it rested on democratic foundations with regard to the election of representatives of the *pievi* (basic administrative units of the island) to the legislative Diet, while, on the other, it maintained an aristocratic structure in the administration of the executive power. Moreover, despite the constitutional statute inviting all Corsicans to vote, in the majority of the *pievi* of Pumonte (corresponding roughly to western Corsica) and of Cismonte (eastern Corsica) only nobles participated in the direct election of their representatives (Dal Passo 2007: 45–6).

Paoli was undoubtedly aware of the fact that in Pumonte, which was dominated by a clan structure, it was necessary to involve a number of patrician families in roles within the state machinery in order to ensure their support. It should also be pointed out that in the Pumonti *pievi*, especially in the internal pasturelands, Paoli did everything within his power to ensure that the representatives of the people participated in the Diet despite regulating everything under his supervision. As noted by Dal Passo, 'control was the only way of maintaining unity and order on the island in this specific historical period: Paoli's contribution was particularly innovative in the organization of the three powers, conciliating the unitary principle with respect for the regional autonomies' (2007: 46).

The Corsican question was of great interest to many of Paoli's contemporaries, from Jean-Jacques Rousseau to James Boswell, from Vittorio Alfieri to Johann Wolfgang von Goethe, who saw him as one of the foremost representatives of the Age of Enlightenment. To mention just a few, Rousseau considered Corsican self-government to be the concrete manifestation of the ideas developed in his *Du contrat social: ou principes du droit politique* (1762); while the Italian dramatist Vittorio Alfieri dedicated his tragedy *Timoleone* to Paoli, describing him as 'the magnanimous advocate of the Corsicans' ([1788] 1946: 111). Marie Anne de Vichy-Chamrond, marquise du Deffand, hostess of some of the foremost literary salons of her day, described Paoli in very flattering terms, drawing attention to his legislative skills with the words 'Goodness, truth, reason, and justice' and comparing him to Horace Walpole (Dal Passo 2007: 51). Voltaire included a chapter titled 'De la Corse' in his *Précis du siècle de Louis XV*, presenting Paoli as 'a legislator more than a warrior: his courage lay in his spirit' ([1768] 1893: 355).

But it was James Boswell's description of Paoli that would resonate the most with foreign observers. Boswell travelled to Centuri in October 1765 and met Paoli in Sollacaro, spending eight days together with him. Drawing inspiration from his conversations with the general, he would later write *An Account of Corsica, The Journal of a Tour to That Island, and Memoirs of Pascal Paoli* (1768), which turned out to be a publishing success: 'the first edition of Corsica in February 1768 was sold out in six weeks and the second (also of 3,500 copies) in a year' ([1768] 2006: V). Boswell's portrait was hagiographic: 'I take the liberty to repeat an observation made to me by that illustrious minister, whom Paoli calls the Pericles of Great Britain: "It may be said of Paoli, as the Cardinal de Retz said of the great Montrose, 'He is one of those men who are no longer to be found but in the lives of Plutarch'" ([1768] 2006: 219). Boswell, like other British intellectuals, saw clear similarities between the administrative structure created by Paoli and that of the British liberal government. Paoli was considered to be both the sole illuminated despot of the eighteenth century and the leader of the first democratic government of the modern age (Dal Passo 2007: I). Instead of focusing on his role in Corsican independence, international public opinion included Paoli among the Philosophes proposing illuminated reforms.

The events taking place in Corsica during Pasquale Paoli's generalship are generally classified under three headings (1755–69): 'nationalist', 'mythical' and 'despotic' (Dal Passo 2007: I–II). The 'Republican' vision proposed by part of French historiography sought a connection between the Corsican revolution and the French revolution, pointing out the profound connection between the island and the French monarchy embodied by the figure of Napoleon. Historians Antoine Casanova and Ange Rovere have noted that, from the time of 1789 Revolution onwards, the fundamental characteristic of the 'Corsican ethnic community' was the 'remarkable, strong feeling of belonging to the French nation' (1979: 9). The nationalistic and specifically irredentist vision of Italian historiography in the 1930s and 1940s described the island as 'Italian territory' that had fallen into foreign hands (Paci 2015a: 34–41). Corsican and British historiography, on the other hand, has focused on the 'mythical' vision of Paoli's generalship, the Constitution and democratic system. This interpretation has tended to exalt the results and to emphasize its passing due to the expansionist aims of the European powers (Dal Passo 2007: V). Lastly, the 'despotic' vision of the Corsican revolution tends to minimize Paoli's achievements and the birth of a national consciousness among Corsicans. According to this latter interpretation – proposed by the more recent historiography – although he acted as an 'illuminated despot', Paoli was ultimately incapable of actively involving the popular masses and his actions need to be reassessed (Dal Passo 2007: II). This perspective has points of contact with the analysis proposed by Franco Venturi, author of *La rivoluzione di Corsica. Le grandi carestie degli anni sessanta. La Lombardia delle riforme* (1987).

'Paolist' Corsica

On 16 August 1756, the first treaty of Compiègne authorized the return of French troops to Corsica and awarded a subsidy to Genoa. During the Seven Years' War, the French forces were stationed in Ajaccio, Calvi and Saint Florence with the aim of preventing the British from using those ports. However, in 1759, after the victories of the British fleet at Toulon and Brest, the French king, Louis XV, decided to withdraw his troops (Beri 2011: 36). Although Genoa lost its subsidy, its attitude over the following years tended to waver: on the one hand, it stubbornly wished to retain its possession of the island, on the other, it was incapable of putting up resistance to the impact of Paolist forces. By 1764, the Republic of Genoa was so deeply in debt that it was forced to make massive cuts to its military presence on the island, making surrender to the Paolist troops inevitable. Under the second treaty of Compiègne signed on 6 August 1764, Genoa ceded control of the island – apart from Bonifacio and the island of Capraia – to the French troops. The treaty contained a clause providing for the withdrawal of the French if they failed to come to an agreement with Paoli's government within four years. The French did not fight the Paolist troops but waged war against the Genoese fleet and in 1767, they occupied the island of Capraia, which became the main base for their corsair fleet (Beri 2011: 38).

In 1755 and in 1763, Paoli attempted to reach an agreement with Louis XV that would have involved making the island a French protectorate in exchange for a number of ports. Paoli and the French foreign minister, duke de Choiseul, engaged in an intense correspondence: the duke offered Paoli nominal sovereignty and the crown of the kingdom of Corsica 'under the sovereignty of Genoa and with the guarantee of France', asking for the cession of some ports in exchange. Paoli could not accept these conditions because Genoa would have had to renounce all claims on the island. As stated in a letter dated 18 May 1766, the island was 'a completely free and independent State'. In January 1768, the Duke de Choiseul occupied Bastia, Saint-Florence and Cap Corse, putting an end to negotiations with Paoli (Dal Passo 2007: 53). The Republic of Genoa soon recognized that it would be impossible to ever reach an agreement with Paoli. It therefore decided to cede the island to France under the treaty of Versailles of 15 May 1768. It was more like a sale than a cession of territory: under the treaty Genoa formally retained its right of sovereignty. France took possession of Bastia, Ajaccio, Calvi and Bonifacio, along with other garrisons, forts and towers, with full sovereignty, as a pledge for the expenses that it would have to meet to occupy and maintain them (Ettori 1987: 5–30); the treaty also had two secret subsections establishing that the French would undertake not to grant independence to the Corsicans and would pay Genoa an annual subsidy of 200000 lire for ten years (Dal Passo 2007: 54). Although it also provided for the possibility of Genoa reclaiming the island at any time provided it repaid all the expenses met by France until that time, the treaty of Versailles marked the definitive transfer of the island to France.

Voltaire later wrote in his *Précis du siècle de Louis XV* that

> Genoa has done well in this affair but France has done even better given that it is powerful enough to ensure that it is respected in Corsica, powerful enough to control it, populate it, make it rich, causing its agriculture and trade to flourish. [...] It remains to be determined if men have the right to sell other men, this is a question that will never be examined in any treaty.
>
> ([1768] 1893: 354–5)

However, the Corsicans, on their part, could not accept a treaty that sanctioned the transfer of their island to France. On 22 May 1768, the Diet met in Corte to introduce enlistment of able-bodied men aged between sixteen and sixty. Although very short-lived, the military campaign took place in the open

Figure 8. The battle of Ponte Novu has become a symbol of Corsican nationalism. Every year, on 8 May, the commemoration of this event takes place with the participation of many people.
Ruines du pont Génois sur le Golo (Haute Corse) sur la commune de Castello-di-Rostino, hameau de Ponte-Novo. En cours de restauration by Piero Montesacro on Wikimedia Commons.

field: Paoli decided not to use guerrilla warfare, which would probably have allowed him to take some positions, but to tackle the French head on. His decision was motivated by the need not to cause internal divisions on the national front and not to appear as an outlaw in the eyes of international observers (Dal Passo 2007: 55). On 8 May 1769, Paoli launched a counter-offensive at Ponte Novu where the Corsicans underwent a complete defeat.

The Battle of Ponte Novu marked the end of Paoli's rule. Paoli went into exile in London where he was met with a warm welcome, receiving a generous pension from King George III and being feted in London's literary and artistic circles. His former companions kept him up to date on developments at home in Corsica.

French Corsica

In 1770, just three years after their acquisition of the island, the French began to create a cadastre providing a detailed, accurate description of the country, its lands and its inhabitants. Between 1770 and 1795, they drew up the Plan Terrier (land survey) so that the government could become as familiar with 'the entire island as an individual is with their own home' (Archives départementales de Corse-du-Sud 2016: 4). The twenty years between 1769 and 1789 resulted in a superficial assimilation that was limited to the coastal towns, ports and defended sites and mainly involved prominent citizens, nobles and the military. Among those embracing this new political direction was the formerly pro-Paolist Bonaparte family. The popular masses, farmers and shepherds, living in the villages were excluded from this process of francization. Hostile to the presence of the Genoese, they also perceived the French as outsiders. The motives for their widespread discontent included excessive regulations and bureaucracy; the hostility and contempt shown by officials to the people but also with regard to the Corsican language, which the French were seeking to replace by enforcing the use of French in all official acts, edicts, in the official gazettes, and in juridical and educational institutions; high taxation on imports of materials and goods; the wish of the French to favour local notables who were pro-French; and last but not least in importance, the memory of the Paolist period.

The island's aristocracy, on the other hand, saw integration with France as a means of obtaining ancient legal and economic privileges (Dal Passo 2007: 173–4). Corsican notables who were deputies at the General States repeatedly underlined the island's loyalty to France while making a number of demands: a request to gain access to all the public functions that was accepted by the king; criticisms of the inadequacies of the justice system and administration; equal treatment for French and Corsican officials; the reopening of the University of Corte; and the extension of tax relief (Dal Passo 2007: 175). On 30 November 1789, at the height of the revolution, the National Assembly passed the proposal put forward by the Corsican deputy Cristoforo Saliceti by recognizing that Corsica belonged to France while the Royal Decree of 4 December 1789 made it possible for Corsican exiles to return home. On 14 July 1790, Paoli landed on the island, and soon after, in September 1790, the *consulta* of Orezza elected him President of the Departmental Congress and commander-general of the National Guard. In early 1793, the French sent an expedition to Sardinia that ended in abject failure; the disastrous outcome was blamed on Paoli, accused of not having been able to mobilize the number of volunteers required. It is true that Paoli had expressed his firm opposition to a plan that was entirely contrary to his ideas: 1) 'it represented a danger to Corsica which "had need neither of war or conquests but only of liberty and peace"; 2) it was an act of unfair aggression towards the Kingdom of Sardinia, for which he had the highest esteem, given that it had always been Corsica's natural ally' (Dal Passo 2007: 181).

Paoli also called for the intervention of the battalion of volunteers under the command of Napoleon Bonaparte. It has been suggested that 'Paoli may have sought a way to rid himself of Napoleon or to destroy his incipient fame with a defeat' (Dal Passo 2007: 181). The fact remains that the French fleet remained in the port of Ajaccio for at least two months, only weighing anchor in January 1793. On 2 April 1793, the Convention suspended Paoli from his military duties and recalled him to Paris. In July of that same year, the Convention declared him a traitor of the fatherland and outlaw. The general swiftly turned to his dense network of contacts with the British – especially with Sir Gilbert Elliot, the British Commissioner – hoping to make the island a 'protectorate whose autonomy could be guaranteed by a Country "with liberal institutions making it particularly suited to this role"'(Dal Passo 2007: 186). Corsica would be a formidable base for the British fleet and a stopping point on the routes to the east Mediterranean and Africa. These communications with his contacts resulted in the decision to carry out a campaign in Corsica in February 1793 that saw the British defeat the French troops who were forced to abandon the island. On 10 June 1794, the *consulta* was convened in Corte, promulgating the birth of an Anglo-Corsican Kingdom. The *consulta*, which legislated from 10 to 21 June 1794, approved a constitution 'guaranteeing the liberty of the nation' and providing for 'the "absolute and definitive" separation from France and passage of Corsica beneath the direct protection of the English government with a Constitution guaranteeing the freedom of the nation' (Dal Passo 2007: 187).

While Elliot was appointed viceroy, Paoli was not given any institutional role. The relationship between the two men soon became strained and Paoli was forced into exile in Great Britain where he remained until his death in 1807. In October 1796, the British evacuated the island and Napoleon's army occupied the island, which was divided into two departments – Golo and Liamone – with the aim of preventing new uprisings. In 1811, Ajaccio was designated administrative capital, a decision that led to dualism with Bastia, the island's traditional cultural and economic capital (Cini 2009: 52). 'The little Paolist "Nabulione", with his Italian accent, who had become the symbol of a country that he now considered his homeland, wanted to transform Corsica into a French land come what may. Even at the cost of authoritarian integration' (Dal Passo 2007: 192). In 1798, the anti-religious fury of the revolutionaries of the Directory triggered a revolt known as the 'Crociata della Crocetta' (Crusade of the Little Cross), which was brutally suppressed, taking the 'notorious name of *francisata*, it was the final act of the religious wars that had poisoned the island's political life for so many years' (Dal Passo 2007: 191).

Corsica between France and Italy

Corsica's Napoleonic period ended with an extreme 'Bonapartist flare-up' (Dal Passo 2007: 197) known as the War of Fiumorbo (1816). The phase of the Restoration saw a return to power of the notables willing to enter into a dialogue with the new French government. In actual fact, the Restoration 'coincided with a situation of latent tension' (Cini 2009: 17) involving two actors: on the one hand, the French officials sent to the island to carry out the process of 'francization' by raising the flag of *civilization*; on the other, part of the Corsican ruling class had become the mouthpiece of an idea of 'progress' that would consider aspects vital to the island's economic and social development, that is, the matter of language, the problem of the administration of justice and of land fragmentation (Cini 2009: 17).

Starting in the early 1730s, the elite of Bastia began to cultivate assiduous cultural relationships with the Grand Duchy of Tuscany, especially with the Florentine group led by Giovan Pietro Vieusseux, Gino Capponi and Raffaello Lambruschini. In those circles, Corsica evoked the idea of a constant striving towards liberty and a spirit of independence expressed, throughout its history, by a people that had never accepted foreign rule. As revealed by the work of Niccolò Tommaseo, the representation of Corsican history by Italian literati placed Corsica and Tuscany in the same cultural context, that of Italy, a political subject that had yet to come into being. Although Italian history, due to its particularism and divisions, had never produced a unitary sentiment, one of a people, 'Corsica's past revealed the persistence [...] of an uncorrupted moral propensity immune to the yoke of tyranny placed on its neck by foreigners and constantly projected towards the attainment of national independence' (Cini 2009: 83).

Bastia's elites used this rose-tinted image of the island to emphasize a '"diversity" from the population of continental France that needed to be vindicated and defended as something that could be exploited by regional institutional powers and by the far more devious powers of the large *patrons* in their search for political autonomy' (Cini 2009: 84). Bastia's elite, beginning with one of its most illustrious exponents, the poet and magistrate Salvatore Viale, collaborated with Italian journals, including the prestigious *Antologia* founded by Vieusseux in Florence in 1829 (Paci 2012: 17–25). During their stays in Corsica, writers Niccolò Tommaseo and Francesco Domenico Guerrazzi entered into the heart of the debate on Pasquale Paoli, who was considered an example and model of democracy: in their eyes the Paolist period was the first war of Italian independence and therefore an anticipation of the Italian Risorgimento

(Cini 1998). The language used by the Corsican elite was Italian, specifically Tuscan, which was attacked by the government as part of its francization campaign: from 1820 onwards, it was forbidden to use Italian in the public administration and university degrees awarded by Italian universities were no longer recognized. 1822 saw the abolition of the Société Centrale d'Instruction Publique, an institution founded four years earlier, representing Bastia's Italian-speaking elites and the merchant bourgeoisie. This elite sought to carve out its own space within a context dominated by administrators sent from Paris but also by families of local notables who could count on the support of the French authorities and who exercised their authority upon the island's society thanks to a system of patronage (Briquet 1997). The University of Pisa, the preferred higher education institution for Corsican students, provided a base for the dialogue between the Tuscan and Corsican elites. Tuscany was a pole of attraction for the Corsican elites who soon built up close links to the group of moderate liberals frequenting the scientific and literary reading room of Vieusseux, who became the leading interlocutor for the development of economic growth projects for Corsica. As pointed out by Marco Cini, 'the project for an economy based on agriculture maintaining its role as the main source of revenues [...] would inevitably meet with the approval of the landowners and intellectuals of Bastia' (2003: 9). Until the fall of the Second French Empire, three languages were in use on the island: Italian, Corsican and French.

Although Corsican was the main spoken language, written Italian enjoyed a similar official status to French throughout the nineteenth century. Tuscan was in fact the official language used by the administration and by the authorities representing central power. On 18 March 1805, an imperial decree was passed to recognize Italian and French bilingualism given the impossibility of immediately implementing the resolution that required all official documents to be drawn up in French. The use of Corsican was limited to spoken communications: Corsican was the language of the people, the language representing the people but also the language used by the elites in their relationships with the grassroots base. During the period between the rule of Napoleon III and the early years of the Third Republic, the island elites with Bonapartist sympathies were Italian-speaking and culturally close to Italy, as revealed by the large number of literary and journalistic writings published in Italian. The birth of the Third Republic was accompanied by a process of francization and 'republicization' of Corsica brought about through schooling and the introduction of the military service, factors that allowed French to be recognized as the sole official written language. During the Third Republic, the Corsican elites gradually became aware that they belonged to a current of Republican ideas (Pellegrinetti and Rovere 2004). The dialogue between the Tuscan and Corsican elites was interrupted in the late 1840s, following the establishment of the Second Republic and the empire of Napoleon III, as the integration of Corsica into the French national context accelerated sharply.

Various elements helped to undermine the hegemonic project of the Corsican elite including the consolidation of the French institutions on the island and the Corsican origins of the imperial family which, as Marco Cini has pointed out, acted 'as a factor of liberation from the complex of "colonized" people that affected large sectors of the island's elites, favouring a more rapid assimilation in the composite French political world' (2009: 10). Taking shape alongside the Republican model and sociality being diffused in the late 1800s was a form of Corsican regionalism that categorically rejected the centralizing State and used the Corsican language as one of the main vectors for its ideas (Ravis-Giordani 2003: 451–8). The defence of the Corsican language revealed a wish to replace the use of the French language, esteemed as a synonym for national unity. The island's nationalism countered the 'one nation, one language' formula with 'my homeland is my language', in other words, my identity (Pellegrinetti 2003: 1). The birth of Corsican regionalism coincided with the foundation of the first newspaper in the Corsican language and was facilitated by the stagnation of the Corsican economy. The island's underdevelopment worsened steadily throughout the nineteenth century.

Between 1890 and the First World War, Corsica became increasingly depopulated, revealed by the high percentage of annual departures, which were on average around 1800 per 300,000 inhabitants (Pellegrinetti 2003: 8). This encouraged the rhetoric of the anti-Republican movements, which never failed to describe Corsica as *île oubliée* or *île abandonnée*, in other words, as an island either forgotten or abandoned by the state authorities. The birth of *A Tramuntana fresca e sana*, a weekly satirical literary journal entirely in Corsican, on 11 October 1896, took place in a setting distinguished by economic scarcity and social backwardness aggravated by the diffusion of links of patronage. Founded by Pierre-Toussaint Casanova, known as Santu Casanova, *A Tramuntana* intended to expose the economic, social and political situation on the island. Its criticism of the Republic often verged on xenophobia, anti-semitism, anti-Masonry, defending religion against the secularization of society (Pellegrinetti 2003: 2). According to Casanova, the written formalization of the Corsican language was the first step in the process of construction of the identity of the 'Corsican people'. His reiterated wish to affirm this identity-defining particularism on the basis of the recognition of a 'Corsican race' was taken up by the journal *A Cispra* in 1914 (Pellegrinetti 2003: 4) and, some years later, by the journal *A Muvra*, founded in Paris in 1920 by two brothers, Petru and Matteo Rocca. Edited by Petru Rocca with the collaboration of several decorated veterans, *A Muvra* presented itself to public opinion as an organ for the defence of the island's demands. In 1922, thanks also to funding provided by businessman François Coty, the *A Muvra* head office was transferred to Ajaccio with the hope of bringing together all of the regionalist elements willing to embrace the Corsican cause (Pomponi 1977: 398).

In October 1922, Petru Rocca, together with other Corsists, founded the Partitu corsu d'azione, initially based on a small membership of journalists, writers, poets, officials and students. Influenced by the ideas of Santu Casanova, Petru Rocca used the columns of his newspaper to showcase many of the key themes covered by *A Tramuntana* in the late nineteenth century. The watchword of the Corsist movement was 'a Nation, a People, a Language, a History, and a Religion' (Paci 2015a: 22). Among the demands put forward by Petru Rocca was for the Corsican language to be taught at all levels of education, for the institution of a university, and for bilingualism in public administration. In November 1926, the Partitu corsu d'azione changed its name to Partitu corsu autonomista: this was followed by articles in *A Muvra* appealing to the principles of Woodrow Wilson regarding the right of all peoples to self-determination in order to justify the autonomist aspirations of the Corsicans.

After an initial phase, in which the Partitu corsu autonomista focused all of its efforts on autonomy, the party began building a unity of purpose with Mussolini's regime. In the course of the 1930s, Rocca's party developed closer relationships with Italian Fascism, embracing the cause of Corsican irredentism. The number of Partitu corsu d'azione militants was rather small and never obtained a wide consensus from the people. Many of them used scholarships granted by the Italian government (Paci 2014b: 150) to go to Italy where they joined the Corsican irredentist action groups founded by Petru Giovacchini (Paci 2010: 89–119). Although the Fascist regime had reinterpreted insularist discourses in an irredentist light, drawing attention to Corsica's Italian identity (*italianità*), the Corsican elites feared they might lose their insular specificity along with the economic and social advantages acquired through their inclusion in the French national context, first and foremost, their access to public posts. The majority of the Corsican population steadfastly opposed Italian imperialism: it was clear to everyone that their eventual inclusion in the Italian state apparatus would not have resulted in recognition of their autonomous status. Cultural links with Italy, gradually weakened by the policies introduced by the French government, were not enough by themselves to justify full adhesion to Fascism.

The francization of the island that took place in the late nineteenth century had led to the progressive disappearance of the use of Italian in the institutions. At the same time, popular contexts continued to use the Corsican language, which the island's autonomist groups sought to defend from those seeking to reduce its use in favour of French and which Fascists considered the most glaring proof of the island's Italian identity. From the viewpoint of Corsica's irredentist elites, equating *corsitude* with *italianità* would provide them with bargaining powers with Paris. They hoped that the threat of adhesion to the fascist annexation project would induce France to grant the island greater autonomy. Mussolini himself was well aware that the island's population was hostile to an eventual Italian annexation. The directives issued by the Duce provided for the temporary occupation of the island (12 November 1942), so as to avoid increasing friction with the local population. This measure proved to be inadequate given the numerous anti-Italian protests throughout the Italian occupation. In fact, the Corsicans reaffirmed their loyalty to Free France, rebelling against the fascist occupation by carrying out acts of vandalism against the Italian consular seats and by joining the Resistance.

During the post–Second World War period, the Corsicans who felt excluded from the national Republican context would again call for autonomy, (Dottelonde 1984) drawing on the narrative of insularism in order to once more oppose French centralism (Paci 2015a: 224–5).

Conclusion

The case studies involved in our analysis have evidenced both common traits and differences that distinguish them from each other. One of the features common to the islands – or archipelagos – being examined was their past experience of different forms of domination, giving rise to a relationship with the cultural and institutional reference centre/s, which sometimes was conflictual. We might consider, for the Mediterranean area, the complex relationship between Sardinia and Sicily on one hand and the central government on the other. The same holds for the relationship between Corsica and the République française, and Malta and Great Britain prior to Maltese independence. In the same way, if we move to the Baltic area, we will encounter similar dynamics in the Åland islands, which have cultural ties to Sweden but are part of Finland, and in Ruhnu, a small island contested by Estonia and Latvia that had cultural relations with the Kingdom of Sweden.

In the cases we have studied in the pages of this book, Mediterranean islands suffer from a rhetoric that holds island regions to be in a position of subordinacy with respect to continental regions. In this regard, we might consider Corsica, the *île oubliée* or forgotten island, or Sicily and Sardinia, which are both dominated by prejudices rooted in the dualist metaphor of North versus South that overlap with progress and backwardness. According to Marcel Farinelli, while Gotland, Saaremaa and Hiumaa are described by Estonian and Swedish historians 'as places that have played an important role in the histories of their respective countries, and not as exotic isles', this is not the case with regard to Corsica and Sardinia, because they do not share a common cultural and historical tradition with the mainland state to which they belong 'or at least not entirely' (2017: 31).

Another element common to the cases here examined regards the narrative of a mythicized past. Corsica keeps alive the memory of heroes – most importantly of all, Sampiero da Bastelica, Pasquale Paoli, and Napoleon Bonaparte – while in Sardinia, they tend to exalt the figure of Giovanni Maria Angioy, hero of the

'Sardinian revolution'. Malta celebrates the 8th September, a national holiday recalling the 'Great Siege' of 1565, which saw the Order of the Knights Hospitaller of St John of Jerusalem resist the Ottoman advance. In Gotland, the Hanse period is described as a golden age because at that time Visby was at the heart of an international trade network. This medieval legacy runs like a thread through narratives of the past in Gotland as well as in Saaremaa, Hiumaa and in the Åland islands. According to Samuel Edquist and Janne Holmén 'the dominant topic in the island's regional history writing from the nineteenth century and well into our own age, is the stress on the perceived peaceful, prosperous and independent "peasant republic" of the early Middle Ages' (2012: 77).

Yet another aspect present in all of these case studies regards their strategic relevance, which was more intense in some periods, less so in others, but continues to represent a trait common to all of these islands in the Mediterranean and Baltic. Just consider, for example, the role played by Malta in the modern age, when it was a Christian outpost ruled by the Knights of St John, and, moving forward to the contemporary period, its function during the Second World War. The same might be said of the Åland islands, whose demilitarization and neutralization is proof of their strategic importance, and of Gotland, which was remilitarized following the Russian invasion of Crimea in 2014 because 'there's always been good reason to practice defending this geostrategic gem: Seize the Baltic Sea island of Gotland and you control the airspace and sea access to Estonia, Latvia and Lithuania along with Finland' (Mudge 2022).

On 7 May 2022, at the height of the Ukrainian war, just before Finland formally submitted its request to join NATO, when asked, during an interview, about the eventual threat of a Russian invasion of the Åland islands, Pekka Haavisto, the Finnish foreign minister, compared the strategic importance of the islands to that of Gotland:

> Well, of course if you look from the strategic point of view, the control of the Baltic Sea, the Åland islands are important, just as Gotland is. We are very aware of this issue or potential issue. For us it is important that we have our military planning regarding Åland, but of course that is only put in place if there is any threat against the islands.
>
> (Sander 2022)

In April, the Speaker of Parliament Matti Vanhanen stated that current international events would lead the Aland islanders to assess whether to launch a process to modify the region's status as a neutral, demilitarized province (Yle

2022). In the same period, the Gotland regiment of the Swedish Army grew exponentially with the aim of rebuilding Sweden's defences. On 13 May 2022, the commander of the Gotland regiment, Col. Magnus Frykvall, declared that 'if you own Gotland, you can control sea and air movement in the whole of the south Baltics (Erlanger 2022)'. Finnish and Swedish public opinion is overwhelmingly in support of the request to join support Nato, aware of the fact that 'Russia's fleet in Kaliningrad is only 200 miles away, and so are its Iskander nuclear-capable missiles' (Erlanger 2022).

We can also see how some of these islands have served as laboratories in which to test policies and models suitable for application elsewhere: in the Mediterranean area, Malta provided Risorgimento exiles with a place to develop and diffuse their ideas, with important consequences for the development of a national awareness on the island. Corsica saw instead the development of the so-called Paolist Constitution, whose pioneering contents anticipated ideas that would be developed in the future. Islands – like the Åland islands, for example – may be testing grounds for eco-sustainable solutions or for forms of government aiming to ease situations of conflict.

We cannot ignore the fact that the Åland islands belong to the Baltic region, and this leads us to consider how the islands' self-descriptions relate to the features and commonplaces of the Baltic/Nordic regionalism on one hand and Mediterranean-ness on the other. Åland's self-perception inserted the archipelago's reality into the wider Nordic area where 'the idea of the "Nordic exception" and of a particular Nordic way of doing things has been a central element in Nordic and national *identity* construction for the Nordic states' and 'the "idea" of the Nordic *model* has also been presented as something that can be copied and implemented elsewhere' (Browning 2007: 2). The Nordic model drew strength from a system distinguished by transregional cooperation. In an interview given in 2015, Barbro Sundback, Social Democrat and co-founder of the Ålandsfredsinstitut, looks back at the period immediately after the collapse of the Soviet Union, suggesting that 'the optimism was very strong' at a time when cooperation projects were being launched to bring the two Baltic shores closer (Paci 2015b). While cooperation between Nordic countries was relatively problem-free given that 'everyone identified with a Nordic identity. They wanted to be Nordic; in other words, proud to be an example of democracy, of Welfare State, of equal opportunities for men and women', the same could not be said of the Baltic countries (Paci 2015b). 'Having worked in Lithuania for many years, I can say that its inhabitants were and still are completely immersed in the Soviet system' (Paci 2015b).

In 1992, Ole Wæver, like many observers of the period, claimed that the Baltic Sea region, this new Hanseatic region, would soon become a reality. He believed that he could see the emergence of a new identity in Northern Europe – a Baltic regional identity (Wæver 1992: 77–102). Nonetheless, as Sundback has pointed out, 'the Baltic States are very different [...] Estonia is connected to Finland because of the language, which belongs to the Finnish branch of the Uralic languages. Russia has a great influence on Latvia. Lithuania is a Catholic country' (Paci 2015b). Sundback believes that 'they don't share the same historical experiences [...] Sweden and Finland have not had to endure the Russian presence in the same way as the Baltic states' (Paci 2015b).

'Mediterranean-ness' takes second place in the way that these islands represent themselves because it is their insularity that prevails; it is no coincidence that people speak of *sicilitudine* or *corsitude*.

But the common thread running through the cases regards the rhetoric of insularity, which in turn becomes a paradigm. The use of this paradigm of insularity as a key criterion for an understanding of insular dynamics means adopting a line of interpretation based on geographic determinism: this means that human factors, like human behaviour and inclinations, are explained through physical factors such as climate, geology, and so on. The adoption of a criterion of geographic determinism means mistaking something that is a manifestation of the physical environment for something that is an expression of a feeling of collective belonging. By way of example, we might mention the theory put forward by Ellsworth Huntington in *Civilization and Climate* (1915), which claims that the degree of civilization of American society depended upon the north American climate; however, this theory does not explain why native Americans would not have been capable of civilizing Europe (Berque 1996: 37). As Giuseppe Dematteis has pointed out, if we decide to explain historic facts by means of a deterministic approach, thereby conferring a 'spatial order' upon them, we are carrying out a tautological operation, deluding ourselves that we have discovered the same spatial relations in reality that we have used to represent that same reality (Dematteis 2002).

Given that from an EU perspective the underdevelopment of islands is caused by geographical isolation, the ultimate resolution of their specific problems would be achieved by creating a 'geographical continuity' (Vieira 2016: 6–7) that 'bridges' the distance both in a literal sense, through the implementation of infrastructure, and metaphorically, through the provision of more funding. In February 2008 the former Italian Prime Minister Silvio Berlusconi announced plans to build the Strait of Messina bridge: this project would have destroyed the symbolic meaning of the passage across the Strait of Messina which was perceived, in the 1960s and 1970s, as the point of separation from Sicily, a symbol in which 'the memories of all periods were concentrated together with unsubdued ancestral fears' (Angelini 2011: 117). From the Unification of Italy onwards, projects for the construction of a bridge across the Strait were the expression of a rhetoric driven by the desire to create a tangible link between Sicily and the mainland in order to reduce the inequality between the northern and southern Italy. In 2018, Silvio Berlusconi drew upon the rhetoric of the Marshall Plan to underline the urgency of planning a bridge across the Strait: 'We have to do it. The logistical costs associated with the lack of territorial continuity with Italy makes Sicilian businesses less competitive. We need to build roads and railways, and a casino in Taormina. What we need, in short, is a Marshall Plan for Sicily that would bring 5–10 billion a year, and a plan for the South' (*la Repubblica* 2018). And during his electoral campaign in 2013, Berlusconi, who was a guest on a television programme, decreed, 'If we win, we'll build a bridge across the Strait to make Sicilians 100% Italian' (2013).

In Saaremaa too, the construction of a bridge to connect the island to the mainland has caused much debate in the public discourse over the past decade even though the project was first aired in 1997, shortly after the 100-year anniversary celebration of a causeway between Muhu Island and Saaremaa. The construction of a land link with the mainland met the expectations of a State that was re-acquiring its independence after the Soviet period. As outlined by Jana Raadik Cottrell and Stuart P. Cottrell, '"Crossing that bridge" is a theme of development and notion of progress in the present-day political landscape of Estonia, where democracy was restored under the slogans "Clear that place!" and "A fresh start"' (2020: 276).

The rhetoric around the construction of the bridge in Sicily – as in Saaremaa – is sparked by the paradigm of insularity. For example, when reading the pages on Sardinia in the *Guida d'Italia* published by the Touring Club Italiano, we are immediately aware of a deterministic approach to the island's history: 'Was the island's geographic reality instrumental in conditioning historic events taking place in Sardinia and in its communities? The answer can only be yes' (*Guida d'Italia* 2002: 24). We also read, 'the natural setting appears to play a decisive role in the fate of a human group, in the formation of a unique historical character. In fact, Sardinia's insularity, its isolation in the middle of the western Mediterranean, the characteristics of its coasts and its relief and the appeal of some of its riches have endowed it with an originality that is sometimes very subtle, sometimes emphatic' and 'what emerges is a violent, hostile nature that has heavily conditioned the possibilities of development of the human communities' (*Guida d'Italia* 2002: 24).

As pointed out by Marcello Tanca during the 'Insulab' workshop held by Roma Tre University in April 2021, the resulting picture is one in which geographic determinism and the paradigm of insularity are presented as the key to explaining the history of Sardinia, when, in fact, there is no equivalence between isolation and insularity (Loi 2006). In order to avoid the paradigm of insularity, Tanca (2018: 5) identifies three levels of geographic reality: the things ('discovering'), the representations ('inventing') and the practices ('participating'). While the attributes of things are spatiality and presence, representations are distinguished by the symbolic and intentionality: lastly, the characteristics of practices are corporeity and non-intentionality. There are three levels: the object, the symbol and the performance. Tourism, therefore, does not depend upon the beauty of the coastlines but is explained within a chain of expectations that nourishes the desire for Mediterranean-ness and Baltic-ness, but then there are the practices, which take place in different contexts.

So, we will have an island, which is undeniably a geographic notion but also an object of representation and expectation: for some it will be a place of refuge and projection of tourist expectations, while for others, like migrants, it will be a place of passage that is reached after overcoming the perils of the sea. As we have seen in all of the cases examined, the insular imaginary contains the indissoluble combination of island-nature, an unspoiled nature (Saaremaa, Hiiumaa, Åland, Gotland) but also a nature resulting in backwardness, especially in the Mediterranean islands, and in the development of forms of organized and unorganized violence that may take the shape of banditry in Corsica and Sardinia and mafia in Sicily.

The islands are a source of attraction for visitors: all of the case studies presented reveal the extreme affection that tourists have for island regions. Tourists seek an elsewhere that is different from their place of origin, somewhere exerting an irresistible pull. Islands are also places where the tourist industry rediscovers an idealized past, as in the case of Gotland and its historic medieval legacy, in order to attract visitors. As Claudio Minca points out, the act of travelling leads us to a mythical world, 'to a spatially limited environment that reproduces tangibly ideal conditions in which to "re-create" ourselves in the broadest sense' (1994: 384).

This gives rise to forms of 'island branding', that is, the use of a series of branding theories and techniques aiming to promote the island space (Mitropoulou and Spilanis 2020: 32). International treaties from the mid-1990s are the first to make use of the expression 'islands of peace', in reference to Åland; 'Peace was at the top of agenda'. The tourist sector sought to present the islands of peace as a brand in order to attract visitors 'hoping to find a pleasant, quiet place' (Paci 2015b). From the 1800s onwards, Corsica was associated with a series of stereotypes outlining the innate hospitality of the islanders, their spirit of freedom, their sense of honour and the practice of the vendetta, all of which propagated through travel accounts, the Parisian press and tourist guides. It was then that the 'bandit of honour' emerged, a figure idealized to the point that it was considered to represent the soul of the Corsican people (Tatasciore 2022: 36). In nineteenth-century travel guides, the image of Corsican 'banditry of honour' became such a recurrent stereotype in the travel experience of tourists that the link between the representation of the geographic space and its inhabitants, and that of the bandit could no longer be unravelled (Tatasciore 2013: 17). Corsica was represented as the island of bandits, a long-lived image fated to survive until the present day. Travelling along the island roads, it is not unusual to see road signs with place names riddled with bullet-holes; at the same time, tourist shops now sell such signs as souvenirs, indicating a desire to reinforce the image of the island as a land of bandits (Paci 2021: 93–4).

Similar discourses contribute to a kind of pseudo-authenticity produced in a process of folklorization to be conveyed to *homo turisticus* (Martinetti 2007: 34). Tourists are motivated by a desire for the discovery of places of authenticity which allow them to encounter otherness and the allegedly original local dimension. They flee from non-places or 'ephemeral spaces' (Minca 1996), yet they contribute to creating such places because they seek confirmation for their vision of the world. This comes about because the tourist space is, above all, an image, a representation made by guides, by travel agencies, but also by the media who influence the offer as well as the demand. According to Baldacchino, '[they] are now, unwittingly, the objects of what may be the most lavish, global and consistent branding exercise in human history' (2012: 55). Islands are also landing places for migrants, as in the cases of Sicily and Lampedusa. Or even of Malta, where, as pointed out by Mark-Anthony Falzon, 'this sense of threat is based on a set of orthodoxies that posit Malta as small, vulnerable and isolated' (2012: 1664). We should not forget, however, that islands are also places of emigration; consider, for example, the Sicilian community in the United States or the Maltese in Australia. Tanca invites us to bear in mind these three levels but not to 'give in to the temptation to normalize them, reducing them to a common denominator' (Tanca 2018: 16).

To sum up on the question of 'insularity', we may depart from Jean-François Staszak's observation according to which the physical, geomorphological or biological conditions of insularity are a premise, not the determinant, of cultural insularity, as the latter does not refer to islands but humans (1997: 354). Therefore, insularity in its cultural dimension should not be considered as a stable condition (Sanguin 1997; Cavallo 2013a: 183). As a social phenomenon it boils down 'to the self-image of a group, which might be based on certain shared beliefs or a shared historical tradition' (Ratter 2018: 14). The characteristics and contents of 'insularity' therefore remain uncertain and change over time. This makes the insularity paradigm a valuable political instrument.

As we have seen with regard to the European institutions, the recognition of 'insularity' constitutes a *conditio sine qua non* for requesting the enactment of measures to serve the specific needs of island areas. No wonder, then, that the representatives of islands at the European Parliament conform to this thesis to enhance their bargaining power within the EU. On 4 February 2016, Salvatore Cicu, the Sardinian Member of the European Parliament from the European People's Party (EPP), called to establish 'a principle of territorial continuity: for example, the transport systems of Sicily and Sardinia will finally be entitled to the economic benefits that they require to cover a geographical gap without encountering EU bans' (*L'Unione Sarda* 2016). Along this line, the two Italian islands created a common 'front'. In 2019, the President of the Region of Sardinia, Christian, Solinas, lobbied the European Union and Commission to introduce measures to combat the natural and structural disadvantages of insularity. In 2020, an agreement was drawn up between Sardinia and Sicily with the aim of 'pursuing a common path for the submission to the European Parliament and Commission of claims linked to a condition of insularity' (*sardiniapost* 2020). The Sicilian regional government insisted that the condition of 'insularity' created 'specificities leading to an objective disadvantage with respect to continental territories' (Regione Siciliana 2021). In 2022, the Italian Senate even approved a constitutional amendment 'regarding the recognition of the peculiarity of the Islands and the overcoming of the disadvantages deriving from insularity' (Senato della Repubblica 2022).

In both the Baltic and the Mediterranean context, the paradigm of insularity has been used to reinforce a particularism in search of recognition and to further political claims. The Åland movement in the 1920s reveals how the insularist rhetoric has been used to negotiate an autonomous status in a Finnish institutional context. Similarly, in Ruhnu, the role of Swedish culture in this small Estonian region is evoked to lay claims to the existence of an insularity that is as linguistic as it is geographical; in the narrative of the islanders, it is their geographic isolation that allows them to maintain their unique Swedish identity.

On the whole, while among the Baltic Sea islands aspects of insularity were on the whole mitigated by reassuring reliance on the more equal and equitable conditions of the Nordic region, the case of the two Italian islands confirms how in the Mediterranean context the political use of insularity has remained massive.

The reliance on the language of insularity is furthered by the main addressee of claims for financial support, the European Union. The EU itself relies on the concept of insularity and its underlying geographical determinism. In this way the EU can present itself as a 'charitable' institution ready to intervene with the provision of structural funds in order to satisfy the requests of their inhabitants. They continue to fuel an insularist mentality, and the propensity of islanders to over-cultivate their insular specificities in order to confirm a particular cultural identity that legitimates their claims for specific benefits (Brunet, Ferras and Théry 1993). However, in the effort of the construction of an insular identity a variable linked to the island imaginary comes into play that 'does not determine, but contours and conditions physical and social events in distinct, and distinctly relevant, ways', as Godfrey Baldacchino explains (2004a: 278). In other words, 'islandness' rather than just 'insularity' co-determines de facto the political negotiation, whatever the prevalent rhetoric of this negotiation may consist of.

All cases studied in this book reveal that every natural limit – including maritime limits – result in a demand for legitimization. Borders play a vital role in our recognition of the existence of an 'Us' and in the definition of the 'Other', who is thereby excluded (Petri 2005: 89–90). The entrenchment of islanders in a local traditional position should not lead us to believe that the line traced by the border is a dichotomous division between Us and the Other. On the contrary, as Rolf Petri has pointed out, the border is evidence of a relationship of sharing and communication:

> The duplicity of separation is well-understood, for example, in the German verb *teilen* which means both "to divide" and "to share" while – and this is also important – the literal translation of sharing is *mitteilen*, "to communicate". In fact, every practical form of sharing creates and presupposes some form of communication – through gestures, words, embraces, weapons – between those who are separated or who are about to separate. Each line of demarcation is always also a shared line, which must necessarily unite what it must separate.
>
> (2005: 90)

Despite the 'appearance of hard boundaries and insularity', the insular condition is described more through connectedness than isolation given 'that apparently emphatic boundary is the most permeable of membranes' (Hay 2006: 23). Aware of the pitfalls involved in a geographically deterministic approach, we should hope that in the future islands will 'stop pursuing and emulating the model of the mainland' and choose to draw upon their 'insular expertise and experience' (Staniscia 2012: 25).

In writing this book, we have aimed to move away from the paradigm of insularity, instead accepting Adam Grydehøj's invitation to expand the reach of island studies and of wider archipelagic and regional dynamics, given that insularity 'risks missing the forest for the trees, the archipelago for the islands' (2017: 8).

References

Abulafia, D. (ed.) (2003), *The Mediterranean in History*, Los Angeles: The J. Paul Getty Museum

Abulafia, D. (2011), *The Great Sea: A Human History of the Mediterranean*, London: Allen Lane

Adorni, D. (1994), 'Lettere ai potenti: I siciliani che scrivevano a Crispi e a Rudiní (1887–1898)', *Studi Storici* 35 (2): 327–403

Agamben, G. (1996), *Mezzi senza fine. Note sulla politica*, Torino: Bollati Boringhieri

Åkermark Spiliopoulou, S. (2009), 'L'exemple des îles Åland ou les vicissitudes d'un concept en flux', in M. Chillaud (ed.), *Les Îles Åland en mer Baltique. Héritage et actualité d'un régime original*, 229–41, Paris: L'Harmattan

The Åland Question (1920), Helsinki: Valtioneuvoston Kirjapaino

Alenius, K. (2006), 'Unification with Sweden, autonomy, federal self-government? The dilemma of the Swedish minority of Estonia during the period between the world wars', *Scandinavian Journal of History*, https://www.tandfonline.com/doi/full/10.1080/03468750600777337?needAccess=true (accessed 7 August 2021)

Alfieri, V. ([1788] 1946), *Tragedie*, vol. 2, Bari: Laterza

Anderson, B. ([1983] 1991), *Imagined Communities: Reflections on the Origin and Spread of Nationalism*, London-New York: Verso

Andersson, O. (1920), *Les origines de la question d'Åland. Åland en 1917–1918*, Helsinki: Imprimerie du gouvernement

Angelini, A. (2011), *Il mitico Ponte sullo Stretto di Messina. Da Lucio Cecilio Metello ai giorni nostri: la storia, la cultura, l'ambiente*, Milano: Franco Angeli

Apostolopoulos, Y., and D. J. Gayle (eds.) (2002), *Island Tourism and Sustainable Development: Caribbean, Pacific and Mediterranean Experiences*, Westport, CT: Greenwood Publishing Group

Archives départementales de Corse-du-Sud (2016), *Les documents du Terrier général de l'île de Corse, étude et histoire du fonds*, http://www.corsedusud.fr/wp-content/uploads/2017/01/Def_Terrier-g%C3%A9n%C3%A9ral_les_documents_V02.pdf> (accessed 27 January 2021)

Arcifa, L. (2020), 'Scontro di civiltà', in G. Barone (ed.), *Storia mondiale della Sicilia*, 114–17, Roma-Bari: Laterza

Åselius, G. (2005), *The Rise and Fall of the Soviet Navy in the Baltic 1921–1941*, London-New York: Routledge

Askey, N. (2014), *Operation Barbarossa: The Complete Organisational and Statistical Analysis, and Military Simulation*, vol. II, Lulu Publishing

The Associated Press (2020), 'Sweden ups defense budget 40% due to regional tensions', *DefenseNews*, https://www.defensenews.com/global/europe/2020/12/15/sweden-ups-defense-budget-40-due-to-regional-tensions/ (accessed 8 June 2021)

Astuto, G. (2009), 'Crispi e la Sicilia: tra cospirazioni e rivoluzioni', in A. G. Ricci and L. Montevecchi (eds.), *Francesco Crispi. Costruire lo Stato per dare forma alla Nazione*, 3–39, Roma: Ministero per i beni e le attività culturali Direzione generale per gli archivi

Atzeni, F., and L. Del Piano (1993), *Intellettuali e politici tra sardismo e fascismo*, Cagliari: Cuec

Atzeni, F. (2015), 'Studi sulla Sardegna nel Risorgimento', in F. Atzeni (ed.), *Un archivio digitale del Risorgimento Politica, cultura e questioni sociali nella Sardegna dell'"800*, 49–72, Cagliari: Grafica del Parteolla

Avagliano, L. et al. (eds.) (1983), *La modernizzazione difficile. Città e campagne nel Mezzogiorno dall'età giolittiana al fascismo*, Bari: De Donato

Aymard, M., and G. Giarrizzo (eds.) (1987), *La Sicilia*, Torino: Einaudi

B7 Baltic Islands (2014), *B7 25. 25 years of the B7 Baltic Islands Network*, https://issuu.com/pelagis/docs/b7-25_brochure_pages (accessed 18 October 2021)

Baldacchino, G. (2002), 'A nationless state? Malta, national identity and the EU', *West European Politics* 25 (4): 191–206

Baldacchino, G. (2004a), 'The coming of age of island studies', *Tijdschrift voor Economische en Sociale Geografie* 95 (3): 272–83

Baldacchino, G. (2004b), 'Autonomous but not sovereign? A review of island sub-nationalism', *Canadian Review of Studies in Nationalism* 21 (1): 77–91

Baldacchino, G. (2005a), 'Successful small-scale manufacturing from small islands: Comparing firms benefiting from locally available raw material input', *Journal of Small Business & Entrepreneurship* 18 (1): 21–37

Baldacchino, G. (2005b), 'Editorial: Islands: objects of representation', *Geografiska Annaler. Series B, Human Geography* 87 (4): 247–51

Baldacchino, G. (2006), 'Islands, island studies, island studies journal', *Island Studies Journal* 1 (1): 3–18

Baldacchino, G. (2008), 'Studying islands: On whose terms? some Epistemological and Methodological challenges to the Pursuit of island studies', *Island Studies Journal* 3 (1): 37–56

Baldacchino, G. (2010), *Island Enclaves: Offshoring Strategies, Creative Governance and Subnational Island Jurisdictions*, Montreal: McGill-Queen's University Press

Baldacchino, G. (2012), 'The Lure of the island: A spatial analysis of power relations', *Journal of Marine and Island Cultures* 1: 55–62

Baldacchino, G., and E. Hepburn (2012), 'A different appetite for sovereignty? Independence movements in subnational island jurisdictions', *Commonwealth & Comparative Politics* 50 (4): 555–68

Baldacchino, G. (ed.) (2013), *The Political Economy of Divided Islands: Unified Geographies, Multiple Polities*, New York: Springer

Baldacchino, G. (2016), *Archipelago Tourism: Policies and Practices*, London: Routledge

Baldacchino, G. (2018), 'Preface', in *The Routledge International Handbook of Island Studies*, 173–201, New York: Routledge

Baldacchino, G., and N. Starc (2021), 'The virtues of insularity: Pondering a new chapter in the historical geography of islands', *Geography Compass* 15 (12): e12596

Baldoli, C. (2008), 'The Northern Dominator and the Mare Nostrum: Fascist Italy's cultural war in Malta', *Modern Italy* 13: 5–20

Ballif, F., and S. Rosière (2009), 'Le défi des «teichopolitiques». Analyser la fermeture contemporaine des territoires', *L'Espace géographique* 38 (3): 193–206

Baltic Orthodoxy 'Swedish conversions', https://www.balticorthodoxy.com/swedish-conversions (accessed 22 July 2021)

Barone, G. (1978), 'Storia della Sicilia e sicilianismo storiografico', *Archivio storico per la Sicilia orientale* 74 (2–3): 309–30

Barone, G. (1987), 'Egemonie urbane e potere locale (1882–1913)', in M. Aymard and G. Giarrizzo (eds.), *La Sicilia*, 191–370, Torino: Einaudi

Barone, G. (2003), 'Sicilianismo, meridionalismo, revisionismo. Note sulla "modernizzazione difficile" della Storia Contemporanea in Sicilia', in F. Benigno and C. Torrisi (eds.), *Rappresentazioni e immagini della Sicilia tra storia e storiografia*, 171–87, Caltanissetta-Roma: Sciascia

Barone, G. (ed.), (2020), *Storia mondiale della Sicilia*, Roma-Bari: Laterza

Basile, M. (2015), 'La pubblicistica politica siciliana durante i moti del 1820: alcune riflessioni di un "veterano della libertà"', *Le Carte e la Storia* 1: 52–66

Basile, M. (2017), 'Il dibattito politico-costituzionale nel 1848', *Foro, Nueva época* 20 (2): 195–211

Bauman, Z. (2000), *Liquid Modernity*, Cambridge: Polity Press

Benigno, F. (2009), 'Il Mediterraneo', *Treccani*, https://www.treccani.it/enciclopedia/il-mediterraneo_%28XXI-Secolo%29/ (accessed 4 January 2022)

Benigno, F. (2013), *Parole nel tempo. Un lessico per pensare la storia*, Roma: Viella

Bergman Rosamond, A., and A. Kronsell (2020), 'Cosmopolitanism and individual ethical reflection – the embodied experiences of Swedish veterans', *Critical Military Studies*, 1–20, https://www.tandfonline.com/doi/pdf/10.1080/23337486.2020.1784639?needAccess=true (accessed 9 June 2021)

Bernardie-Tahir, N. (2010), 'Immobiles îles Temporalités et altérités insulaires', *Géographie et cultures* 75: 1–13, http://journals.openedition.org/gc/1647 (accessed 11 February 2022)

Bernardie-Tahir, N. (2011), *L'usage de l'île*, Paris: Petra

Bernardie-Tahir, N., and C. Schmoll (2014), 'Opening up the island: A "counter-islandness" approach to migration in Malta', *Island Studies Journal* 9 (1): 43–56

Bernardie-Tahir, N., and C. Schmoll (2015), 'Îles, frontières et migrations méditerranéennes: Lampedusa et les autres', *L'Espace politique* 15 (1): 1–13

Beri, E. (2011), *Genova e il suo regno. Ordinamenti militari, poteri locali e controllo del territorio in Corsica fra insurrezioni e guerre civili (1729–1768)*, Novi Ligure: Città del silenzio edizioni

Beri, E. (2013a), '"L'irregolare agire di monsieur de Cursay". Controllo del territorio, ordine pubblico e amministrazione della giustizia in Corsica (1748-1753)', in L. Antonielli and S. Levati (eds.), *Controllare il territorio. Norme, corpi e conflitti tra medioevo e prima guerra mondiale*, 315-30, Soveria Mannelli: Rubettino Editore

Beri, E (2013b), '"Far le marce per le esecuzioni di giustizia". La truppa regolata genovese e l'ordine pubblico nel Regno di Corsica (1741-1745)', in L. Antonielli (ed.), *Polizia Militare Military Policing*, 147-74, Soveria Mannelli: Rubettino Editore

Beri, E. (2014), 'Contrabbandieri, faccendieri e mediatori fra Toscana e Corsica (1729-1768)', *Études corses* 78: 43-60

Beri, E. (2017), 'La Corsica, frontiera marittima genovese (secc. XVI-XVIII)', in a cura di A. Gallia, L. Pinzarrone and G. Scaglione (eds.), *Isole e frontiere nel Mediterraneo moderno e contemporaneo*, 283-96, Palermo: New Digital Frontiers

Berlinguer, L., and A. Mattone (1998), *La Sardegna*, Torino: Einaudi

Berlusconi, S. (2013), In onda [television program], La7, 9 febbraio 2013

Berque. A. (1996), *Etre humains sur la Terre: principes d'éthique de l'écoumène*, Paris: Gallimard

Bialasiewicz, L., P. Giaccaria, A. Jones, and C. Minca (2013), 'Re-scaling "EU"rope: EU macroregional fantasies in the Mediterranean', *European Urban and Regional Studies* 20 (1): 59-76

Biazzo Curry, C. (2001), 'La sicilianità come teatralità in Sciascia e Bufalino', *Quaderni d'italianistica: revue officielle de la Société canadienne pour les études italiennes* 22 (2): 139-57

Billig, M. (1995), *Banal nationalism*, Los Angeles: Sage

Bilmanis, A. (1945), *Baltic Essays*, Washington, DC: Latvian Legation

Birocchi, I. (1992), *La carta autonomistica della Sardegna tra antico e moderno. Le leggi fondamentali nel triennio rivoluzionario (1793-96)*, Torino: G. Giappichelli Editore

Bitossi, C. (1997), *Il Regno di Corsica 1700-1768*, Milano: F. M. Ricci

Blanc-Noël, N. (2002), *La Baltique, une nouvelle région en Europe*, Paris: L'Harmattan

Bondin, R. (1980), *Deportation, 1942: The Internment and Deportation of Maltese Nationalists*, Malta: Rama Publications

Bonnemaison, J. (1990), 'Vivre dans l'île. Une approche de l'îléité océanienne', *L'Espace Géographique* 19-20 (2): 119-25

Bono, S. (2016), 'Mediterraneo, storie di una idea liquida', *Mediterranea. Ricerche storiche* 13: 119-32

Borioni, P. (2005), *Svezia*, Milano: Unicopli

Borutta, M., and S. Gekas (2012), 'A colonial sea: The Mediterranean, 1798-1956', *European Review of History/ Revue européenne d'histoire* 19 (1): 1-13

Boswell, J. ([1768] 2006), *An Account of Corsica: The Journal of a Tour to That Island, and Memoirs of Pascal Paoli*, Oxford: Oxford University Press

Bourdieu, P. (1980), 'Le Nord et le Midi: Contribution à une analyse de l'effet Montesquieu', *Actes de la recherche en Sciences sociales* 35: 21-5

Brambilla, C. (2015), 'Exploring the critical potential of the borderscapes concept', *Geopolitics* 20 (1): 14-34

Braudel, F. ([1949] 1995), *The Mediterranean and the Mediterranean World in the Age of Philip II*, 2 vol., Berkeley: California University Press

Brazzelli N. (2012), *Isole: Coordinate geografiche e immaginazione letteraria*, Milano: Mimesis

Brigand, L. (1991), *Les îles en Méditerranée. Enjeux et perspectives*, Paris: Économica

Briguglio, L. (1995), 'Small island developing states and their economic vulnerabilities', *World Development* 23 (9): 1615–32

Briquet, J. L. (1997), *La tradition en mouvement: clientélisme et politique en Corse*, Paris: Belin

Brogini, A. (2005), *Malte, frontière de chrétienté (1530–1670)*, Roma: Publications de l'École française de Rome

Brotton, J. (2013), *A History of the World in 12 Maps*, London: Penguin

Browning, C. S. (2007), 'Branding nordicity models, identity and the decline of exceptionalism', *Cooperation and Conflict: Journal of the Nordic International Studies Association* 42 (1): 27–51

Brown, P. M. (1921), 'The Aaland islands question', *The American Journal of International Law* 15: 268–72

Brunet, R., R. Ferras, and H. Théry (eds.) (1993), *Les mots de la géographie. Dictionnaire critique*, Montpellier-Paris: RECLUS-La Documentation Française

Bufalino, G. (1996), 'Io contro Stupidania', *Corriere della Sera*

Butera, S. (1998), 'L'ideologia sicilianista e mediterranea', *Rivista economica del Mezzogiorno* 12 (1): 185–91

Cabouret, M. (1992), 'Öland et Gotland, court essai sur le degré d'insularité dans une mer intérieure, la Baltique', *Hommes et Terres du Nord* 4: 190–6

Cabouret, M. (1994), 'Notes sur la vie insulaire en Estonie', *Norois* 162: 315–31

Caldwell, J. C., G. E. Harrison, and P. Quiggin (1980), 'The demography of micro-states', *World Development* 8 (12): 953–62

Canale Cama, F., D. Casanova, and R. M. Delli Quadri (2009), *Storia del Mediterraneo moderno e contemporaneo*, Napoli: Guida

Cancila, O. (2008), *I Florio: storia di una dinastia imprenditoriale*, Milano: Bompiani

Cao, M. L. (1928), *La fine della Costituzione autonoma sarda in rapporto col Risorgimento e coi precedenti storici*, Cagliari: Ed. Collana di Mediterranea

Capasso, S., G. Corona, and W. Palmieri (2020), 'Il valore del mare. Riflessioni sul Mediterraneo', in S. Capasso, G. Corona, and W. Palmieri (eds.), *Il Mediterraneo come risorsa. Prospettive dall'Italia*, 11–30, Bologna: Il Mulino

Cardia, M. (1992), *La nascita della regione autonoma della Sardegna: 1943–1948*, Milano: Franco Angeli

Carta, L. (2000), 'L'insurrezione cagliaritana del 28 aprile e la vittoria del partito patriottico', in L. Carta (ed.), *ActaCuriarum Regni Sardiniae. L'attività degli Stamenti nella 'Sarda Rivoluzione'*, 120–73, Cagliari: Consiglio regionale della Sardegna

Carta, L. (2019), 'I moti angioiani della fine del Settecento in Sardegna interpretati dallo storico di Torralba Sebastiano Pola', *Fondazione Sardinia*, http://www.fondazionesardinia.eu/ita/?p=16229 (accessed 24 December 2020)

Carta, S. (2012), 'L'Occidente in antropologia: Occidentalismo', *Visual Ethnography* 1 (1): 54–63

Cassano, F. (1996), *Il pensiero meridiano*, Roma-Bari: Laterza

Cassano, F. (2004), *Homo civicus: la ragionevole follia dei beni comuni*, Bari: Edizioni Dedalo

Casanova, A., and A. Rovere (1979), *Peuple corse, révolutions et nation française*, Paris: Editions sociales

Castelain, J. P. (2006), 'Approches de l'île, *Ethnologie française* 36 (3): 401–6

Cavallo, F. L. (2013a), 'Oggetti geografici, soggetti simbolici. Isole e insularità in geografia culturale', in A. Paolillo (ed.), *Luoghi ritrovati. Itinerari di geografia umana tra natura e paesaggio*, 177–205, Vidor: ISTHAR Editrice

Cavallo, F. L. (2013b), 'Insularità e portualità come dialettica spaziale tra apertura e chiusura', *Portus. The Online Magazine of RETE* 13: 1–7

Cavallo, F. L., and G. Di Matteo (2021), 'Volunteer tourism and lived space: Representations and experiences from Lesvos', *Tourism Recreation Research* 46 (1): 19–33

Chabot, G. (1935), 'La vie maritime en Estonie d'après Mme Olga Gallin', *Annales de géographie* 248: 203–6

Chevalier, M. (1832), 'Système de la Méditerranée', in *Politique industrielle et système de la Méditerranée: Religion Saint-Simonienne*, 101–50, Paris

Chillaud, M. (2009), *Les Îles Åland en mer Baltique: héritage et actualité d'un regime original*, Paris: L'Harmattan

Cimino, M. (1988), *Un'inchiesta sul separatismo siciliano*, Palermo: Istituto Gramsci Siciliano

Cini, M. (1998), *La nascita di un mito: Pasquale Paoli tra '700 e '800*, Pisa: BFS

Cini, M. (2003), *Une île entre Paris et Florence. Culture et politique de l'élite corse dans la première moitié du XIXe siècle*, Ajaccio: Albiana

Cini, M. (2009), *Corsica e Toscana nell'Ottocento. Relazioni politiche, economiche e culturali fra due regioni del Mediterraneo*, Genova: ECIG

Clark, E., and T. L. Clark (2009), 'Isolating connections –connecting isolations', *Geografiska Annaler: Series B, Human Geography* 91 (4): 311–23

Congregalli, M. (2018), 'Gotland, da isola degli artisti a prima linea contro la Russia', *Esquire*, https://www.esquire.com/it/lifestyle/viaggi/a21727897/gotland-da-isola-degli-artisti-a-prima-linea-contro-la-russia/ (accessed 9 June 2021)

Contu, G. (ed.) (1994a), *Emilio Lussu e il sardismo*, Sassari: Edizioni Fondazione Sardinia

Contu, G. (1994b), *Il federalismo nella storia del sardismo*, Sassari: Edizioni Fondazione Sardinia

Cosgrove, D. (1984), *Social Formation and Symbolic Landscape*, London: Croom Helm

Council of the European Communities, Commission of the European Communities (1992), *Treaty on European Union*, Luxembourg: Office for Official Publications of the European Communities

Crispi, F. ([1855] 2001), *Dei diritti della Corona d'Inghilterra sulla Chiesa di Malta*, Roma: Montagnoli Editori

Cubeddu, S. (1993), *Sardisti. Viaggio nel Partito Sardo d'Azione tra cronaca e storia*, vol. 2, Sassari: Editrice Democratica Sarda

Cubeddu, S. (1999), 'I dirigenti della Sardegna moderna e gli appuntamenti della storia', in S. Cubeddu (ed.), *L'ora dei Sardi*, 323–38, Sassari: Edizioni Fondazione Sardinia

Cuppini, N. (2018), 'Paesaggio terracqueo: il Mediterraneo come spazio urbanizzato?', in D. Paci, P. Perri and F. Zantedeschi (eds.), *Paesaggi mediterranei. Storie, rappresentazioni, narrazioni*, 33–45, Roma: Aracne

Cuttitta, P. (2012), *Lo spettacolo del confine: Lampedusa tra produzione e messa in scena della frontiera*, Milano: Mimesis

Daftary, F. (2000), *Insular Autonomy: A Framework for Conflict Settlement? A Comparative Study of Corsica and The Åland Islands*, Flensburg: European Centre for Minority Issues

Dal Passo, F. (2007), *Il Mediterraneo dei lumi. Corsica e democrazia nella stagione delle rivoluzioni*, Napoli: Bibliopolis

Davies, N. (1997), *Europe: A History*, London: Pimlico Random House

de Angelo Laky, L., and E. Angliker (2021a), 'Questions of insularity in the ancient mediterranean', *Mare Nostrum* 12 (2): IX–XVI

de Angelo Laky, L., and E. Angliker (2021b), 'Mare Nostrum interview: Jonathan Pugh – The power of thinking with islands', *Mare Nostrum* 12 (2): 265–77

De Certeau, M. ([1980] 1984), *The Practice of Everyday Life*, vol. 1, Berkeley: University of California Press

De Bono, P. (1899), *Breve compendio della storia di Malta*, Malta: Stamperie del Governo

De Felice, R. (ed.) (1974), *La Carta del Carnaro nei testi di Alceste De Ambris e di Gabriele D'Annunzio*, Bologna: Il Mulino

De Montesquieu, Ch. L. ([1748] 1989), *The Spirit of the Laws*, Cambridge: Cambridge University Press

Debord, G. (1983), *La société du spectacle*, Paris: Champ libre

Debrune, J. (2001), 'Le Système de la Méditerranée de Michel Chevalier', *Confluences Méditerranée* 36 (1): 187–94

Del Piano, L. (1995), *Regionalismo e autonomismo in Sardegna e in Sicilia (1848–1914)*, Sassari: Edizioni Fondazione Sardinia

Del Piano, V. (1996), *Giacobini moderati e reazionari in Sardegna. Saggio di un dizionario biografico 1793–1812*, Cagliari: Edizioni Castello

DeLoughrey, E. (2001), '"The litany of islands, the rosary of archipelagoes": Caribbean and Pacific archipelagraphy', *ARIEL: A Review of International English Literature* 32 (1): 21–51

Dematteis, G. (2002), *Progetto implicito: il contributo della geografia umana alle scienze del territorio*, Milano: Franco Angeli

Depraetere, C. (1990–1991), 'Le phénomène insulaire à l'échelle du globe: tailles, hiérarchies et formes des îles océanes', *L'Espace Géographique* 2: 126–34

Depraetere, C. and A. L. Dahl (2007), 'Island locations and classifications', in G. Baldacchino (ed.), *A World of Islands*, 57-106, Charlottetown: Institute of Island Studies

Depraetere, C. (2008), 'The challenge of Nissology. A global outlook on the world archipelago. Part II: The global and scientific vocation of Nissology', *Island Studies Journal* 3 (1): 17-36

Deprest, F. (2002), 'L'invention géographique de la Méditerranée: éléments de réflexion', *L'Espace géographique* 31 (1): 73-92

Denier, J. (1919), *L'attribution des îles d'Åland*, Paris: Impr. Lahure

Diamond, J. (1997), *Guns, Germs, and Steel: The Fates of Human Societies*, New York: W. W. Norton & Company

Diamond, J., and J. A. Robinson (eds.) (2010), *Natural Experiments of History*, Cambridge, MA: Harvard University Press

Di Falco, S. (2003), *La cooperazione regionale in ambito UE: il caso della Corsica*, dissertation, Torino: Università degli studi di Torino

Di Gregorio, P. (1994), 'Nobiltà e nobilitazione in Sicilia nel lungo Ottocento', *Meridiana. Rivista di storia e scienze sociali* 19: 83-112

Di Tucci, R. (1922), *Manuale di storia della Sardegna*, Cagliari: Società Tipografica Sarda

Diegues, A. C. (1997), 'As ilhas e arquipélagos tropicais brasileiros: práticas sociais e simbólicas', in A. C. Diegues (ed.), *Ilhas e sociedades insulares*, 3-36, São Paulo: Nupaub

Diegues, A. C. (1998), *Ilhas e mares: simbolismo e imaginario*, São Paulo: Editora Hucitec NUPAUB

Dommen, E. (1980), 'Some distinguishing characteristics of island states', *World Development* 8 (12): 931-43

Dottelonde, P. (1984), *Histoire de la revendication corse 1959-1974*, PhD thesis, Paris: IEP de Paris

Drolet, M. (2015), 'A nineteenth-century Mediterranean union: Michel Chevalier's Système de la Méditerranée', *Mediterranean Historical Review* 30 (2): 147-68

Dühr S., C. Colomb, and V. Nadin (2010), *European Spatial Planning and Territorial Cooperation*, London-New York: Routledge

Eckstein, L., and A. Schwarz (2019), 'The making of Tupaia's map: A story of the extent and mastery of Polynesian navigation, competing systems of wayfinding on James Cook's endeavour, and the invention of an ingenious cartographic system', *The Journal of Pacific History* 54 (1): 1-95

Edquist, S., and J. Holmén (2012), 'Identities and history writing on islands in the Baltic Sea', in K. Topsø Larsen (ed.), *From One Island to Another - a Celebration of Island Connections*, 73-82, Nexø: CRT

Edquist, S. (2015), 'In the shadow of the Middle Ages? Tendencies in Gotland's history-writing, 1850-2010', in S. Edquist and J. Holmén (eds.), *Islands of Identity. History-Writing and Identity Formation in Five Island Regions in the Baltic Sea*, 39-142, Huddinge: Södertörn university

Edquist, S., and J. Holmén (2015), *Islands of Identity: History-Writing and Identity Formation in Five Island Regions in the Baltic Sea*, Stockholm: Sodertorn University

Eesti Kultuurfilm, 'Konstantin Päts Saaremaal (1939)', https://www.dailymotion.com/video/x2ooh0d (accessed 29 August 2021)

Eesti Saarte Kogu (2017), https://saared.ee/wp-content/uploads/2019/10/AEI-review-ENG.pdf (accessed 6 January 2022)

Elfving, J. (2017), 'Gotland: Sweden's crown jewel in the Baltic', *Eurasia Daily Monitor* 14, https://jamestown.org/program/gotland-swedens-crown-jewel-baltic/ (accessed 9 June 2021)

Eriksson, S., L. I. Johansson, and B. Sundback (1995), *The Åland Islands Demilitarized Region*, Mariehamn: Åland Islands Peace Institute

Eriksson, S., L. I. Johansson, and B. Sundback (2006), *Islands of Peace: Åland's Autonomy, Demilitarisation and Neutralization*, Mariehamn: Åland Islands Peace Institute

Erlanger, S. (2022), 'After 200 years of neutrality, Sweden weighs joining NATO', *The New York Times*, https://www.nytimes.com/2022/05/13/world/europe/sweden-finland-nato-putin.html (accessed 19 May 2022)

Escach, N. (2011), 'La "Nouvelle Hanse" de Björn Engholm a-t-elle vraiment été un échec?', *Eurostudia* 7 (1–2): 73–86

ESIN (2021), 'Origins and aims', https://europeansmallislands.com/origins-and-aims/ (accessed 6 January 2022)

ESPON (2013), 'The development of the Islands – European Islands and cohesion policy (EUROISLANDS)', https://www.espon.eu/sites/default/files/attachments/FinalReport_foreword_CU-16-11-2011.pdf (accessed 7 January 2022)

ESPON (2019), 'ESPON Bridges. Balanced regional development in areas with geographic specificities', https://www.espon.eu/sites/default/files/attachments/BRIDGES%20-%20Final%20Report.pdf (accessed 7 January 2022)

Estonian World (2021), 'Estonia remembers the Soviet deportations', https://estonianworld.com/life/estonia-remembers-the-soviet-deportations/ (accessed 29 August 2021)

Estonica. Encyclopedia about Estonia (1919), 'Saaremaa uprising', http://www.estonica.org/en/Saaremaa_Uprising/ (accessed 29 August 2021)

Estonica. Encyclopedia about Estonia (1941), 'Summer war (1941)', http://www.estonica.org/en/Summer_War_1941/ (accessed 29 August 2021)

Ettori, F. (1987), 'Peuple, nationalité, nation: pour une réévaluation de l'histoire de la Corse', *Peuples méditerranéens* 38–39: 5–30

EUR-Lex (2015), 'EU strategy for the Baltic Sea region', https://eur-lex.europa.eu/legal-content/EN/LSU/?uri=celex:52009DC0248 (accessed 6 January 2022)

European Commission (2019), 'The European green deal', https://eur-lex.europa.eu/legal-content/EN/TXT/?qid=1576150542719&uri=COM%3A2019%3A640%3AFIN (accessed 7 January 2022)

European Committee of the Regions (2020), 'We need a new EU strategy for Mediterranean islands to build higher resilience to health and environmental crises', https://cor.europa.eu/en/news/Pages/We-need-a-new-EU-strategy-for-Mediterranean-islands-to-build-higher-resilience-to-health-and-environmental-crises.aspx (accessed 7 January 2022)

The European Council (1988), 'Rhodes 2–3 December 1988', http://aei.pitt.edu/1483/1/rhodes_june_1988.pdf (accessed 2 October 2021)

European MSP Platform (2021), 'Baltic sea', https://maritime-spatial-planning.ec.europa.eu/sea-basins/baltic-sea-0 (accessed 5 January 2022)

European Parliament (2016), 'European parliament resolution of 4 February 2016 on the special situation of islands', https://www.europarl.europa.eu/doceo/document/TA-8-2016-0049_EN.html (accessed 7 January 2022)

European Union (2012), 'Consolidated version of the treaty on the functioning of the European Union', *Official Journal of the European Union*, https://eur-lex.europa.eu/LexUriServ/LexUriServ.do?uri=CELEX:12012E/TXT:en:PDF (accessed 21 October 2021)

European Union (2021), 'Sustainable blue economy - questions and answers', https://ec.europa.eu/commission/presscorner/detail/it/qanda_21_2346 (accessed 21 October 2021)

EUROSTAT (2018), 'Methodological manual on territorial typologies', https://ec.europa.eu/eurostat/documents/3859598/9507230/KS-GQ-18-008-EN-N.pdf (accessed 7 January 2022)

EUSBSR (2009), 'Action plan', https://www.balticsea-region-strategy.eu/action-plan?Task=document.viewdoc&id=17 (accessed 6 January 2022)

Fabei, S. (2007), *Carmelo Borg Pisani (1915–1942). Eroe o traditore?*, Bologna: Editrice Lo Scarabeo

Facineroso, A. (2013), *Il cavaliere errante. Pasquale Calvi tra rivoluzione ed esilio*, Acireale-Roma: Bonanno Editore

Falzon, M. A. (2012), 'Immigration, rituals and transitoriness in the Mediterranean island of Malta', *Journal of Ethnic and Migration Studies* 38 (10): 1661–80

Farinelli, M. A. (2017), 'Island societies and mainland nation-building in the Mediterranean: Sardinia and Corsica in Italian, French, and Catalan nationalism', *Island Studies Journal* 12 (1): 21–34

Faucci, R. (1972), 'Lotta di classe e crisi della classe dirigente in Sardegna', *Quaderni storici* 7 (19): 351–5

Fazi, A. (2009), *La recomposition territoriale du pouvoir: les régions insulaires de la Méditerranée occidentale*, Ajaccio: Albiana

Feldgrau, 'The naval war in the Baltic sea 1941–1945', https://www.feldgrau.com/WW2-German-Baltic-Sea-Naval-War/ (accessed 29 August 2021)

Feldmann, B. (2010), 'Garrisons towns in the Baltic Sea area', *Baltic Worlds*, 12 February 2010, http://balticworlds.com/wp-content/uploads/2010/02/27-29-%C3%B6ar.pdf (accessed 9 June 2021)

Feldmann, L. (1990), 'Saaremaa', *The Christian Science Monitor*, https://www.csmonitor.com/1990/0921/zsaar.html (accessed 29 August 2021)

Ferlazzo Ciano, G. (2018), *I discendenti dei felici. Il piccolo Risorgimento di Malta (1814–1880)*, Pisa: Pacini Editore

Ferretti, F. (2011), *L'Occident d'Elisée Reclus: l'invention de l'Europe dans la Nouvelle Géographie Universelle (1876–1894)*, thesis, Paris-Bologna: Paris la Sorbonne-University of Bologna

Fiorentini, B. (1966), *Malta rifugio di esuli e focolare ardente di cospirazione durante il Risorgimento italiano*, Malta: Ed. Casa S. Giuseppe

Fiorentini, B. (1982), 'Il giornalismo a Malta durante il Risorgimento italiano', in V. Bonello, B. Fiorentini and L. Schiavone (eds.), *Echi del Risorgimento a Malta*, 23–177, Milano: Cisalpino-Goliardica

Fogu, C. (2010), 'From Mare Nostrum to Mare Aliorum: Mediterranean theory and mediterraneism in contemporary Italian thought', *California Italian Studies Journal* 1 (1): 1–23

Fogu, C. (2020), *The Fishing Net and the Spider Web: Mediterranean Imaginaries and the Making of Italians*, London: Palgrave Macmillan

Fois, G. (2006), *Storia della Brigata Sassari*, Cagliari: Edizioni della Torre

Formosa, D. (2017), *The 1836 Austin and Lewis Commission. An Analytical Review of Private Correspondences and Reports*, Malta: University of Malta.

Foschi, A. D., X. Peraldi, and M. Rombaldi (2005), 'Inter-island links in Mediterranean Short Sea Shipping Networks', *Discussion Paper* 52: 1–27, http://www.ec.unipi.it/documents/Ricerca/papers/2005-52.pdf (accessed 18 October 2021)

'The fortification of the Åland islands' (1908), *The American Journal of International Law* 2: 397–8

Foxlee, N. (2010), *Albert Camus's 'The New Mediterranean Culture': A Text and Its Contexts*, Oxford: Peter Lang

Franceschi Leonardi, M. (2014), 'Paoli, Pasquale', *Dizionario Biografico degli Italiani* 81, https://www.treccani.it/enciclopedia/pasquale-paoli_%28Dizionario-Biografico%29/ (accessed 18 January 2021)

Franchetti, L. ([1876] 2011), *Condizioni politiche e amministrative della Sicilia*, Roma: Donzelli

Frasca, F. (2004), 'Malta isola fortezza nel Mediterraneo in età moderna', *Informazioni della difesa* 4: 44–54

Frascani, P. (2008), *Il mare*, Bologna: Il Mulino

The free dictionary by Farlex, 'Saaremaa Uprising of 1919', https://encyclopedia2.thefreedictionary.com/Saaremaa+Uprising+of+1919 (accessed 29 August 2021)

Frendo, H. (1989), *Malta's Quest for Independence. Reflections on the Cours of Maltese History*, Malta: Valletta Publishing

Friggieri, O. (1995), *Il-Kuxjenza Nazzjonali Maltija. Lejn definizzjoni Storika-Kulturali*, Malta: P.E.G

Fucito, L. (2020), 'Dossier del Servizio Studi sul riconoscimento degli svantaggi naturali derivanti dall'insularità (A.S. n. 865)', https://www.senato.it/service/PDF/PDFServer/BGT/01155127.pdf (accessed 13 February 2022)

Gabriele, N. (2003), 'L' «Imperfetta» fusione', *Studi Sardi* 33: 499–520

Gaja, F. (1962), *L'esercito della lupara*, Milano: AREA Editore

Gallia, A. (2012), 'La valorizzazione dei beni culturali e ambientali per lo sviluppo delle isole minori italiane', *Rivista giuridica del Mezzogiorno* 26 (4): 929–59

Ganci, M. ([1978] 1986), *La Nazione Siciliana*, Siracusa: Ediprint

Gerner, K. (2002), 'How to construct a Baltic history?', in W. Maciejewski (ed.), *The Baltic Sea Region: Cultures, Politics, Societies*, 50–4, Uppsala: The Baltic University Press

Giaccaria, P., and C. Minca (2010), 'The Mediterranean alternative', *Progress in Human Geography* 35 (3): 345–65

Giarrizzo, G. (1968), 'La Sicilia nel 1812. Una revisione in atto', *Archivio storico per la Sicilia orientale* 64 (1): 53–66

Giarrizzo, G. (1987), 'Introduzione', in M. Aymard and G. Giarrizzo (eds.), *La Sicilia*, XIX–LVII, Torino: Einaudi

Gillis, J. R. (2001), 'Places remote and islanded', *Michigan Quarterly Review* 40, https://quod.lib.umich.edu/cgi/t/text/textidx?cc=mqr;c=mqr;c=mqrarchive;idno=act2080.0040.107;g=mqrg;rgn=main;view=text;xc=1 (accessed 9 June 2021)

Glete, J. (2013), 'Naval power and control of the sea in the Baltic in the sixteenth century', in J. B Hattendorf and R. W. Unger (eds.), *War at Sea in the Middle Ages and the Renaissance*, 217–32, Cambridge: Cambridge University Press

Goethe, J. W. ([1816] 2013), *Viaggio in Italia*, Milano: Mondadori

Gotkowska, J., anch P. Szymański (2016), 'Gotland and Åland on the Baltic chessboard – Swedish and Finnish concerns', *Analyses*, https://www.osw.waw.pl/en/publikacje/analyses/2016-10-26/gotland-and-aland-baltic-chessboard-swedish-and-finnish-concerns (accessed 9 June 2021)

Gotlands Kommun (1994), *White Paper: Gotland in the Baltic Sea, in Sweden and in Europe*, Visby: Gotlands Kommun

Götz, N. (ed.) (2014), *The Sea of Identities. A Century of Baltic and East European Experiences with Nationality, Class and Gender*, Huddinge: Södertörns Högskola

Götz, N. (2016), 'Spatial politics & Fuzzy regionalism. The case of the Baltic Sea area', *Baltic Worlds* 9 (3–4): 55–67

Gramsci, A. ([1916] 2019), *La questione meridionale*, Raleigh: Aonia edizioni

Gras, P. (2013), *Le temps des ports. Déclin et renaissance des villes portuaires (1940–2010)*, Paris: Éditions Tallandier

Graumann, O., and S. Affeldt (2020), 'The Hanseatic league and education – A neglected chapter in European and German history', *International Dialogues on Education* 7 (1): 10–30

Graziani, A. M. (1997), *La Corse génoise: économie, société, culture; période moderne 1453–1768*, Ajaccio: Piazzola

Graziani, A. M. (2017), 'Sampiero di Bastelica', *Dizionario Biografico degli Italiani* 90, https://www.treccani.it/enciclopedia/sampiero-di-bastelica_(Dizionario-Biografico)/ (accessed 6 January 2021)

Gregory, C. N. (1923), 'The neutralization of the Åaland islands', *The American Journal of International Law* 17: 63–76

Grießner, D. B. (2012), 'The Åland islands and the construction of ålandishness', in K. Topsø Larsen (ed.), *From One Island to Another. A Celebration of Island Connections*, 85–93, Nexø: CRT

Grimaldi, A. (2016), 'L'insurrezione di Palermo del 1820. Aspetti politico-costituzionali', *Rivista di diritto e storia costituzionale* 1: 1–6

Grimaldi, A. (2017), 'La Costituzione siciliana del 1812', *Revista de derecho* 48: 208–33

Grimaldi, A. (2018), 'L'insurrezione siciliana del 1820. Aspetti politico-costituzionali', *Revista de estudios histórico-jurídicos* 40: 213–35

Grzechnik M. (2012), 'Making use of the past: The role of historians in the Baltic Sea region building', *Journal of Baltic Studies* 43 (3): 329–43

Grzechnik M., and H. Hurskainen (eds.) (2015), *Beyond the Sea. Reviewing the Manifold Dimensions of Water as Barrier and Bridge*, Köln-Weimar-Wien: Böhlau

Grzechnik M. (2016), 'Space of failed expectations? Building a Baltic Sea region after the end of the cold war', *Comparativ. Zeitschrift für Globalgeschichte und vergleichende Gesellschaftsforschung* 26 (5): 29–42

Grydehøj, A. (2017), 'Editorial. A future of island studies', *Island Studies Journal* 12 (1): 3–16

Guarracino, S. (2007), *Mediterraneo. Immagini, storie e teorie da Omero a Braudel*, Milano: Bruno Mondadori

Guida d'Italia (2002), *Sardegna*, Milano: Touring club italiano

Haase, D., and A. Maier (2021), *Islands of the European Union: State of Play and Future Challenges*, Brussels: European Parliament, Policy Department for Structural and Cohesion Policies

Hache, J. D. (1998), 'Towards a political approach to the island question', in G. Baldacchino and R. Greenwood (eds.), *Competing Strategies of Socio-Economic Development for Small Islands*, 31–68, Charlottetown: Institute of Island Studies

Hache, J. D. (ed.) (2000), *Quel statut pour les Îles d'Europe?*, Paris: L'Harmattan

Hägerhäll Aniansson, B. (1992), *Co-operation in the Baltic Sea Area: The Second Parliamentary Conference on Co-operation in the Baltic Sea Area; Report form a Conference Arranged by the Nordic Council at Stortinget, Oslo, Norway, 22–24 April 1992*, København: The Nordic Council

Hall, C. M. (2012), 'Island, islandness, vulnerability and resilience', *Tourism Recreation Research* 37 (2): 177–81

Hannikainen, L. A. (1994), 'The continued validity of the demilitarised and neutralised status of the Åland islands', *Zeitschrift für ausländisches öffentliches Rechtund Völkerrecht* 54: 614–51

Hay, P. (2006), 'A phenomenology of islands', *Island Studies Journal* 1 (1): 19–42

Hau'ofa, E. (1994), 'Our sea of islands', *The Contemporary Pacific* 6 (1): 147–61

Hayward, P. (2012), 'Aquapelagos and aquapelagic assemblages. Towards an integrated study of island societies and marine environments', *Shima: The International Journal of Research into Island Cultures* 6 (1): 1–11

Hegel, G. W. F. ([1837] 2001), *The Philosophy of History*, Kitchener: Batoche Books

Hepburrn, E. (2012), 'Recrafting sovereignty: Lessons from small island autonomies?', in M. G. Gagnon and M. Keating (eds.), *Political Autonomy and Divided Societies: Imagining Democratic Alternatives in Complex Settings*, 118–33, Basingstoke: Palgrave Macmillan

Hermanson, R. (1921), *La question des Îles d'Åland*, Helsinki: Imprimerie du governement

Herzfeld, M. (1984), 'The horns of the Mediterraneanist dilemma', *American Ethnologist* 11 (3): 439–54

Hobsbawm, E. J. ([1959] 1963), *Primitive Rebels, Studies in Archaic Forms of Social Movement in the 19th and 20th Centuries*, New York: Praeger

Holmén, J. (2014), 'A small separate fatherland of our own: Regional history writing and regional identity on islands in the Baltic Sea', *Island Studies Journal* 9: 135–54

Holmén, J. (2020), 'Time and space in time and space: Mapping the conceptual history of mental maps and historical consciousness', *Contributions to the History of Concepts* 15 (2): 105–29

Horden, N., and P. Purcell (2000), *The Corrupting Sea: A Study of Mediterranean History*, Hoboken: Wiley-Blackwell

Hull, G. (1993), *The Malta Language Question. A Case History in Cultural Imperialism*, Malta: Said International

Huntington, S. P. (1996), *The Clash of Civilizations and the Remaking of World Order*, New York: Simon & Schuster

I documenti diplomatici italiani, Quinta serie: 1914–1918 (1916a), vol. 5 (24 October 1915–17 June 1916), n. 704, Roma: Istituto poligrafico dello Stato, Libreria dello Stato

I documenti diplomatici italiani, Quinta serie: 1914–1918 (1916b), vol. 5 (24 October 1915–17 June 1916), n. 770, Roma: Istituto poligrafico dello Stato, Libreria dello Stato

I documenti diplomatici italiani, Sesta serie: 1918–1922 (1919), vol. 1 (4 November 1918–17 January 1919), n. 751, Rome: Istituto poligrafico dello Stato, Libreria dello Stato

Iachello, E. (2018), 'Giuseppe Giarrizzo, politico e storico. Una conversazione in Sicilia', *Studi Storici* 3: 611–39

Ibba, R. (2019), 'Abitare la Sardegna rurale nella lunga età moderna', in L. Boi, A. Cannas and L. Vargiu (eds.), *Abitare. Approcci interdisciplinari e nuove prospettive*, 65–81, Cagliari: UNICApress

Il Programma Italia-Francia Marittimo, http://interreg-maritime.eu/programma (accessed 16 February 2021)

Isabella, M. (2009), *Risorgimento in Exile. Italian Émigrés and the Liberal International in the Post-Napoleonic Era*, Oxford-New York: Oxford University Press

Isabella, M. and K. Zanou (eds.) (2016), *Mediterranean Diasporas. Politics and Ideas in the Long 19th Century*, London-New Delhi-New York-Sydney: Bloomsbury

Isin, E. F., and G. M. Nielsen (ed.) (2008), *Acts of Citizenship*, London: Zed Books

Ivetic, E. (2019), *Storia dell'Adriatico. Un mare e la sua civiltà*, Bologna: Il Mulino

Jackson, R. E. (2008), *Islands on the Edge: Exploring Islandness and Development in Four Australian Case Studies*, PhD thesis, Tasmania: University of Tasmania

Johansson, L. I. (1984), 'The autonomy of Åland – basis of a flourishing society', in M. Isaksson and L. I. Johansson (eds.), *The Åland Islands: Autonomous Demilitarized Region*, 20–39, Mariehamn: Åland Islands Peace Institute

Joenniemi, P. (2014), 'The Åland islands: Neither local nor fully sovereign', *Cooperation and Conflict* 49: 80–97

Jussila, O., S. Hentilä, and J. Nevakivi (2004), *Storia politica della Finlandia 1809–2003*, Milano: Guerini e Associati

Kettunen, P. (2006), 'Le modèle nordique et le consensus sur la compétitivité en Finlande', *Revue internationale de politique comparée* 13 (3): 447–67

Ķibilds, M. (2018), 'Ruhnu rumpus: How the tiny Baltic island came under Estonian control', *Public Broadcasting of Latvia*, https://eng.lsm.lv/article/culture/history/ruhnu-rumpus-how-the-tiny-baltic-island-came-under-estonian-control.a279652/ (accessed 7 August 2021)

Kirby, D. (1995), *The Baltic World 1772–1993. Europe's Northern Periphery in an Age of Change*, London: Routledge

Klinge, M. (1994a), *Breve storia della Finlandia*, Helsinki: Otava

Klinge, M. (1994b), *The Baltic World*, Helsinki: Otava

Koselleck, R. ([1979] 2004), *Futures Past: On the Semantics of Historical Time*, New York: Columbia University Press

Kranking, G. E. (2009), *Island People: Transnational Identification, Minority Politics, and Estonia's Swedish Population*, dissertation, Columbus: The Ohio State University

Kreem, J. (2011), 'Seasonal isolation in the communication in Livonia', in T. Jørgensen and G. Jaritz (eds.), *Isolated Islands in Medieval Nature, Culture and Mind*, 120–7, Budapest-New York: Central European University Press

Kuldkepp, M. (2015), 'Hegemony and liberation in World War I: The plans for new Mare Nostrum Balticum', *Ajalooline Ajakiri* 3 (153): 249–86

Kurunmäki, J. (2016), 'Challenges of transnational regional democracy: Baltic Sea Parliamentary Conference, 1991–2015', *Comparativ. Zeitschrift für Globalgeschichte und vergleichende Gesellschaftsforschung* 26 (5): 43–57

L'Unione Sarda (2016), 'Ue, approvata la risoluzione Cicu sull'insularità: "Un voto storico per Sardegna e Sicilia"', *L'Unione Sarda.it*, https://www.unionesarda.it/politica/ue-approvata-la-risoluzione-cicu-sull-insularita-un-voto-storico-per-sardegna-e-sicilia-ygx0u2xc (accessed 18 October 2021)

La Manna, F. (2020), 'Soggetti e contesto. Nobili, notabili e dimensione urbana nella Sicilia del 1848', *Studi Storici* 61 (3): 681–707

La Repubblica (2018), 'Berlusconi: "Ponte sullo Stretto e casinò, serve un piano Marshall per la Sicilia"', *la Repubblica*, https://palermo.repubblica.it/politica/2018/02/20/news/berlusconi_ponte_sullo_stretto_e_casino_serve_un_piano_marshall_per_la_sicilia_-189304135/ (accessed 18 October 2021)

Lando, F. (2012), 'La geografia umanista: un'interpretazione', *Rivista Geografica Italiana*, 119: 259–89

Le Goff, J. (1988), *Histoire et mémoire*, Paris: Gallimard

Lefebvre, H. (1991), *The Production of Space*, Oxford: Blackwell
Lemaire, L. (2014), 'Islands and a carceral environment. Maltese policy in terms of irregular migration', *Journal of Immigrant and Refugee Studies* 12 (2): 143–60
Léouzon Le Duc, L. A. (1854), *Les Îles d'Åland avec une carte et deux gravures*, Paris: Hachette
Licata, G. (1965), 'Le origini del fascismo in Sicilia', *Vita e Pensiero* 39 (1–2): 164–71
Lindberg, F. A. (1961), 'La Baltique dans l'historiographie scandinave, problèmes et perspectives', *Annales. Economies, Sociétés, Civilizations* 16: 425–40
Loel, R. (2008), 'Esimese Eesti presidendi ametlik visiit Saare maakonda', *Saarte Hääl*, https://arhiiv.saartehaal.ee/2008/02/23/esimese-eesti-presidendi-ametlik-visiit-saare-maakonda/ (accessed 29 August 2021)
Loi, A. (2006), *Sardegna: geografia di una società*, Cagliari: AV
Lott, A. (2018), *The Estonian Strait: Exceptions to the Strait Regime of Innocent or Transit Passage*, Leiden: Brill Nijhoff
Lundberg, D., K. Malm, and O. Ronström (2003), *Music Media Multiculture. Changing Musicscapes*, Stockholm: Svenskt visarkiv
Lupo, S. (1977), 'La questione siciliana a una svolta. Il sicilianismo fra fascismo e dopoguerra', in G. Barone et al. (eds.), *Potere e società in Sicilia nella crisi dello Stato liberale*, 151–222, Catania: Pellicanolibri
Lupo, S. (1981), *Blocco agrario e crisi in Sicilia tra le due guerre*, Napoli: Guida
Lupo, S., and R. Mangiameli (1983), 'La modernizzazione difficile: blocchi corporativi e conflitto di classe in una società "arretrata"', in L. Avagliano et al. (eds.), *La modernizzazione difficile. Città e campagne nel Mezzogiorno dall'età giolittiana al fascismo*, 217–62, Bari: De Donato
Lupo, S., and R. Mangiameli (1990), 'Mafia di ieri, mafia di oggi', *Meridiana. Rivista di storia e scienze sociali* 7–8: 17–44.
Lupo, S. (1993), *Storia della mafia: dalle origini ai giorni nostri*, Roma: Donzelli.
Lupo, S. (2015), *La questione. Come liberare la storia del Mezzogiorno dagli stereotipi*, Roma: Donzelli.
Lussana, F. (2006), 'Gramsci e la Sardegna. Socialismo e socialsardismo dagli anni giovanili alla grande guerra', *Studi Storici* 47 (3): 609–35
Madau Diaz, G. (1979), *Un Capo Carismatico. Giovanni Maria Angioy*, Cagliari: Ettore Gasperini Editore
Malkin, I. (2013), *A Small Greek World: Networks in the Ancient Mediterranean*, Oxford: Oxford University Press
Malmros, P., and M. Hallberg (2012), 'A short history of the world heritage site of Visby', in H. Martinsson-Wallin and A. Karlström (eds.), *World Heritage and Identity: Three Worlds Meet*, 49–58, Visby: Gotland University Press
Mangiameli, R. (1980), 'Separatismo e autonomismo in Sicilia fra politica e storiografia', *Italia contemporanea*, 141: 89–98
Mangiameli, R. (1987), 'La regione in guerra (1943–50)', in M. Aymard and G. Giarrizzo (eds.), *La Sicilia*, 485–600, Torino: Einaudi

Mangiameli, R. (2000), *La mafia tra stereotipo e storia*, Caltanissetta-Roma: Sciascia

Mangiameli, R. (2020), '1943. La ri-scoperta della Sicilia', in G. Barone (ed.), *Storia mondiale della Sicilia*, 435–39, Roma-Bari: Laterza

Manno, G. (1842), *Storia moderna della Sardegna da 1773 al 1799*, Torino: Fratelli Favale

Mantovani, M. L. (2021), 'DDL insularità, approvato al Senato. La dichiarazione di voto del M5S', https://www.marialauramantovani.it/2021/11/03/ddl-insularita-approvato-al-senato-la-dichiarazione-di-voto-del-m5s/ (accessed 13 Febraury 2022)

Marimoutou, J. C. and J. M. Racault (eds.) (1995), *L'insularité: thematique et representations*, Paris: Harmattan

Marino, G. C. (1971), *L'ideologia sicilianista: dall'età dei lumi al Risorgimento*, Palermo: Flaccovio

Marino, G. C. (1979), *Storia del separatismo siciliano: 1943–1947*, Roma: Editori riuniti

Martinetti, J. (2007), 'Les tourments du tourisme sur l'île de Beauté', *Hérodote* 127 (4): 29–46

Martinetti, J. (2014), 'Quel rôle aujourd'hui pour les grandes îles en Méditerranée? Une géopolitique «comparée» de l'insularité méditerranéenne', *Cahiers de la Méditerranée* 89, https://journals.openedition.org/cdlm/7752#bodyftn23 (accessed 6 January 2022)

Martini, P. (1852), *Storia di Sardegna dall'anno 1799 al 1816*, Cagliari: Tipografia di A. Timon

Mattone, A., and P. Sanna (2007), *Settecento sardo e cultura europea. Lumi, società, istituzioni nella crisi dell'antico regime*, Milano: Franco Angeli

Matvejević, P. ([1987] 1991), *Breviario Mediterraneo*, Milano: Garzanti

Matvejević, P. (1998), *Il Mediterraneo e l'Europa*, Milano: Garzanti

McAlinden, T. (2007), 'Estonian-Swedes embrace cultural autonomy rights', *Network Europe*, https://web.archive.org/web/20070306165348/http://networkeurope.radio.cz/feature/estonian-swedes-embrace-cultural-autonomy-rights (accessed 7 August 2021)

McCall, G. (1994), 'Nissology: A proposal for consideration', *Journal of the Pacific Society* 17 (2–3): 1–14

Meistersheim, A. (1988), 'Insularité, insularisme, îléité, quelques concepts opératoires', *Cahiers de l'institut de développement des îles méditerranéennes* 1: 96–120

Mertelsmann, O. (2016), *The Baltic States under Stalinist Rule*, Köln: Böhlau Verlag

Meyer, P. (2013), *Histoire d'une mer d'ambre*, Paris: Perrin

Miccichè, A. (2019), 'Tra autonomismo e Stato democratico: i linguaggi repubblicani in Sicilia (1944–1947)', *Diacronie. Studi di storia contemporanea* 40 (4): 1–18

Michel, E. (1932), 'Gaffori, Giovan Pietro', *Enciclopedia Italiana*, https://www.treccani.it/enciclopedia/giovan-pietro-gaffori_%28Enciclopedia-Italiana%29/ (accessed 10 January 2021)

Michel, E. (1937), 'Teodoro re di Corsica', *Enciclopedia Italiana*, https://www.treccani.it/enciclopedia/teodoro-re-di-corsica_%28Enciclopedia-Italiana%29/ (accessed 8 January 2021)

Michel, E. (1948), 'Esuli italiani a Malta nel 1848', *Nuova Rivista Storica* 32 (6): 232–62

Migliorini, E. (1930), 'Bellingshausen, Fabian Gottlieb von', *Enciclopedia Italiana*, https://www.treccani.it/enciclopedia/fabian-gottlieb-von-bellingshausen_%28Enciclopedia-Italiana%29/ (accessed 29 August 2021)

Mikaberidze, A. (2005), *The Russian Officer Corps in the Revolutionary and Napoleonic Wars: 1792–1815*, Staplehurst: Spellmount

Minca, C. (1994), 'Le isole tropicali: luoghi reali o luoghi-immagine?', in Laboratoire d'Ethnologie (ed.), *Le tourisme international entre traditions et modernité: actes du colloque international, Nice, 19–21 novembre 1992*, 383–8, Nice: Université de Nice Sophia-Antipolis

Minca, C. (1996), *Spazi effimeri: geografia e turismo tra moderno e postmoderno*, Padova: CEDAM

Mirwaldt, K., I. McMaster, and J. Bachtler (2010), 'The concept of macro-regions: Practice and prospects', *Discussion Paper*, http://eu.baltic.net/The%20Concept%20of%20Macro-Regions%20Practice%20and%20Prospects_Background_Paper.pdf, (accessed 6 October 2021)

MIS (1946), 'La beffa dell'autonomia', *Trinacria*

Mitropoulou, A., and I. Spilanis (2020), 'From insularity to islandness: The use of place branding to achieve sustainable island tourism', *International Journal of Islands Research* 1 (1): 31–41

Moles, A. A., and E. Rohmer, (1978), *Psychosociologie de l'espace*, Paris: Casterman

Moles, A. A. (1982), 'Nissonologie ou sciences des îles', *L'Espace géographique* 11 (4): 281–9

Monina, G. (2008), *La Grande Italia marittima. La propaganda navalista e la lega navale italiana 1866–1918*, Soveria Mannelli: Rubbettino

Monmonier, M. (2018), *How to Lie with Maps*, Chicago: University of Chicago Press

Moro, A. (1964), 'Storico Messaggio di amicizia di Aldo Moro alla Nazione Maltese in occasione dell'indipendenza di Malta', *Ambasciata d'Italia La Valletta*, https://amblavalletta.esteri.it/ambasciata_lavalletta/it/ambasciata/news/dall_ambasciata/2009/07/messaggio-aldo-moro.html (accessed 6 May 2021)

Mudge, R. (2022), 'Sweden's Gotland gets ready for anything amid rising Russian threats', *Deutsche Welle*, https://www.dw.com/en/swedens-gotland-gets-ready-for-anything-amid-rising-russian-threats/a-60620892 (accessed 12 February 2022)

Mudimbe, V. Y. (2007), *L'invenzione dell'Africa*, Roma: Meltemi

Myrberg, N. (2009), 'An island in the middle of an island. On cult, laws and authority in Viking age Gotland', in E. Regner, C. von Heijne, L. Kitzler Åhfeldt, and A. Kjellström (eds.), *From Ephesos to Dalecarlia. Reflections on Body, Space and Time in Medieval and Early Modern Europe*, 101–277, Stockholm: The Museum of National Antiquities

Nadarajah, Y., and A. Grydehøj (2016), 'Island studies as a decolonial project', *Island Studies Journal* 11 (2): 437–46

Nasone, A. (2014), 'La guerra come strumento di emancipazione di un popolo. Il caso del Sardismo', *Politics* 2 (2): 71–88

Newspaper Index, http://homepages.gac.edu/~kranking/Aiboland/Newspaper/NewspaperIndex.html (accessed 23 July 2021)

Nordic Co-operation (2007), 'Ålandsdokumentet', https://www.norden.org/en/node/4826 (accessed 5 January 2022)

Norman J., N. J. Padelford, and K. G. A. Andersson (1939), 'The Aaland islands question', *The American Journal of International Law* 33: 465–87

North, M. (2015), *The Baltic: A History*, Cambridge, MA: Harvard University Press

Novacco, N. (2005), 'Intervista al dott. Nino Novacco', *Rivista economica del Mezzogiorno* 19 (2–3): 549–73

Office of the Historian, 'Press release issued by the department of state on July 23, 1940', https://history.state.gov/historicaldocuments/frus1940v01/d412 (accessed 29 August 2021)

Ojalo, H. (2019), 'Saaremaa metsavennad 1941. aasta Suvesõjas', https://forte.delfi.ee/artikkel/86508751/katkend-raamatust-saaremaa-metsavennad-1941-aasta-suvesojas (accessed 29 August 2021)

Olausson, M. (2007), *Autonomy and Islands. A Global Study of the Factors That Determine Island Autonomy*, Åbo: ÅboAkademisFörlag

Olivesi C. (1995), 'La Corse et la construction européenne', *Annuaire des collectivités locales* 15 (1): 55–65

Olsson, J., and J. Aström (2004), 'Régionalisation et régionalisme en Suède', *Annuaire des collectivités locales* 24: 335–52

Orioles, V. (2010), 'Tra sicilianità e similitudine', *Linguistica* 49: 227–34

Paci, D. (2010), 'L'archivio della Natio Còrsa. Petru Giovacchini e i Gruppi di Cultura Còrsa', *Etudes corses* 71: 89–119

Paci, D. and F. Pietrancosta (2010), 'Il separatismo siciliano (1943–1947)', *Diacronie. Studi di storia contemporanea* 3 (2): 1–27

Paci, D. (2011), '"Proudhon in esilio". La ricezione del pensiero proudhoniano negli ambienti del fuoruscitismo italiano in Francia (anni venti e trenta)', *Società e Storia* 131: 104–31

Paci, D. (2012), 'Le dialogue des élites méditerranéennes à travers les médias au XIXe siècle: le cas de Malte et de la Corse', *Cahiers de la Méditerranée* 85: 11–30

Paci, D. (2014a), 'Is history the strongest weapon? Corsica in the Fascist mare nostrum', *Journal of Modern Italian Studies* 19 (5): 625–40

Paci, D. (2014b), 'Francesco Guerri e il movimento irredentista còrso in Italia', *Etudes corses* 78: 149–65.

Paci, D. (2014c), '«Lingua di Dante, fede di Roma». La battaglia per l'italianità a Malta tra le due guerre', *Contemporanea* 17: 551–76.

Paci, D. (2015a), *Corsica fatal, Malta baluardo di romanità. L'irredentismo fascista nel mare nostrum (1922–1942)*, Firenze-Milano: Le Monnier-Mondadori

Paci, D. (2015b), Interview with Barbro Sundback. Personal interview. Marienham, 28 October 2015.

Paci, D. (2016a), *L'arcipelago della pace. Le isole Åland e il Baltico (XIX-XXI sec.)*, Milano: Unicopli

Paci, D. (2016b), 'From isolation to connectivity? The views of the European Union on Mediterranean and Baltic islands in the 20th and 21th century', *Comparativ. Zeitschrift für Globalgeschichte und vergleichende Gesellschaftsforschung* 26 (5): 14–28

Paci, D. (2018), 'La région baltique et ses îles: un modèle régional de cooperation', *Revista História: Debates E Tendências* 18 (2): 194–203

Paci, D., P. Perri, and F. Zantedeschi (2018), 'Introduzione', in D. Paci, P. Perri and F. Zantedeschi (eds.), *Paesaggi mediterranei. Storie, rappresentazioni, narrazioni*, 9–14, Roma: Aracne

Paci, D. (2021), 'Pianificazione territoriale, turismo ed ecoturismo nell'Île de Beauté. Immagini, politiche e pratiche', in D. Paci and F. L. Cavallo (eds.), *Il tesoro dell'isola. Ecoturismo e insularità in Europa*, 91–111, Milano: Unicopli

Palamenghi Crispi, G. (2009), 'Crispi nella tradizione familiare', in A. G. Ricci and L. Montevecchi (eds.), *Francesco Crispi. Costruire lo Stato per dare forma alla Nazione*, 379–82, Roma: Ministero per i beni e le attività culturali Direzione generale per gli archivi

Paniga, M. (2017), *Mario Berlinguer: Avvocato, magistrato e politico nell'Italia del Novecento*, Milano: Franco Angeli

Papa, E. (1996), 'Meridionalismo e insularità negli scrittori siciliani contemporanei', *Belfagor* 51 (5): 582–7

Partito repubblicano siciliano (1945), 'Autonomia-Separatismo', *Sicilia Repubblicana*

Peel, C. (2009), *Guta Lag. The Law of the Gotlanders*, London: Viking Society for Norther Research-University College London

Pellegrinetti, J. P. (2003), 'Langue et identité: l'exemple du corse durant la troisième république', Cahiers de la Méditerranée', *Cahiers de la Méditerranée* 66: 1–11, http://journals.openedition.org/cdlm/116 (accessed 19 February 2021)

Pellegrinetti, J. P., and A. Rovere (2004), *La Corse et la République. La vie politique de la XXIe du Second Empire au début du XXIe siècle*, Paris: Le Seuil

Peresso, G. (2013), 'The establishment of broadcasting in Malta', *Arkivju* 2: 1–7

Peresso, G. (2015), *Giuseppe Donati and Umberto Calosso. Two Italian Anti-fascist Refugees in Malta*, Malta: SKS

Péron, F. (1993), *Des îles et des hommes*, Rennes: Édition de la Cité/Ouest

Perotti, S. (2017), *Atlante delle isole del Mediterraneo. Storie, navigazioni, arcipelaghi di uno scrittore marinaio*, Milano: Bompiani

Perrin, T. (2021), 'De l'Arc méditerranéen à la Méditerranée occidentale: vers une macro-région?', *Méditerranée. Revue géographique des pays méditerranéens* 132, https://journals.openedition.org/mediterranee/12224 (accessed 6 January 2022)

Petri, R. (2005), 'Gerarchie culturali e confini nazionali. Sulla legittimazione delle frontiere nell'Europa dei secoli XIX e XX', in S. Salvatici (ed.), *Confini. Costruzione, attraversamenti, rappresentazioni*, 79–99, Soveria Mannelli: Rubettino

Petri, R. (2016a), 'Region building around the Baltic Sea, 1989-2016: Expectations and disenchantment', *Comparativ. Zeitschrift für Globalgeschichte und vergleichende Gesellschaftsforschung* 26 (5): 7-13

Petri, R. (2016b), 'The Mediterranean metaphor in early geopolitical writings', *History* 101 (348): 671-91

Petrogiannis, V. (2020), *European Mobility and Spatial Belongings. Greek and Latvian Migrants in Sweden*, Huddinge: Södertörns högskola

Petrusewicz, M. (2018), 'Il Mediterraneo dopo Braudel: quale nuova storiografia?', in D. Paci, P. Perri, and F. Zantedeschi (eds.), *Paesaggi mediterranei. Storie, rappresentazioni, narrazioni*, 15-30, Roma: Aracne

Pirandello, L. ([1913] 1918), *I vecchi e I giovani*, Milano: Treves

Pirenne, H. (1937), *Mahomet et Charlemagne*, Paris: PUF

Podestà, A. (1940), 'Alle fonti della storia nordica', *Sapere* 6, http://www.viagginellastoria.it/archeoletture/archeologia/1940nordica.htm (accessed 8 June 2021)

Pomponi, F. (1977), 'Le régionalisme en Corse dans l'entre-deux-guerres (1919-1939)', in C. Gras and G. Livet (eds.), *Régios et régionalisme en France du XVIIIème siècle à nous jours*, 393-415, Paris: PUF

Pontieri, E. (1935), 'Carlo Felice al governo della Sardegna (1799-1806)', *Archivio Storico Italiano* 93 (356): 187-231

Popovici, J. (1923), *La question îles d'Åland*, Paris: Librairie Le François

Prodi, R. (2002), 'Europe and the Mediterranean: Time for action', https://ec.europa.eu/commission/presscorner/detail/en/SPEECH_02_589 (accessed 6 January 2022)

Public broadcasting of Latvia (2020), 'Documentary examines the curious fate of Ruhnu island', https://eng.lsm.lv/article/features/video/documentary-examines-the-curious-fate-of-ruhnu-island.a361465/ (accessed 7 August 2021)

Pugh, J. (2013), 'Island movements: Thinking with the Archipelago', *Island Studies Journal* 8 (1): 9-24

Pugh, J., and D. Chandler (2021), *Anthropocene Islands: Entangled Worlds*, London: University of Westminster Press

Pulvirenti, C. M. (2013), *Biografia di una rivoluzione. Nicola Fabrizi, l'esilio e la costruzione dello stato italiano*, Acireale: Bonanno Editore

Pulvirenti, C. M. (2014), 'La rivoluzione immaginata. Gli esuli a Malta e l'iniziativa meridionale per il Risorgimento italiano', *Meridiana* 81: 169-88

Quammen, D. (2012), *The Song of the Dodo: Island Biogeography in an Age of Extinctions*, New York: Random House

Quartararo, M. R. (1980), *Roma tra Londra e Berlino. La politica estera fascista dal 1930 al 1940*, Roma: Bonacci

Raadik Cottrell, J., and S. P. Cottrell (2020), 'In spaces in between–From recollections to nostalgia: Discourses of bridge and island place', *Island Studies Journal* 15 (2): 273-90

Ratka, E. (2010), 'La politique méditerranéenne de Nicolas Sarkozy: une vision française de la civilisation et du leadership', *L'Europe en Formation* 356 (2): 35–51

Ratter, B. M. W. (2018), *Geography of Small Islands. Outposts of Globalisation*, Cham: Springer

Raukas, A. (2009), *Geotourism Highlights of the Saaremaa and Hiiumaa Islands*, Tallinn: GEOGuide Baltoscandia

Ravis-Giordani, G. (2003), 'La Corse: culture régionale? Culture régionalisée?', *Ethnologie française* 33 (3): 451–8, https://www.cairn.info/revue-ethnologie-francaise-2003-3-page-451.htm (accessed 19 February 2021)

Rebas, H. (2012), 'Frustration and revenge? Gotland strikes back – during the long 15th Century, 1390's–1525', in M. F. Scholz, R. Bohn and C. Johansson (eds.), *The Image of the Baltic a Festschrift for Nils Blomkvist*, 229–54, Visby: Gotland University Press

Regione Autonoma della Sardegna (1993), 'Legge Regionale 14 settembre 1993, n. 44 Istituzione della giornata del popolo sardo "Sa Die de sa Sardinia"', *Regione Autonoma della Sardegna*, http://www.regione.sardegna.it/j/v/86?v=9&c=72&s=1&file=1993044 (accessed 24 December 2020)

Regione Siciliana (2021), 'Stima dei costi dell'insularità per la Sicilia', http://pti.regione.sicilia.it/portal/pls/portal/docs/152986797.PDF (accessed 13 February 2022)

Renda, F. (1987), 'La «questione sociale» e i Fasci (1874–94)', in M. Aymard and G. Giarrizzo (eds.), *La Sicilia*, 159–88, Torino: Einaudi

Republic of Estonia. Ministry of Foreign Affairs (2020), 'Tartu Peace Treaty 2 February 1920', https://vm.ee/en/tartu-peace-treaty-2-february-1920 (accessed 29 August 2021)

Ricci, A. G. (2009), 'Presentazione', in A. G. Ricci and L. Montevecchi (eds.), *Francesco Crispi. Costruire lo Stato per dare forma alla Nazione*, V–XII, Roma: Ministero per i beni e le attività culturali Direzione generale per gli archivi

Richards, J. (1982), 'Politics in small independent communities: Conflict or consensus?', *Journal of Commonwealth & Comparative Politics* 20 (2): 155–71

Ricoeur, P. (1986), *Du texte à l'action. Essais d'herméneutique II*, Paris: Éditions du Seuil

Ricotti, C. R. (2005), *Il costituzionalismo britannico nel mediterraneo (1794–1818)*, Milano: Giuffrè

Romeo, R. (1961), 'Amari, Michele', in Istituto dell'Enciclopedia italiana (ed.), *Dizionario Biografico degli Italiani*, 637–54, Roma: Istituto dell'Enciclopedia italiana

Rönnby, J. (2007), 'Maritime durées: Long-term structures in a coastal landscape', *Journal of Maritime Archaeology* 2 (2): 65–82

Ronström, O. (2005), 'Memories, tradition, heritage', in O. Ronström and U. Palmenfelt (eds.), *Memories and Visions. Studies in Folk Culture IV*, 1–15, Tartu: University of Tartu http://owe.ompom.se/pdf/106-Memories_tradition_heritage.pdf (accessed 8 June 2021)

Ronström, O. (2008), '"KUBB" Local identity and global connectedness in a Gotland parish', Refereed papers from the 4th International Small Island Cultures Conference the Turku archipelago, June 17th -20th 2008, https://sicri-network.org/ISIC4/g.%20ISIC4P%20Ronstrom.pdf (accessed 8 June 2021)

Rose-Redwood, R., N. Blu Barnd, A. H. E. Lucchesi, S. Dias and W. Patrick (2020), 'Decolonizing the map: Recentering Indigenous mappings', *Cartographica: The International Journal for Geographic Information and Geovisualization* 55 (3): 151–62

Rotkirch, H. (1986), 'The demilitarization and neutralization of the Åland islands: A regime "in European Interests" withstanding changing circumstances', *Journal of Peace Research* 23: 357–76

Rotondo, B. M. (2014), 'La Brigata Sassari nella storia del Sardismo', *Humanities* 3 (5): 56–81

Royle, S. A., and D. Scott (1996), 'Accessibility and the Irish islands', *Geography: Journal of the Geographical Association* 81 (2): 111–20

Royle, S. A. (2001), *A Geography of Islands: Small Island Insularity*, London-New York: Routledge

Rudas, N. (1999), 'L'interazione arcana. Alla radice della creatività dei sardi', in S. Cubeddu (ed.), *L'ora dei Sardi*, 255–91, Sassari: Edizioni Fondazione Sardinia

Rudling, A. (2006), 'Jörgen Hedman, Lars Åhlander. Runö: Historien om svenskön i Rigabukten [Runö: The History of the Swedish Island in the Bay of Riga]', *Scandinavian-Canadian Studies / Études scandinaves au Canada*, https://scancan.net/rudling_1_16.htm (accessed 22 July 2021)

Rudolf, U. J. (2018), *Historical Dictionary of Malta*, London: Rowman & Littlefield

Rumford, C. (2008), *Citizens and Borderwork in Contemporary Europe*, London: Routledge

Saaremaa Turism (2021), *Saaremaa. Journey Plans*, Saaremaa Turism

Said, W. E. (1978), *Orientalism*, London: Penguin

Salice, G. (2011), *Dal villaggio alla nazione. La costruzione delle borghesie in Sardegna*, Cagliari: AM&D

Salice, G. (2012), 'L'invenzione della frontiera. Isole, Stato e colonizzazione nel Mediterraneo del Settecento', *Ammentu* 2: 93–113

Salice, G. (2015a), *Colonizzazione sabauda e diaspora greca*, Viterbo: Sette Città

Salice, G. (2015b), 'The Greek mirror: Philhellenism and southern Italian patriotisms (1750–1861)', *Journal of Modern Italian Studies* 20 (4): 491–507

Salice, G. (2016), 'La rivoluzione immaginata. Lo sguardo britannico sulla "sarda rivoluzione" (1793–1796)', in P. Carta, F. Falchi and G. Salice (eds.), *Sardinia. Un'isola nell'immaginario anglo-americano*, 9–30, Napoli: Edizione Scientifica

Salice, G. (2020), '28 aprile "Die de Sa Sardigna". Una rilettura', *Storia Digitale UniCA Il portale della Storia Digitale dell'Università degli Studi di Cagliari*, https://storia.dh.unica.it/2020/04/28/28-aprile-1794-sa-die-de-sa-sardigna/ (accessed 1 February 2021)

Salsano, R. (2019), 'La dimensione cronotopica della Sicilia nell'immaginario di Pirandello', *Verbis* 1: 137–45

Sander, G. F. (2022), 'Finland's foreign minister on why Helsinki is moving toward NATO now', *Foreign Policy*, https://foreignpolicy.com/2022/05/07/finland-nato-foreign-minister-haavisto/ (accessed 19 May 2022)

Sanguin, A. L. (1997) (ed.), *Vivre dans une île. Une géopolitique des insularités*, Paris: L'Harmattan,

Sanguin, A. L. (2007), 'Périphéricité et ultra périphéricité insulaires dans l'Union européenne', *L'Espace politique* 2 (2): 1–23

Sardiniapost (2019), 'Le isole del Mediterraneo si alleano. Solinas: "Rivendichiamo i nostri diritti"', *Sardiniapost,* https://www.sardiniapost.it/politica/alleanza-per-le-isole-del-mediterraneo-solinas-rivendichiamo-i-nostri-diritti/ (accessed 13 February 2022)

Sardiniapost (2020), 'Sardegna e Sicilia, battaglia in Europa. Fronte unico su trasporti e insularità', *Sardiniapost*, https://www.sardiniapost.it/politica/sardegna-e-sicilia-battaglia-in-europa-fronte-unico-su-trasporti-e-insularita/ (accessed 13 February 2022)

Savelli, A. (1943), *Storia di Malta. Dai primordi ai giorni nostri*, Milano: ISPI

Schaub, M. K. (2020), *Natural and Cultural Heritage in Tourism on Gotland Heritage Tourism Characteristics and the Relation of Natural and Cultural Heritage*, dissertation, Uppsala: Uppsala Universitet

Schmitt, C. ([1942] 2002), *Terra e mare*, Milano: Adelphi

Schofield, J. (2016), 'Why Sweden is putting troops on this idyllic holiday island', *The Local*, https://www.thelocal.se/20160914/why-is-sweden-stationing-troops-on-gotland-important/ (accessed 9 June 2021)

SEArica (2020), 'Marine biodiversity in a changing climate: How do we best enable the Baltic Sea ecosystem to be part of the solution?', http://www.searica.eu/sea-basins-and-islands/baltic/marine-biodiversity-in-a-changing-climate-baltic-sea-event (accessed 7 January 2022)

SEArica (2021a), 'Baltic Sea ports as drivers of the sustainable blue economy: Making the Green Deal a reality', http://www.searica.eu/sea-basins-and-islands/baltic/baltic-sea-ports-as-drivers-of-the-sustainable-blue-economy-making-the-green-deal-a-reality (accessed 7 January 2022)

SEArica (2021b), 'Towards an EU strategy for sustainable tourism: Building forward smarter and greener in the EU coastal & insular regions', http://www.searica.eu/sea-basins-and-islands/mediterranean (accessed 7 January 2022)

Sedda, F. (2019) 'Il pianeta delle isole', in F. Sedda (ed.), *Isole. Un arcipelago semiotico*, 9–57, Milano: Meltemi

Senato Della Repubblica (2022), 'Atto Camera n. 3353 XVIII Legislatura', https://www.senato.it/leg/18/BGT/Schede/Ddliter/54546.htm (accessed 13 February 2022)

Serpentini, A. L. (ed.) (2006), *Dictionnaire historique de la Corse*, Ajaccio: Albiana

Sciascia, L. (1971), *Intervista a Leonardo Sciascia*, http://www.teche.rai.it/2019/11/leonardo-sciascia/ (accessed 10 February 2021)

Shell, M. (2014), *Islandology. Geography, Rhetoric, Politics*, Stanford: Stanford University Press

Signorelli, A. (2015), *Catania borghese nell'età del Risorgimento. A teatro, al circolo, alle urne*, Milano: Franco Angeli

Siotto-Pintòr, G. (1877), *Storia civile dei popoli sardi dal 1798 al 1848*, Torino: Tipografia Bellardi e Appiotti

Söderhjelm, J. O. (1928), *Démilitarisation et neutralisation des iles d'Åland en 1856 et 1921*, Helsinki: Söderström & C.o Förlagsaktiebolag

Sooväli, H. (2004), *Saaremaa Waltz. Landscape Imagery of Saaremaa Island in the 20th Century*, Tartu: Tartu University Press

Sotgiu, G. (1986), *Storia della Sardegna dopo l'Unità*, Roma-Bari: Laterza

Ståhl, M. (2014), 'Öland lämnar B7-samarbetet', *Ölandsbladet*, https://www.olandsbladet.se/ettan/oland-lamnar-b7-samarbetet/ (accessed 6 January 2022)

Stanbridge, K. (2002), 'Master frames, political opportunities, and self-determination: The Åland islands in the post-WWI Period', *The Sociological Quarterly* 43: 527–52

Staniscia, S. (2012), 'Island-ness', in G. De Luca and V. Lingua (eds.), *Arcipelago mediterraneo. Strategie di riqualificazione e sviluppo nelle città-porto delle isole*, 19–25, Firenze: Alinea editrice

Staszak, J. F. (1997), 'L'insularité de Zanzibar, de l'empire des boutres aux nouvelles utopies', in A. L. Sanguin (ed.), *Vivre dans une île*, 339–55, Paris: L'Harmattan

Staszak, J. F. (2003), *Géographies de Gauguin*, Rosny-sous-Bois: Bréal

Stöcker, L. F. (2018), *Bridging the Baltic Sea: Networks of Resistance and Opposition during the Cold War Era*, Lanham: Lexington Books

Stratford, E. (2008), 'Islandness and struggles over development: A Tasmanian case study', *Political Geography* 27: 160–75

Stratford, E., G. Baldacchino, E. McMahon, C. Farbotko, and A. Harwood (2011), 'Envisioning the archipelago', *Island Studies Journal* 6 (2): 113–30

Stratford, E., G. Baldacchino, and E. McMahon (2023), *Rethinking Island Studies: Methodologies for Studying Islands*, Lanham, MD: Rowman & Littlefield International

Stråth, B. (2000), 'The Baltic as an image and illusion: The construction of a region between Europe and the nation', in B. Stråth (ed.), *Myth and Memory in the Construction of Community: Historical Patterns in Europe and beyond*, 199–214, Bruxelles: Peter Lang

Sulis, F. ([1857] 1987), *Dei moti politici dell'isola di Sardegna dal 1793 al 1821. Narrazioni storiche*, Bologna: Forni

Suwa, J. I. (2007), 'The space of Shima', *Shima: The International Journal of Research into Island Cultures* 1 (1): 6–14

Svedjemo, G. (2014), *Landscape Dynamics: Spatial Analyses of Villages and Farms on Gotland AD 200–1700*, Uppsala: Uppsala universitet

Taglioni, F. (2011), 'Insularity, political status and small insular spaces', *Shima: The International Journal of Research into Island Cultures* 5 (2): 45–67

Tallinna Rootsi-Mihkli kogudus, (2021), 'Island folk', http://www.stmikael.ee/index.php/en/ajalugu/2-1/112-estonian-swedes (accessed 22 July 2021)

Tanca, M. (2018), 'Cose, rappresentazioni, pratiche: uno sguardo sull'ontologia ibrida della Geografia', *Bollettino della Società Geografica Italiana* 14 (1): 5–17

Tatasciore, G. (2013), ' Il banditismo d'onore in Corsica nell'immaginario di viaggio francese (1815–1915)', *Diacronie. Studi di Storia Contemporanea* 15 (3): 1–20, http://www.studistorici.com/wp-content/uploads/2013/10/04_TATASCIORE.pdf (accessed 13 February 2022)

Tatasciore, G. (2022), *Briganti d'Italia. Storia di un immaginario romantico*, Roma: Viella

Temine, E. (2000), 'Repenser l'espace méditerranéen. Une utopie des années trente?', *La pensée de midi* 1 (1): 56–61

Thordeman, B. (1939), *Armour from the Battle of Wisby 1361*, Uppsala: Almquist & Wiksells Boktryckeri A.B

Togliatti, P. (1965), *La questione siciliana*, Palermo: Edizioni Libri Siciliani

Tøllefsen, T. O., and J. M. White (2021), 'Navigating an orthodox conversion: Community, environment, and religion on the Island of Ruhnu, 1866-7', *Scandinavian Journal of History*, https://www.tandfonline.com/doi/ref/10.1080/03468755.2021.1921840?scroll=top (accessed 22 July 2021)

Tomasi Di Lampedusa, G. ([1958] 1961), *The Leopard*, London: Reprint Society

Torre, A. (2011), 'Comunità e località', in P. Lanaro (ed.), *Microstoria. A venticinque anni da L'eredità immateriale*, 25–58, Milano: FrancoAngeli

Trabelsi, M. (2005), *L'insularité*, Clermont-Ferrand: Presses universitaires Blaise Pascal

Trampus, A. (2008), *Il diritto alla felicità. Storia di un'idea*, Roma-Bari: Laterza.

Trampus, A. (2014), 'Tra Corsica e Toscana: Emer de Vattel e i percorsi del costituzionalismo settecentesco', *Études corses* 78: 61–79

Treaty of Amsterdam (1997), https://www.cvce.eu/content/publication/1999/1/1/578ebb8e-d641-4650-b1e3-3b3a795e01c9/publishable_en.pdf (accessed 2 October 2021)

Trizzino, A. (1945), *Che vuole la Sicilia?*, Roma: STEI

Turco, A. (1980), *Insularità e modello centro-periferia: l'isola di Creta nelle sue relazioni con l'esterno*, Milano: Unicopli

Tuveri, G. B. (1860), *Il Governo e i Comuni*, Cagliari: Tipografia nazionale

Üldentsüklopeedia (2013), 'Uniting Ruhnu with the Republic of Estonia', http://entsyklopeedia.ee/article_eng/uniting_ruhnu_with_the_republic_of_estonia1# (accessed 7 August 2021)

Üldentsüklopeedia (2014), 'Ruhnu during the Soviet period', http://entsyklopeedia.ee/article_eng/ruhnu_during_the_soviet_period1 (accessed 7 August 2021)

Uppsala Universitet (2021), 'About the Baltic University Programme', https://www.balticuniv.uu.se/about-us/ (accessed 5 January 2022)

Van Lierop, C. (2020), 'Implementation of macro-regional strategies', https://www.europarl.europa.eu/RegData/etudes/BRIE/2017/608717/EPRS_BRI(2017)608717_EN.pdf (accessed 6 January 2022)

Van Lierop, C. (2021), 'Working towards a macro-regional strategy for the Mediterranean', https://www.europarl.europa.eu/RegData/etudes/BRIE/2021/698064/EPRS_BRI(2021)698064_EN.pdf (accessed 6 January 2022)

Vassallo, I. (2012), *Enrico Mizzi: Between Nationalism and Irredentism*, dissertation, Malta: University of Malta

Västrik, R. (2015), 'Constructing national identity in Soviet Estonian documentary cinema: A case study of the documentary Ruhnu (1965) by Andres Sööt', *Baltic Screen Media Review* 3: 4–29

Venturi, F. (1987), *Settecento riformatore. L'Italia dei Lumi (1764–1790). La rivoluzione di Corsica. Le grandi carestie degli anni sessanta. La Lombardia delle riforme*, Torino: Einaudi

Verga, G. ([1881] 1972), *I Malavoglia*, Manchester: Manchester University Press

Vergé-Franceschi, M. (1996), *Histoire de la Corse. Le pays de la grandeur*, Paris: Editions du Felin

Vieira, A. (2010), 'As Ilhas: Da Nissologia à Nesologia', *Anuário do Centro de Estudos des História do Atlântico* 2: 1–26

Vieira, A. (2016), 'Il discorso dell'anti-insularita e il poio maderense come sua negazione', *Diacronie. Studi di Storia Contemporanea* 27 (3): 1–34, http://www.studistorici.com/wp-content/uploads/2016/09/15_VIEIRA.pdf (accessed 13 February, 2022)

Villari, R. (1975), *Storia contemporanea*, Bari: Laterza

Virkkunen, J. (1999), 'The politics of identity: Ethnicity, minority and nationalism in Soviet Estonia', *GeoJournal* 48: 83–9

Voltaire ([1759] 1947), *Candide*, West Drayton: Penguin Books

Voltaire ([1768] 1893), *Précis du siècle de Louis XV*, Paris: A. Colin

Wæver, O. (1992), 'Nordic nostalgia: Northern Europe after the Cold War', *International Affairs* 68 (1): 77–102

Walcott, D. (2014), *Omeros*, Farrar: Straus and Giroux

Warrington, E., and D. Milne (2007), 'Island governance', in G. Baldacchino (ed.), *A World of Islands. An Island Studies Reader*, 379–427, Charlottetown: Institute of Islands Studies

Warrington, E., and D. Milne (2018), 'Governance', in G. Baldacchino (ed.), *The Routledge International Handbook of Island Studies*, 173–201, New York: Routledge

Wawrzeniuk, P. (2014), 'The making of Gammalsvenskby 1881–1914 – identity, myth and imagination', in P. Wawrzeniuk and J. Malitska (eds.), *The Lost Swedish Tribe: Reapproaching the History of Gammalsvenskby in Ukraine*, 89–110, Huddinge: Södertörn University

Wawrzeniuk, P., and J. Malitska (2014), 'Approaching the "Lost Swedish Tribe" in Ukraine', in P. Wawrzeniuk and J. Malitska (eds.), *The Lost Swedish Tribe: Reapproaching the History of Gammalsvenskby in Ukraine*, 13–38, Huddinge: Södertörn University

Wedin, L. (2017), 'Gotland: île stratégique', *Revue Défense Nationale* 800: 139–45

Weibull, J. (1996), *Storia della Svezia*, Stockholm: Svenska Institutet

Williams, R. (2009), 'Excluding to protect: Land rights and minority protection in international Law', in S. Åkermark (ed.), *The Right of Domicile on Åland*, 95–136, Mariehamn: The Åland Islands Peace Institute & The Åland Parliament

Yle (2022), 'Parliament speaker Vanhanen clarifies Åland comments', *Yle*, https://yle.fi/news/3-12416456 (accessed 19 May 2022)

Zanella, R. (1989), 'Elezioni e partiti a Malta prima e dopo l'indipendenza', *Quaderni dell'Osservatorio Elettorale* 22: 7–70

Zichi, G. (2008), *I cattolici sardi e il Risorgimento*, Milano: Franco Angeli

Zucchetto, J., and A. M. Jansson (1985), *Resources and Society a Systems Ecology Study of the Island of Gotland, Sweden*, New York: Springer-Verlag

Index

Abulafia, David XI, 28, 33
Aceto Cattani, Giovanni 125–6
Adorni, Daniela 128–9
Affeldt, Sören 21
Agamben, Giorgio 59
Åhlander, Lars 110
Ahtisaari, Martti Oiva Kalevi 76
Akel, Friedrich 109
Alatri, Paolo 120
Alenius, Kari 108
Alexander I 63–4, 92, 139
Alfieri, Vittorio 179
Amari, Michele 120, 127
Andersen, Knud 46
Anderson, Benedict 13, 70
Andersson, Otto 63–71
Angelini, Aurelio 195
Angioy, Giovanni Maria 159–62, 191
Angliker, Erica 11–12
Apostolopoulos, Yorghos X
Arcifa, Lucia 127
Armengol, Francina 55
Åselius, Gunnar 100
Askey, Nigel 100
Astuto, Giuseppe 143
Aström, Joachim 86
Atzeni, Francesco 162, 165
Audisio, Gabriel 31
Avagliano, Lucio 122
Aymard, Maurice 122

Bachtler, John 44
Bakhtin, Mikhail Mikhailovich 117
Balbiano, Vincenzo 156
Baldacchino, Godfrey X, 2–3, 7–9, 12, 197, 199
Baldoli, Claudia 150
Ball, Alexander 138–40
Ballard, Jean 30
Ballif, Florine 58
Barbaro, Ramiro 147
Barone, Giuseppe 119–23, 129

Barrault, Émile 29
Basile, Maria Concetta 125–7
Bauman, Zygmunt 31, 58
Bellieni, Camillo 153, 165–6
Benigno, Francesco 16, 30, 32–3, 36–7
Bentnick, William 139
Bergman Rosamond, Annika 84
Beri, Emiliano XII, 172, 174–7, 180–1
Berlinguer, Luigi 153–5
Berlinguer, Mario 167
Berlusconi, Silvio 194–5
Bernardie-Tahir, Nathalie 3, 7–8, 58
Berque, Augustin 194
Bialasiewicz, Luiza 18
Biazzo Curry, Corrada 118
Bīlmanis, Alfrēds 25
Birocchi, Italo 155
Bitossi, Carlo 170
Björkman, Carl 69
Blanc-Noël, Nathalie 22
Blees, Nikolai 108, 112
Blumfeldt, Evald 94, 96
Bodisko, Nikolay 82
Boffa, Paul 149
Bondin, Ray 151
Bonnemaison, Joël 3
Bono, Salvatore 28, 33–4, 140
Borioni, Paolo 65
Borutta, Manuel 29
Boswell, James 179
Bourdieu, Pierre 9
Brambilla, Chiara 60
Brancato, Francesco 121
Braudel, Fernand IX, 8–9, 25–6, 30–3
Brazzelli, Nicoletta 11
Brigand, Louis 3
Briguglio, Lino 42
Briquet, Jean-Louis 186
Brogini, Anne 31
Brotton, Jerry VIII
Brown, Philip Marshall 74
Browning, Christopher S. 20

Bruix, Etienne Eustache 139
Brunet, Roger 6, 199
Bufalino, Gesualdo 118
Butera, Salvatore 120

Cabouret, Michel 78, 86, 90, 102
Cabras, Vincenzo 157
Caldwell, John C. X
Calosso, Umberto 150
Calvi, Pasquale 143
Camus, Albert 30
Canale Cama, Francesca 31
Cancila, Orazio 129
Cane, Crescenzio 118
Canepa, Antonio 129–30
Cao, Maria Luisa 162
Cao, Umberto 165
Capasso, Salvatore 33
Capponi, Gino 185
Caracciolo, Domenico 120
Carta, Luciano 157, 159
Carta, Silvio 17
Caruana, Francesco Saverio 137–8
Casanova, Antoine 180
Casanova, Daniela 31
Casanova, Pierre-Toussaint (Santu) 187–8
Cassano, Franco 36
Castelain, Jean-Pierre 7
Catherine I 93
Catherine II 93
Catherine de' Medici 171
Cavallo, Federica Letizia 8, 60, 198
Cavendish Ponsonby, Frederick 141
Chamberlain, Joseph 146
Chandler, David XI
Charles V 135, 171
Charles VI of France 170
Charles Albert 163
Charles Emmanuel IV 160, 162
Charles Felix 162
Chevalier, Michel 29–30
Chillaud, Matthieu 24, 63–5, 68
Chirac, Jacques 35
Christian II 81
Ciampi, Carlo Azeglio 60
Cicu, Salvatore 198
Cimino, Marcello 130
Cini, Marco XII, 184–7
Ciusa, Francesco 164

Clark, Eric 48
Clark, Thomas L. 48
Cocco Ortu, Francesco 164
Colomb, Claire 45
Congregalli, Matteo 83
Contu, Gianfranco 154, 166–8
Corona, Gabriella 33
Cosgrove, Denis E. 9
Cosimo I de' Medici 171
Cossiga, Francesco 153
Cottrell, Jana Raadik 90, 195
Cottrell, Stuart P. 90, 195
Coty, François 188
Crispi, Francesco 129, 143
Croce, Benedetto 120
Cubeddu, Salvatore 165–6, 168
Cuppini, Niccolò 31
Cuttitta, Paolo 58

Daftary, Farimah 62–3, 72, 75
Dahl, Arthur 7
Dal Passo, Fabrizio 172–5, 178–85
Darwin, Charles X
Davies, Norman 80
De Angelo Laky, Lilian 11–12
De Belgrand Vaubois, Claude-Henri 137–9
De Bono, Paolo 140
De Certeau, Michel 9
De Campredon, Jacques 173
De Chauvelin, Germain-Louis 173
De Choiseul, Étienne François 181
De Cursay, Gallimard Marc 176
De Felice, Renzo 166
De la Gardie, Axel Julius 93
De la Gardie, Jakob 92
De Retz (de Gondi, Jean-François Paul) 179
De Rocca Serra, Camille 44
De Stefano, Francesco 121
Debord, Guy 58
Debrune, Jérôme 30
Deffenu, Attilio 164–6
Del Piano, Lorenzo 165–6
Del Piano, Vittoria 158
Deledda, Grazia 154, 164
Delli Quadri, Rosa M. 31
Delors, Jacques 41
DeLoughrey, Elizabeth X

Dematteis, Giuseppe 164
Denier, Jean 69
Depraetere, Christian 7, 11
Deprest, Florence 29–30
Depretis, Agostino 127–8, 164
Di Falco, Sara 45
Di Gregorio, Pinella 116–17, 124
Di Matteo, Giovanna 60
Di Tucci, Raffaele 162
Diamond, Jared X
Diegues, Manuel 7, 46
Dommen, Edward X
Donat, bishop of Riga 105
Donati, Giuseppe 150
Doria, Andrea 171
Dottelonde, Pierre 189
Drolet, Michael 28
Du Deffand (de Vichy-Chamrond, Marie Anne) 179
Dühr, Stefanie 45

Eckstein, Lars VIII
Edquist, Samuel 7, 62, 79, 81–2, 85–7, 89, 91–6, 99–100, 102, 192
Einbund, Karl 109
Elfving, Jörgen 84
Ellemann-Jensen, Uffe 22
Elliot, Gilbert 184
Enfantin, Prosper 29
Engholm, Björn 21–2
Eric of Pomerania 81
Eriksson, Suzanne 62, 64, 66, 69–70, 75–7
Erlandsson, Thoedor 81
Erlanger, Steven 193
Escach, Nicolas 21–2
Ettori, Farrandu 181
Ewart Gladstone, William 141

Fabei, Stefano 152
Fabrizi, Nicola 143
Facineroso, Alessia 143
Falzon, Mark-Anthony 197
Farinelli, Marcel A. 7, 191
Faucci, Riccardo 165
Fazi, André 7
Feldmann, Beate 83, 103
Ferdinand I 124, 126
Ferdinand II 126
Ferdinand IV of Naples 126, 137–8, 140

Ferlazzo Ciano, Giulio XII, 135, 137–42, 145, 147
Ferrari, Giuseppe 131
Ferras, Robert 6, 199
Ferretti, Federico 29
Finocchiaro Aprile, Andrea 130–2
Fiorentini, Bianca 142
Florio, family 129
Fogu, Claudio 36, 58
Fois, Giuseppina 165
Formosa, Daniela 145
Fortunato, Giustino 128
Foschi, Alga Danila 43
Foxlee, Neil 30
Franceschi Leonardi, Mario 178
Franchetti, Leopoldo 128
Frasca, Francesco 135, 138, 140
Frascani, Paolo 31
Frederick II of Denmark 91
Frendo, Henry 141, 144
Friggieri, Oliver 144
Frisella-Vella, Giuseppe 120, 129
Frykvall, Magnus 193

Gabriele, Nicola 162–3
Gaffori, Giovanni Pietro 177
Gaja, Filippo 130
Gallia, Arturo 2
Ganci, Massimo 120–2, 129, 131
Gandolfo, Asclepia 166
Garibaldi, Giuseppe 132
Gauguin, Paul 7
Gayle, Dennis J. X
Gekas, Sakis 29
George III 182
Gerner, Kristian 22
Giaccaria, Paolo 13, 32
Giafferri, Luigi 173
Giarrizzo, Giuseppe 116, 121–2, 124, 134
Gillis, John R. 88
Giolitti, Giovanni 122, 165
Giovacchini, Petru 188
Glenelg, Charles Grant 141
Glete, Jan 81
Gotkowska, Justyna 84
Götz, Norbert XII, 19, 25, 27, 46
Graham Campbell, David 150
Gramsci, Antonio 153, 166, 168–9
Grandell, John 76

Graneri, Pietro Giuseppe 156
Gras, Pierre 80
Graumann, Olga 21
Graziani, Antoine-Marie 170–1, 177
Gregory VII 170
Gregory, Charles Noble 63, 72, 74
Grieco, Ruggiero 166–7
Grießner, Doris 62
Grimaldi, Angelo 123, 125, 139
Grimaldi, Gian Giacomo 177
Grönberg, Carl Gustaf 112
Grydehøj, Adam 12, 200
Grzechnik, Marta 22–3, 25, 27, 46
Guarracino, Scipione 31
Guerrazzi, Francesco Domenico 185
Gustav IV Adolf 64
Gustav I Vasa 82
Gustav V 72
Gustavus II Adolphus 92

Haase, Diána 35, 50, 52, 55–6
Hache, Jean-Didier 2, 40–4
Hackmann, Jörg 19
Hägerhäll Aniansson, Britt 25
Hall, C. Michael IX
Hallberg, Maria 86–7
Haller, Józef 20
Hamilton, William 138
Hannikainen, Lauri Antero 62
Hau'ofa, Epeli XI
Hay, Pete 7, 11, 200
Hayward, Philip 11
Hedman, Jörgen 110
Hegel, Georg Wilhelm Friedrich 28
Henry II of France 171
Henry the Lion 79
Hentilä, Seppo 63, 65, 67, 72–3
Hepburn, Eve 2–3, 6–7
Hermanson, Robert 70–1
Herzfeld, Michael 32
Hitler, Adolf 98
Hobsbawm, Eric 129
Holmén, Janne XII, 7, 17, 62, 85–6, 89, 91–6, 99–100, 102, 192
Horden, Peregrine 32–3
Hull, Geoffrey 146
Humbert of Savoy 131
Huntington, Ellsworth 194
Huntington, Samuel P. 31
Hurskainen, Heta 46

Iachello, Enrico 121
Ibba, Roberto XII, 156
Isabella, Maurizio 124, 142
Isin, Engin F. 59
Ivetic, Egidio 16, 32–3

Jackson, Rebecca Erinn 3
Jakovlev, Tormis 102
Jansson, Ann-Mari 82
Jansson, Roger 24
Joenniemi, Pertti 64, 77
Johannes V von Münchhausen 91
Johansson, Lars Ingmar 62, 64, 66, 69–70, 75–7
John I 90
Jones, Alun 18
Jürgenstein, Anton 109
Jussila, Osmo 63, 65, 67, 72–3

Keenan, Patrick Joseph 146
Kekkonen, Urho 20
Kettunen, Pauli 24
Ķibilds, Martins 106–7, 109
Kirby, David 26
Kjellén, Rudolf 67
Klaar, Jaan 95
Klinge, Matti 26, 64–5
Kokovkin, Reet 47
Körber, Martin 91
Koselleck, Reinhardt 17
Kranking, Glenn Eric 106–8, 110–12
Kreem, Juhan 80
Kronsell, Annica 84
Kuldkepp, Mart 20
Kurunmäki, Jussi XII, 23, 27

La Manna, Fabrizio XII, 126
Lambruschini, Raffaello 185
Lando, Fabio 40
Le Goff, Jacques 97
Lefebvre, Henri VIII
Lemaire, Léa 58
Lember, Jaan 103
Léouzon Le Duc, Louis 65–6
Li Causi, Girolamo 133
Lindberg, Folke 79
Ljubovtsev, Ilya Mikhailovich 99
Lo Vetere, Filippo 129
Loel, Rita 96
Loi, Antonio 196

Lorenz, Tomas 112
Lott, Alexander 109
Louis XV 173, 180–1
Luha, Artur 96
Lundberg, Dan 88
Lundström, Vilhelm 70
Lupo, Salvatore 122–3, 129
Lussana, Fiamma 168–9
Lussu, Emilio 153–4, 165, 167

Mack Smith, Denis 121
Madau Diaz, Antonello 159
Maier, Andreea 35, 50, 52, 55–6
Malitska, Julia 91–4
Malm, Krister 88
Malmros, Pär 86–7
Malkin, Irad 36
Manacorda, Gastone 122
Mangiameli, Rosario XII, 123, 129–32
Mannarino, Gaetano 136
Manno, Giuseppe 160
Mannu, Francesco Ignazio 160
Margaret of Flanders 79
Maria Carolina of Naples 138
Maria Theresa of Austria 176
Marimoutou, Jean-Claude 8
Marino, Giuseppe Carlo 120, 130–1
Marras, Pietro 154
Martinetti, Joseph 41, 58, 60, 197
Martini, Pietro 160
Marx, Karl IX
Mattone, Antonello 153, 155, 157–61
Matvejević, Pedrag 7–8, 37
Maurras, Charles 30
Mertelsmann, Olaf 99
McAlinden, Tom 98, 111
McCall, Grant 11
McMaster, Irene 44
Meistersheim, Anne 2–3
Meyer, Philippe 79
Miccichè, Andrea 130, 133
Michel, Ersilio 143, 175, 177
Mifsud Bonnici, Ugo 143
Migeot, Raymond cfr. Jean Denier
Mikaberidze, Alexander 82
Milne, David 7, 42–4
Minca, Claudio 18, 32, 196–7
Minghetti, Marco 127–8
Mirwaldt, Katja 44
Mitropoulou, Angeliki 196

Mizzi, Enrico 135, 148–50, 152
Mizzi, Fortunato 146–8
Mitrovich, Giorgio 141–2
Moles, Abraham André 10–11
Molotov, Vyacheslav Mikhailovich 96–8, 101
Monina, Giancarlo 29
Monmonier, Mark S. VIII
Montesquieu (de Secondat, Charles-Louis) 9, 174, 176
More O'Ferrall, Richard 145
Mussolini, Benito 31, 130, 148, 150, 166–7, 188–9
Musso, François 41
Myrberg, Nanouschka 78

Nadarajah, Yaso 12
Nadin, Vincent 45
Napoleon I 29, 63, 123, 137, 180, 184
Napoleon III 30, 186–7
Nasone, Antonello 165
Nasser, Gamal Abdel 33
Nelson, Horatio 138
Neumann, Iver 25
Nevakivi, Jukka 63, 65, 67, 72–3
Nielsen, Greg Marc 59
Nihlén, John 82
Nitti, Francesco 167
Norby, Søren 81
North, Michael 79
Novacco, Nino 132

Oddo, Francesco L. 121
Ojalo, Hanno 99–100
Olausson, Pär 41
Olivesi, Claude 41, 43, 45, 47
Olsson, Jan 86
Öpik, Elena 91
Orioles, Vincenzo 118
Orlov, Grigorij Grigor'evič 105
Oskar I 66
Ots, Georg 89
Oxenstierna, Axel 63

Pacciardi, Randolfo 131
Padelford, Norman J. 63–9, 71
Pais Serra, Francesco 164
Palamenghi Crispi, Guido 143
Paliaccio, Gavino 158
Palmieri, Walter 33

Paniga, Massimiliano 164
Paoli, Giacinto 174, 177
Paoli, Pasquale 171, 174, 177–85, 191
Papa, Enzo 118
Pätsand, Konstantin 95
Paul I of Russia 139
Pellegrinetti, Jean-Paul 187–8
Peel, Christine 78
Peraldi, Xavier 43
Peresso, Giorgio XII, 150, 152
Pericles 179
Péron, Françoise 10
Perotti, Simone XII
Perri, Paolo 31
Perrin, Thomas 35–6
Peter I 93
Peter IV of Aragon 170
Petri, Rolf XII, 17, 26, 28–9, 37, 199
Petrogiannis, Vasileios XII, 17
Petrusewicz, Marta 32
Philip II of Spain 171
Philip V of Spain 173
Pietrancosta, Fausto 130
Pinello, Felice 173
Pinna di Pozzomaggiore, Pietro 167
Pintor, Efisio 157
Pirandello, Luigi 116, 133
Pirenne, Henri 31
Pitzolo, Girolamo 157–9
Pius VII 139
Plutarch 179
Podestà, Attilio 85
Pomponi, Francis 188
Pontieri, Ernesto 120, 162
Potëmkin, Grigorij Aleksandrovič 93
Prodi, Romano 28
Pugh, Jonathan XI, 11–12
Pulvirenti, Chiara Maria 142–4
Purcell, Nicholas 32–3

Quartararo, Rosaria 150

Raadik-Cottrell, Jana 90, 195
Racault, Jean-Michel 8
Raffiotta, Giovanni 121
Ratka, Edmund 35
Ratter, Beate M. W. 198
Raudseppa, Johan 100
Raukas, Anto 90–1
Ravis-Giordani, Georges 187

Rebas, Hain 80
Reclus, Élisée 29
Reid, William 143
Renda, Francesco 120, 128
Ricci, Aldo G. 143
Richards, Jeffrey X
Ricoeur, Paul 9
Ricotti, Carlo R. 123
Riis, Vassili 99
Riva, Gigi 153–4
Rivarola, Paolo Battista 174–5
Robinson, James A.
Rocca, Matteo 188
Rocca, Petru 188
Rohmer, Élisabeth 10
Romano, Salvatore Francesco 120–1
Rombaldi, Michel 43
Romeo, Rosario 120, 122, 127
Rönnberg, Lars 98, 111
Rönnby, Johan 30
Ronström, Owe 81–2, 87–8
Rose-Redwood, Reuben VIII
Rosière, Stéphane 58
Rosselli, Carlo 167
Rotkirch, Holger 65–8, 72, 74
Rotondo, Bianca Maria 165
Rousseau, Jean-Jacques 7, 179
Rovere, Ange 180, 187
Royle, Stephen A. X, 3
Rudas, Nereide 154
Rudling, Anders 105, 110–11
Rudolf, Uwe Jens 148
Rumford, Chris 18
Russel, Alfred X
Russwurm, Carl 94

Said, Edward 16, 32
Saint-Simon, Claude Henri de 29–30
Salaris, Francesco 164
Salice, Giampaolo XII, 154–6, 159, 161, 163
Saliceti, Cristoforo 183
Salsano, Roberto 117
Samuelsson, Jörgen 49
Sander, Gordon F. 192
Sanguin, André-Louis 40–1, 198
Sanna, Piero 157–61
Sarkozy, Nicolas 35
Satta, Sebastiano 154, 164
Saumarez, James 138

Säve, Per Arvid 85
Savelli, Agostino 146, 148–9
Sceberras Testaferrata, Camillo 141–2, 147
Sciascia, Leonardo 116–18, 121, 134
Schaub, Mareike 86
Schmitt, Carl 31
Schmoll, Camille 3, 58
Schofield, Jack 84
Schwarz, Anja VIII
Scott, Derek X
Scroccu, Gianluca XII
Sedda, Franciscu 5
Segni, Antonio 153
Serpentini, Antoine Laurent 170
Settimo, Ruggero 143
Shakhovskoi, Sergei 105
Shell, Marc 11
Signorelli, Alfio 124
Siotto-Pintòr, Giovanni 163
Sjoestedt, Erik Valentin 68
Snöbohm, Alfred Theodor 78–9
Söderhjelm, Johan Otto 63
Solinas, Christian 198
Sonnino, Sidney 68, 128, 146
Sööt, Andres 113
Sooväli, Helen 89–90, 92, 96–7, 102–3
Sotgiu, Girolamo 155, 162
Souminem, Ilkka 26
Spilanis, Ioannis 196
Spiliopoulou Åkermark, Sia 24
Ståhl, Michael 49
Stalin (Iosif Vissarionovich) 97
Stanbridge, Karen 72–3
Staniscia, Stefania 200
Stanley, Edward 141
Staszak, Jean-François 7, 198
Starabba di Rudinì, Antonio 129
Starc, Nenad X
Steffens, Hans 108
Stenbock, Karl Magnus 93
Stöcker, Lars Fredrik 26
Stråth, Bo 26
Strickland, Gerald 149–52
Stratford, Elaine X, XI, 3, 7, 11
Suleiman the Magnificient 171
Sulis, Francesco 161
Sundback, Barbro 62, 64, 66, 69–70, 75–7, 193–4
Sundblom, Julius 69–71, 75

Surovtsev, Vladimir Dmitrievich 89
Suwa, Jun'ichiro X
Svedjemo, Gustaf 79
Szymański, Piotr 84

Taglioni, François 42
Tammart, Henno 99
Tammekann, August 96
Tanca, Marcello 196–7
Tasca, Lucio 129
Tatasciore, Giulio 197
Temine, Émile 31, 37
Théry, Hervé 6, 199
Thordeman, Bengt 81
Togliatti, Palmiro 133
Tøllefsen, Trond O. 105
Tomasi di Lampedusa, Giuseppe 119, 120, 132
Tommaseo, Niccolò 185
Tommasi, Giovanni Battista 139
Tommasini, Francesco 68, 73
Torre, Angelo 9
Trabelsi, Mustapha 8
Trampus, Antonio 176, 178
Trizzino, Antonino 130
Turco, Angelo 2
Turri, Mario (cfr. Canepa, Antonio)
Tuveri, Giovanni Battista 163

Ulmanis, Kārlis Augusts Vilhelms 108–9

Valdemar, Atterdag 80
Valéry, Paul 31
Van Lierop, Christiaan 27, 35
Vanhanen, Matti 192
Vassalli, Mikiel Anton 144
Vassallo, Ivan XII, 149
Västrik, Riho 113–14
Venturi, Franco 180
Verga, Giovanni 116
Vergé-Franceschi, Michel 170
Viale, Salvatore 170, 185
Victor Amadeus II of Savoy 155
Victor Amadeus III 155–7, 160
Victor Emmanuel 116, 162
Vidal de La Blache, Paul 30
Vieira, Alberto 3, 194
Vieussieux, Giovan Pietro 185–6
Villari, Rosario 124, 128
Virkkunen, Joni 97–8, 102

Visconti Venosta, Emilio 146
Vitale, Emmanuele 137
Vivalda, Filippo 158
Voltaire (Arouet François-Marie) 175, 179, 181
Von Bellingshausen, Fabian Gottlieb 92
Von Döbeln, Georg Carl 64
Von Goethe, Johann Wolfgang 119, 179
Von Hompesch zu Bolheim, Ferdinand 137
Von Münchhausen, Johannes V 91
Von Neuhoff, Theodore 174–5
Von Ribbetrop, Joachim 96, 101
Von Segebaden, Carl Otto 82

Wæver, Ole 194
Walcott, Derek XI
Walpole, Horace 179
Warrington, Edward 7, 42–4
Wawrzeniuk, Piotr 91–4
Weber, Max 80

Wedin, Lars 83
Weibull, Jorgen 65, 75
Welles, Benjamin Sumner 98
Wellington (Wellesley, Arthur) 140
White, James M. 105
Williams, Rhodri C. 73
Wilson, Woodrow 188

Yeliseyev, Alexej Borisovič 100

Zakrevskij, Arsenjij Andrejevitj 65
Zanardelli, Giuseppe 128
Zanella, Remo 148
Zanou, Konstantina 124, 142
Zantedeschi, Francesca 31
Zauli Sajani, Tommaso 142
Zichi, Giuseppe 163
Zinna, Lucio 118
Zinoviev, Mihail Alekseyevich 89
Zucchetto, James 82

www.ingramcontent.com/pod-product-compliance
Lightning Source LLC
Chambersburg PA
CBHW062138300426
44115CB00012BA/1971